On My Home Ground

By the same author:

SPACE BELOW MY FEET

TWO STAR RED

Gwen Moffat on the Milestone Buttress, North Wales

ON MY
HOME GROUND

by

GWEN MOFFAT

HODDER AND STOUGHTON

Copyright © 1968 by Gwen Moffat
First printed 1968
SBN 340 02681 2

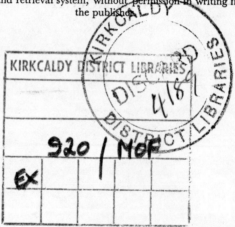

Printed in Great Britain for
Hodder and Stoughton Limited,
St. Paul's House, Warwick Lane, London, E.C.4, by
Cox & Wyman Limited
London, Fakenham and Reading

CONTENTS

ILLUSTRATIONS

KEY TO ACKNOWLEDGEMENTS

[1] S. R. G. Bray
[2] J. A. Jones
[3] Author
[4] B. H. Humble
[5] David M. Morgan Rees
[6] J. Brailsford

[7] J. R. Lees
[8] Robert Armstrong
[9] Jeanne Woodroffe
[10] Sheffield Newspapers Ltd.
[11] A. F. Becker
[12] David Wills

CHAPTER I

The Wild Mountain

COMING HOME TO Maen y Bardd after a day's climbing — particularly a cold, wet day when you'd been fighting all the time — plodding up the mountain in the dusk, you were suddenly aware of the contrast: on one side, danger, on the other, security. And on a stormy night, when you couldn't see the house for the rain or the blizzard, and there was no light because it was empty, it was delightful to think that a few hundred feet higher was this refuge, waiting. In ten minutes there'd be light and warmth, hot food and a dry bed. In ten minutes you'd be home.

The cottage stood at eight hundred feet on the edge of the tree-line. Under the terrace and the sloping garden the ground dropped away to the village six hundred feet below. Beyond the village was the long line of the river, and beyond that, the Denbigh Moors. Northwards you saw the lighthouse flashing off the Great Orme eight miles away, but to the south the view was cut by a spur of little peaks coming down from the main range of the Carneddau, peaks which ended in a rounded fort of a hill where thick old woods crept up the sides but left the top so bare that, even from a distance, you could see the line of the ancient earthworks where invaders were repulsed by jagged splinters of stone embedded in the turf.

Above the house the trees stopped, except for thorns and the occasional hardy sycamore on the site of a ruin. Maen y Bardd was the highest inhabited house above all that stretch of the Conway Valley; coming home at night you could place it easily if someone were there; you looked up and there was the light surrounded by the blackness of the mountain: the highest light. Sometimes I mistook it for a star.

There was no road to the house. A narrow lane climbed up from the village with a parking place for cars near the top. Then there was half a mile of walking, but after one field and a gate I was on my own land. Not mine legally, but Maen y Bardd land, so mine in my mind. And from this gate, on a good evening, you looked up and there were the roof and the upper windows above the hazel coppice but so merged in the gloom of the sycamores that you felt its presence more than saw it.

When the front door closed it shut out not only the elements but all exterior distractions. There was no telephone, no mail waiting behind the door. The postman left letters in a box at the road-end. There were only the fire and the lamp to light, supper to prepare and then a few hours of writing before bed. But I left the curtains undrawn: Johnnie might come after a rescue or on unexpected leave and he liked to see the light from the valley. For the same reason the door was never locked at night. Bumps in the small hours could be cattle rubbing themselves on the walls, but just as likely himself coming upstairs in the dark.

Maen y Bardd marked the end of nine years of living rough. At the start of those years I had done nothing extraordinary; there had been school, a suburban home in Sussex, and then the war and life in the Services. The vague desire to be something different, to live excitingly was temporarily satisfied by riding powerful motor cycles, but when I was transferred to staff cars the old longings came back, intensified. Then I met a climber, was taken climbing, and my world slipped into gear. Nothing mattered now other than mountains. Stationed at Stoke-on-Trent with the Army, I didn't consider deserting. I thought of the mountains I had just climbed, I looked at the empty barrack room, and – a few hours after I returned from leave in Snowdonia – I went back to the hills.

In the next six months I wandered from North Wales to Cornwall and back again, climbing in the mountains, hitching down to Land's End where new friends – all conscientious objectors, mostly artists – eked out a subsistence living as woodsmen. I helped cut down trees, picked spring flowers, modelled for artists. When I thought of a high wind in high places and of rock I went north again, sleeping in barns in bad weather, in the open on good nights. In my rucksack I carried little more than a sleeping bag and my boots. I went barefooted to save my boot nails.

Eventually all climbers want to go abroad – to the Alps – but I had no passport and no means of getting one while I was on the run from the police and the military authorities. I needed that passport, but – perhaps more than this – I needed a goal. I was twenty-one and for six months I had done exactly what I wanted to do. I had been very happy, but six months without an aim was enough. So I went back to the Army, served my time, and in the spring returned to Snowdonia with my freedom and eighty pounds gratuity.

Wales held me for a while. I made new friends: people who had fun yet considered careers; for the most part they were ex-Servicemen waiting to go up to universities. With them I climbed, first in Wales, then in the Lake District, Skye, on Ben Nevis. Scotland captivated me with its vastness, its remoteness, the seemingly interminable ranges of great new mountains. Every peak I hadn't climbed was an unclimbed one.

I worked for the Forestry Commission in the Great Glen, then I moved to the Isle of Skye and lived in a cottage on the shore of one of the western lochs. From the pantry window I saw half the range of the Cuillin, from the kitchen I looked beyond a stark black headland to the Outer Isles. I picked winkles for Billingsgate, read Russian novels and started to write.

A summer in the Alps followed, with an engineer called Gordon Moffat. We lived in a tent in the pine forests below Mont Blanc. Gordon worked on a hydro-electric scheme in the mountains. I lay in the glade and wrote, and sometimes I climbed. It was a hot, lazy world interspersed with those hard, bitter expeditions above the snowline from which I returned, not satiated, but always wanting more.

We married when we returned from France. Gordon went to work for a marine engineer in Conway and we bought a derelict fishing boat for twenty pounds. We had no money except Gordon's wages but he was clever with his hands and within four months the old mud-filled hulk had become a clean and cosy home for a baby. Sheena was born during that first summer on the boat.

By the second summer she was walking, and climbing out of her play pen. The combination of toddler, low gunwales and high tide was too harrowing. We sold the boat and moved to Scotland.

We were living on the Gairloch when the marriage ended. Incompatibility covers less a multitude of sins than a number of explanations that would be boring in the telling, and it all comes down to the same thing in the end: the partners are happier apart than together. Sheena and I went to Sussex and I found a job as property mistress in a Brighton theatre: a life that was intensely different and absorbing — until the spring came and I remembered the hills.

We returned to Wales with all our belongings: a few bags, a cot, a radio and a typewriter. For some weeks we lived in a climbing hut in the Gwynant Valley while I looked for work. Here I met Johnnie Lees who was leader of the R.A.F. Mountain Rescue team at Valley on Anglesey. I met him in a bar one night at Easter and he saw me back to the hut: down the long track that was to lead eventually to Maen y Bardd and my coming home up the mountain after a day's guiding.

He told me of a vacancy for a youth hostel warden in the

Conway Valley. I applied for the job and got it. Rhiw Farm was a self-cooking hostel so I was really only a caretaker and I received a caretaker's wages: one pound a week during the first summer, ten shillings during the winter. Coal and oil were supplied by my employers. I had a rise of fifty per cent at the start of the second year and, since I was starting to sell scripts to the B.B.C., we were managing to live fairly well. But when I fell ill at the start of the second winter I was already wondering if I couldn't do something better, something a little more remunerative. Encouraged by Johnnie and my friends I applied to the British Mountaineering Council to become a guide. There were no women guides and the challenge appealed to me. I wasn't sure about taking up full-time guiding because this would mean Sheena going to boarding school.

When I fell ill the issue was decided. My doctor told me the hostel life was too strenuous, mainly because there was no way up the mountain except on foot and I had to carry everything on my back from the bus stop in the village: provisions, hostel equipment, even Sheena when she was tired.

My mother handed me my guide's certificates as I was coming out of the anaesthetic after the second operation.

I gave up the hostel, Sheena went south to attend a small school near my mother while I moved north to lodgings and a job in Fort William. In my opinion I didn't possess the qualifications of a guide. Through the following winter I set to work to obtain them. During the week I drove a travelling shop but at the weekends I climbed: alone, with friends, or with the Kinloss Mountain Rescue team of which Johnnie was now in charge.

I started guiding in the spring. I was an itinerant guide, travelling from Scotland to the Lakes and Wales and back again. Sheena joined me for the holidays, either in Sussex or in the mountains.

After a year of this, living in tents and barns and furnished cottages, I started to look for a permanent place. Then I remembered Maen y Bardd: the empty house across the fields from the Welsh youth hostel. I started negotiations with the owner and rented the place at fifteen pounds a year.

Until now I had lived in a series of more or less temporary refuges forced on me by circumstances: a barn where I could recover from a broken leg, a rented cottage for the Christmas holiday, a few days in an hotel because my tent had been ripped by a cow. Maen y Bardd was different: I didn't move out to do a job, I went away – and, when engagements were cancelled, and at the end of the season, I came back and picked up the threads: working in the garden, casting an eye over the animals and their progeny. The land was used for grazing cattle, sheep and ponies so I had the fun of living on a farm with just enough responsibility to amuse me. I kept an eye on the animals and rang the bailiff if anything went wrong.

Life assumed a rhythm dominated by the seasons. Summer went out with the first of the autumn gales and the ponies came up to winter on the mountain. Snow appeared on the tops, first a dusting, then a cover, then blizzards and soft white drifts. While the lane was still passable for a tractor, the bailiff brought loads of hay which I fed to the cattle when they could no longer get at the grass. The thaw came, and floods, and at last a day when I was suddenly shocked out of my mental hibernation by the blatant explosion of spring. I had been aware, even in the autumn, that there were tight catkins on the hazels, but I'd forgotten them through the winter. Now, perhaps after a week of driving rain, the sun shone on a still morning with the first celandines on the banks and all the birds singing.

The sheep were taken down to the valley before lambing time, but after the new grass came through (and when the lambs were strong enough to climb the mountain) the flock came back – usually in the afternoon, so that the first night was full of frenzied shouting as the ewes sought their lambs which had become separated in the confusion of the journey.

When I wasn't working there were a hundred diversions to fill the day: watching the long-tailed tits bringing food to their young in the nest beside the barn, getting up at dawn with no more reason than to see the hares feeding, shopping in the village on foot because you missed so much if you went down the lane in a car.

The lane was slightly sunken between banks topped by high hedges. We found the earliest primroses here and later there were foxgloves. After our first summer I suggested to Mr Parry, our wiry little roadman, that he should wait till the foxgloves were past their prime before he came up the lane to tidy the verges with his hook. Mr Parry agreed with his eager smile — but I didn't trust him: the Welsh are too polite to disagree. When, next summer, and all subsequent years, I saw that he waited till the foxgloves had bloomed, there was a new *entente* between us.

There were grass snakes in the lane, which was the main reason for not using the car on hot days. My mother, town bred but of country extraction, said she'd once known a woman in Sussex who could smell snakes. She didn't claim this distinction for herself (no more than she thought it unusual that she should be related to a Sussex witch), but she could find a snake without knowing where it was.

"Go quietly," I'd say, "there's usually one basking behind that big clump of primroses."

But the hollow, so obviously used, would be bare.

Coming back from the village she'd say:

"Don't talk; we may see the snake."

"He's found somewhere else. Actually I haven't seen him for ages. I just thought he might be there."

She'd peer and part the leaves, move away and peer again.

"Come on, you're miles from where I've seen him."

"No, wait. I think he's here."

And she'd find him, coil on gleaming coil, like a miniature python — and fast asleep. We'd go away quietly; it was bad manners to wake sleeping animals.

An old oak stood beside the gate that opened on our land. It was so old its bark was riddled and tubular. Some of these passages ran into the lower limbs, some were blind ends. I found this out when I came on a snake sunning himself at the foot of the trunk. He was startled, but like all wild animals, he had his escape route: one of the tubes up the bark. Now the bark had been rubbed away by cattle for the first few feet but there must have been some rugosities on the exposed wood because the snake seemed to spring upwards straight into the base of a tube. But he'd chosen the wrong one. He disappeared, then to my astonishment, his head appeared at the base of another passage. Seeing me he dived up the next one and these antics continued (at one time the head appeared below one passage while the tail dangled beneath its neighbour) until eventually the correct route was found, all movement stopped and I almost heard the delicate hiss of relief.

Sheena came home for all the holidays. She loved the animals and spent hours playing with the ponies, riding them with a rope bridle I made, trying to tame the calves. She liked organisation so long as she didn't feel organised. Apparent casualness, whims of the moment, were accepted if there was a semblance of motive. "Let's go to the top of the mountain" or "let's explore the ravine" were received in doubtful silence, but if I said we must go to the ravine to pick bluebells because Johnnie was coming, or that if we went up the hill we could see if the wild mare had dropped her foal, these were met with enthusiasm.

The wild ponies were ragged animals compared with the fat ones which wintered at Maen y Bardd, but they *were* wild. They didn't winter on the mountain, they lived there all the time. We watched them through binoculars and if we came

Maen y Bardd

Pipistrella

Jet

on them suddenly, feeding in a sheltered hollow, they galloped. Once, on the high plateau of the Carneddau, I had come on a small herd with a stallion. I knew they were shy as deer, but when the mares clustered together and the stallion came out in front and snorted and stamped his hooves, I went away. He was too noble to challenge.

Not all our leisure time was taken up with exploring. There was a lot to do about the house, particularly in the garden. The ground was dug in the autumn and manured during the winter. During early spring I would be busy carrying bucket-loads of mole-hill earth for seed beds. Then came the sowing: first earlies, second earlies and main crop, with every morning marked by a solemn inspection to see what was coming through. The garden had been untended for so long that none of the resident birds had the slightest interest in seeds. I concentrated on vegetables and there wasn't much room for flowers but I had sweet smelling ones under the windows: night-scented stock and mignonette – and there were lupins: great clustered spires of orange and pink and blue against the old grey walls.

At this time I was doing little serious writing, only the occasional B.B.C. script or magazine feature, and the money I earned would have kept us at subsistence level but for the garden and the land. Greens lasted us till Christmas and then the stored root crops took us through till spring. The kitchen was hung with curious pendulous muddles of spikes and globes which was the nearest I could get to Breton onion strings – but the onions were good. And apart from the traditional jams and jellies I experimented with exotic hedgerow blends and came up with rowan and crab-apple jelly: deliciously tart, and rich flame held against the light. The visual aspect of one's store cupboard is one of its joys.

The days were never long enough and yet there was no feeling of being crowded. If you'd been watching one group of mushrooms you knew you must be there at the right moment to beat the flies to them but you got up earlier to do it. The red squirrels and the jays must be raced to the hazel nuts but you couldn't say we were part of the rat race; after all there were enough nuts — and brambles and wild plums — for all of us on the mountain.

CHAPTER 2

Cats and other Occupational Hazards

AT THE HOSTEL I had a tortoiseshell cat. She came as a kitten to catch mice and when I started guiding she went to live with a woman at the foot of the hill. No one knew what happened to her in the end. She had a litter there but the kittens were eaten by a rat or a weasel, and the cat disappeared and was never seen again.

With my absences from Maen y Bardd I felt it unfair to have another animal so I made no effort to find a successor. They found me.

I was doing the washing in the dairy one winter morning when a little black queen came trotting down the back entrance. She was hungry and pregnant and I fed her. She stayed with me until my next trip to Scotland and when I returned she was gone. I discovered that she belonged to a neighbouring farm. "You took my best mouser," the farmer grumbled at me.

I protested, but anyone who feeds a stray animal in the country is guilty of enticement. I knew the kittens would be drowned so I asked for one; it wasn't that I wanted a kitten; I didn't want the little cat to lose all her litter.

There must have been some emanations going out from me as I left the farm, some wave of feline sympathy of which I was unaware. As I passed the youth hostel, untenanted in winter since I left it, a little black cat came running through the grass. "Pipistrella!" I scolded.

But Pipistrella's eyes were green and this one had yellow

eyes. So Jet arrived, trading on my emanations, and now, ten years later, is still with us.

While she came to me in the first place, she shifted her allegiance almost as soon as she met Johnnie. Perhaps this was because, after her arrival, for four years we seemed always to have kittens. I acquired a shuffling gait through the need, in a rather dim house, to kick kittens out of doorways before treading on them.

Jet was more attached to people than to cats. She was an adequate mother physically but she lost interest after her progeny were weaned. It was I who had to referee their squabbles and supervise their meals. I who looked out on hearing screams from the bog, to see the short-eared owl making dummy runs at a clump of sedges; and I who had to nip down and rescue the most reckless kitten, Eartha Kitt, just before her nerve broke and she was borne off to provide dinner for the owlets. I had no patience with her; we all knew the owl hunted the bog every day in the middle of the afternoon.

In the evenings, as soon as I settled by the fire, the kittens made a concerted rush for my lap. It was no wonder that Jet went to Johnnie.

Pipistrella's kitten, which I'd saved from drowning, came to me when he was weaned: a black and white tom wild with fear. I had to bring him home in a string sack where he lay in the bottom screaming. I shut him in the parlour for a few hours, then went and sat with him all evening. After three days of this enforced propinquity, when he'd got so far as to sit by my feet in front of the fire, I took him out. All his fear returned and I was the only familiar object in a hostile world. A sheep moved and he rushed to crouch on my feet. I picked him up and he snuggled inside my coat. He found very quickly that if fear could be conquered in one direction, you could have it all ways. He began to bully Jet. He was a very personable little cat. He thought like a human – not always to his advantage. When a mouse disappeared down a hole, instead of crouching quietly and waiting, he put his front paw in up to the shoulder and raked about while he stared absently into the middle distance, all concentration on that paw. He took to inspecting any hole in this way and it was inevitable that eventually he should hit on the one the little bees lived in.

I was sitting in the sun on the doorstep drinking coffee, and feeling very much involved with himself exploring the new hole, when suddenly his squint of concentration changed to one of outrage. He did a back somersault and came down with every hair on end, spitting obscenities. The first bee, also very angry, blundered out of the hole. I rolled with my coffee and kicked the door shut. Jake Stoat was quicker: I had one glimpse of a black and white streak curving over the gate and he was gone.

I called him Jake Stoat because of his habit of rearing high with craned neck to see over the tops of tall grasses. Johnnie, briefed beforehand, had found a home for him on Anglesey. I let him go reluctantly.

At Maen y Bardd I saw rather more of Johnnie than I had at the youth hostel. The responsibility of a home – and this particular home – meant that he was needed more often to attend to chores which were beyond my strength and ingenuity. I ran the house but he maintained it – with the exception of the garden which was my province. He made the stile at the bottom of the garden and re-hung gates. The gates weren't our responsibility but since we used them they were our concern. He made an ingenious framework on the principle of a yoke which enabled me to carry the chemical closet and a full bucket of water without the contents slopping over my legs. Sewage was dumped in a seemingly bottomless trough by the ruined pig sties. The lavatory was in a lean-to shed in the garden. A sycamore stood above it which meant that in stormy weather there were distractions, either loud

$$\frac{B}{6}$$

drops plopping on the tin roof, or the constant fear that a branch might come down and crush you, not *in flagrante delicto*, but not decent either. If you left the door open you looked out on the Carneddau.

The path to the lavatory was approached by two uneven slabs of stone below the terrace. If I hadn't cut back the ferns these were slimy in wet weather. For this reason when we had visitors we moved the closet to the old bakehouse which was reached from the back door by way of level cement — dry because this entrance was roofed with slabs. There were little ferns in all the cracks and a wren nested well out of reach of the cats.

In the bakehouse there was a huge oven cater-cornered, and the chimney. At the base of the chimney there was a mound of mortar sent down by nesting jackdaws.

It was gloomy in there and perhaps visitors unused to country life were a little confused by their surroundings. George Sneed, the craftsman in wood, brought his Italian wife to stay and Anna dropped her wedding ring in the closet. It took us an hour to recover it, fishing with sticks. Nor was the bakehouse as private as it might have been. Smokers complained that they felt guilty because their smoke drifted up through chinks in the slates and obviously annoyed the bats which hung from the rafters.

Another small point which the Sneeds found disturbing was that during their visit, when one went to the lavatory one was accompanied by a band of purposeful kittens. All our litters were house-trained, but since mother cats train by example, and I had the fostering of the kittens after weaning, it was only natural that when I went to the lavatory the kittens queued beside me to use the mound at the foot of the bake-house chimney.

"You'll have to do something," George complained, "no one has any privacy."

It was unfortunate that the next day was wet. After break-fast I put on an oilskin and started along the back passage, bound for the open moor. The kittens stopped at the bake-house and waited politely for me to return. Why go and get your feet wet when you could do it in the dry? So we had to wait till the rain stopped before we could go out and squat in a solemn row under a hedge.

Weather affected our lives as much if not more than it affected the farming community. There was the problem of fuel for instance. We agreed with our landlord that no tree should be cut down but we pounced like vultures on those that fell in the gales. We had a cross-cut saw and wedges and once the logs were cut into manageable lengths I could do the rest myself. Splitting logs on an autumn afternoon, stacking the ingle-nook with rows of raw-smelling ash and sycamore, was one of my most primitive satisfactions.

Coal came by the lorry load, once a year. Only Land Rovers and tractors could negotiate our steep track, and the coalman had to make a six-mile detour to come *down* to us. A tarred lane ran below the spur of little peaks to the south and this came out on our mountain about a mile away and four hundred feet higher than Maen y Bardd. The last mile of this journey was on the Roman track that ran above our fields. It was gratifying to think that our fuel came by way of a road that was still good after nearly two thousand years.

The reason why the coalman came once a year was that the fields between us and the Roman road could be traversed by a loaded lorry only when they were bone-dry. So we had to wait for a drought before we could order coal. If we ran short Johnnie brought bags up in the Land Rover.

If dry weather was welcomed for some things (and par-ticularly we needed it for the climbing – most of our climbing and all the rescues were made more hazardous by bad weather) at the same time there were occasions when I longed for rain.

The cottage must have been built on a geological fault; most of the springs emerged on the eight-hundred foot contour line. Our water supply came from a spring, but this wasn't constant. During droughts or periods of low rainfall it dried up. But two fields away, towards the hostel, there was a good stream which never dried out. Washing clothes in cold water is not very satisfactory, but I could compromise. Since I had to carry water during droughts for drinking, on wash-days I carried treble the usual quantity, washed and boiled clothes at the cottage, then carried them across the fields to be rinsed. The bullocks were a hazard here: the stocky black Welsh cattle which had the run of the farm. Since I fed them in winter, not only with hay but with old kale and sprout tops from the garden, they were unduly affectionate and chased me when they were bored. I gave them a run for their money and they danced after me, darting in with tossing heads then sheering off with gay twisting kicks that made one anxious about slipped discs. The bull and the old cows watched with heavy disapproval.

In the summer, as I crossed the fields loaded with wet washing, the bullocks remembered the winter game and came galloping down the mountain for another round. Going across to rinse the washing involved a stealthy undercover skulk along the hedges because they got still more excited if they spotted you. Bullocks, just because they are bullocks, are a little retarded, and they are quite sure any stealth is all part of the game.

After weeks of this sort of lark I welcomed the first storm clouds and set buckets under all the down pipes in case it turned out to be only a shower.

The landlord came to our rescue with a galvanised tank. The water supply, which previously had been just a shallow pool that I'd dammed with sods and which leaked abomin-ably, was connected with the tank and now we had a reser-voir of eight hundred gallons. Nevertheless, we still had to carry water in times of drought when the contents of the tank became so stagnant we couldn't use it even for washing.

The water pipe from the tank to the house was very old. In

frosty weather it sprang leaks, and it was a devil of a job trying to expose these with a man-size pickaxe and the ground
so hard every blow sent a jar right down your spine. I was
lucky in that the leaks usually occurred in the same place so
I knew where to dig. I mended them with plastic sheeting
bound with binder twine.

The water problem was always with us: either the lack of it
or too much. On the mountain itself springs seemed few and
far between, but in our kitchen we had seven. We'd be playing Scrabble in the evening when I'd feel a shadow of uneasiness. Something was wrong: had I heard an unidentified
sound, was a cat crying to come in, were the sheep in the
garden? Something would move in a corner, a little later it
moved again, and gleamed. Sheena would follow my glance.

"The springs are up."

We had two rooms downstairs: the kitchen with its flagged
floor where we lived most of the time, and the parlour
where we camped in times of flood. As the water rose we man-
handled the easy chairs into the other room, then the big
trestle table, the books from the lower shelves of the book-
case, the cats' baskets. We rolled up the mats and put them
in the dairy. Then we lit the parlour fire and resumed our
Scrabble while, in the kitchen, the seven springs came up
one by one until they covered the floor and the water moved
out into the tiny tiled hall then – fortunately – flowed out of
the front door before it reached the parlour.

Some time after the heavy rain stopped, and presumably
when the mountain had drained off, you noticed – as you
cooked in gum boots at the calor-gas stove – that the water
was no longer welling up in the corners. The springs had
stopped; now you had to dispose of the lake on the floor.

Below the range was a grating over a deep ash pit. We
took up the grating and swept the water down the hole where
it seeped away immediately. The house was two hundred
years old and could have had no foundations. Then we lit the
fire and tried to dry out.

The fire was picturesque but not effective. Even when I'd draught-proofed the two doors in the kitchen, it was still one of those fires which roasted you on one side although most of the heat seemed to be escaping up the enormous chimney. We had constant boiling water because a huge iron kettle hung on a chain from a gibbet affair, but obviously the whole arrangement, for all its quaintness, was uneconomical.

Johnnie came up one weekend with Bill Trench, a burly chimney sweep who was the only man I'd trust to wreck and repair my kitchen. They tore out the old range and installed a square, flat-topped ship's stove which had been thrown out by the youth hostel. "To cook for 30 men" it said on a plaque on the copper water tank, and it did. I'd cooked on it for the rescue teams at the hostel.

Various modifications were needed. The stove wouldn't draw and they were forced to run a flue right up the chimney and out of the top, and even then it sooted up quickly and I had to clean the flues every third day, sometimes every day in still weather. But when it was drawing properly we could sit in the kitchen on winter nights in our shirt sleeves.

We were grateful for that warmth on bath nights. Johnnie bathed at the camp, but Sheena and I used a tin tub in front of the stove. Emptying this was rather tricky. With the cold water which we'd added, the bath was too heavy even for both of us, and water had to be ladled into buckets and taken piecemeal to the sink in the dairy.

We were lucky to have the sink. When we first came to Maen y Bardd there were some people in the village who not only carried water from a communal tap in the street, but who carried all their dirty water out and put it on the garden. The village got its main drainage system while we were there though, of course, we weren't included.

At first everyone was excited by the novelty of The Drain: the excavator, the pipes, the magic of purifying tanks, but soon they became *blasé* and stopped walking down after chapel on Sundays to inspect the diggings. Before they reached this stage however, The Drain was the main topic of conversation in the pub. I was given colourful and conflicting accounts of the intricacies of modern sewage disposal, and already the old days, the pre-Drain days, were being recalled with nostalgia. We remembered Mrs Williams Chapel who had a bathroom installed at great expense because she was convinced that she would never see main drainage in her lifetime.

This was in my hostel days. I remember Mrs Owen Jones demanding dramatically:

"And where's all the water going out of Mrs Williams Chapel's toilet, I'd like to know? I'll tell you where it's going. *And* where it's coming up. In Tom Hallelujah's cellar!"

(Hallelujah because he used to drive a steam roller and one Sunday morning drove it up the village street, drunk but singing hymns: "Hallelujah" right through the congregation coming out of chapel.)

"I *like* the Welsh," Johnnie said, stumbling up through the bog after a gay evening, steering by the glow-worms and getting nowhere, "don't you like the Welsh?"

I reflected that when you get a twisted Welshman there are dark things in his soul which seem to be darker with him than with anyone else. Then I thought of some evil Englishmen and John Knox and the Campbells in Glen Coe. Yes, taken generally, I'd sooner live with the Welsh than with any other people.

CHAPTER 3

High Sanctuary

EVERY WINTER Johnnie went to Scotland to train potential team leaders. When the Christmas holiday was over I went too. While she was alive I stayed with a friend near Fort William who was suffering from disseminated sclerosis. I had met her when I was driving my mobile shop. She lived with her husband and family in the Great Glen. I would stay with her for a few weeks helping with the housework.

We sat in the kitchen with Ben Nevis on the other side of the glen while I talked about books and films, people and travel. I was full of despair. I didn't ask why it had to happen — like sceptics asking Christians why God allows babies to be burned by napalm. I knew I had to accept Janet's condition and I couldn't. She had been a fell-walker, and in a day or two I'd be up there on the Ben and she'd be down here, slowly dying — at forty-six — of an incurable disease. Later she was admitted to hospital and because her brain was now affected it had to be a mental hospital. Her ward was approached through dim corridors where listless patients stared at me blankly. I was allowed to go there out of visiting hours and my presence in the ward caused a little excitement. Janet, lying swollen and still in bed (always in bed now; she had lost the use of her legs) was childishly resentful when the nurses asked me to go and take tea with the walking patients. Some of these seemed happy enough but others sat immobile, lost in their own grey world.

After one such visit I went to a doctor friend and confessed my feelings of horror and inadequacy.

"You don't have to be upset," he told me, "she feels nothing. It's a vegetable existence."

"What will happen to her?"

"She'll die soon: pneumonia or septicaemia."

"How — septicaemia?"

"Bed sores."

The mountains were a sanctuary: not just a way of blocking things out, but a positive help too. You went up angry, bewildered, depressed; you went up dirty, feeling that a heap of rock and ice could do no good — but you went because you'd made the arrangement and in any case, there was nothing else to do. And as you topped the first steep rise above the Great Glen the mountain stood up in front and hit you hard and all your love and aggression surged up in response. The mountain was something you could get your teeth into.

On a good day in winter the Ben is all glitter and shadow, diamonds and ermine, and silence so deep you can hear the wind in the ravens' wings. With a gale sweeping the summit plateau it's hell; but behind the blizzard it's worse: an implacable presence in an ambiance of violence. It takes everything you feel, absorbs it and, at the right moment, throws it back. Here you come down to essentials: love and passion, respect and awe, but never indifference.

Johnnie met me one March evening and we slept at a croft outside Fort William. I woke early next morning and lay and listened to the wind. He moved beside me and I knew he was listening too.

"What's it like?"

"Miserable. Snowing."

"The light's wrong for that."

Through a gap in the curtains we could see a strip of cloud. A new calf bleated in the byre.

"It's spring," he said, "hard snow, ice pitches, blue sky. Come on, get cracking."

"What do you think?" he asked as we threaded our way through the boulder fields and the great buttresses came into view one by one, plastered with snow, and the cloud down to three thousand feet.

"Let's do Gardyloo Gully," I said, and he stared at me.

It was past eleven o'clock, there was a strong wind on top and the weather was an unknown quantity.

"It's short," I said, "and only one hard pitch; we can go and look at it."

It was a day for looking; even in the glen you could hear the wind in the summit rocks. We dropped our gear at the hut at the foot of the face and headed up into Observatory Gully. Gardyloo was at the head of this, hidden in the mist. There was avalanche debris underfoot, but it was old and hard, covered with new snow. The latter was inches deep in places, balling in our crampons, so we took to the windswept slopes at the side, and moved easily up the long incline to below the foot of our proposed route where we stopped and uncoiled the rope.

We were in the cloud now. As we climbed, the snow, trapped between the gully walls, became deeper and the angle steepened. We led alternately, sometimes kicking till the crampons found a purchase in the good layer underneath, sometimes cutting steps. It was warm work, and pleasant so long as the rubbish the leader sent down missed the second. In turns we ran out a lot of rope and the clods of ice had a long way to travel; they were rotating fast by the time they passed the one belayed, vulnerable as a sitting duck, on the bare slope below.

It started to snow and the drifting flakes mixed with spindrift blowing off the walls so that we climbed in a strange pale world where even the rope and ourselves were drifted white, and we moved so slowly as to seem immobile in the whirling snowstorm.

We passed under a great arch of rock and knew we were close to the crux. I found a crescent-shaped ledge at the side of the gully and belayed.

I watched Johnnie as he moved away, not far, and saw him stop; he'd be looking for a chockstone — we would need a good anchor here. A wall of grey ice impended above him; I couldn't see its top. I didn't like this at all so I turned to contemplate the view and what Johnnie refers to in ghoulish delight as "the situation". The view was the gully walls coated and bubbled and bulging with ice; the situation was the slope running down to the lip under the arch and then — nothing. I looked back at the great pitch and suddenly I was very cold.

"Come on," he called, and I moved sluggishly towards him, seeing as I approached that he was belayed in a cave, seeing that he'd already started work on the ice pitch.

I stopped a few feet below him and stared at the bulging wall.

"I've cut the first two holds," he said gently.

"Seventy feet?"

"No, not as much as that — and I've got a splendid belay."

When two people have done hard climbs together for a long time there's little they don't know about each other's technical ability, which is one thing, about each other's guts, which is another. A leader's greatest asset is a sympathetic second.

I was aware of my world waiting: Johnnie in the cave, the feel of the axe in my gloved hand, the ice wall — and there was I, the fourth part in this world, and my moving would fuse the parts.

I moved and it all clicked into place; there was the sudden drive of adrenalin, the impatience to be away; my face felt strained as I clenched my jaw hard, clamping down on this fever of anticipation. I took the little hammer from him, adjusted my slings just right, and then I turned and studied the ice. Only the placing of the first holds could be worked out from here, after that I didn't know how I'd be balanced and would have to play it off the cuff.

For the first few feet I was able to wedge myself against the opposite wall and work, not really putting my shoulder into it because I'd looked down and thought how strange it was that a leader could actually hear the thud of a falling body on hard snow, had waited for Johnnie to curse my hesitation, had cursed it myself, and then I'd retracted my nervous tentacles back from the fall, the slide and the drop, back from Johnnie, and I'd focused on the job in hand. Beside me was a great icicle, not pendant but embedded: a pillar of ice.

I put a sling round it and clipped the rope into the carabiner. Now I could fall only a few feet, now I could work.

I forgot the exposure, forgot that I was on the crux of Gardyloo, forgot my second. There was only the bulge and me, and the importance of not skimping the handholds, which was difficult because they were so steeply above my head that I couldn't see where I was cutting. Then, as the bulge pushed me off and out, I turned my head and saw the opposite wall — which had been so friendly below when I was wedged against it — offering itself again for the crucial move. The ice was thin on it but good enough for one small hold. With my gloved left hand frozen in a slot, I leaned sideways and cut the nick that would allow me to step up and past the bulge.

There were a few more holds to cut as the angle lessened, then the fierce overarm swing of the axe, the pick biting deep and steady, and one last heave on the shaft and I was up. With a free hand at last I could rub the spindrift off my frozen eyelashes. I looked up and saw the cornice fifty feet above, hanging in hazy eaves from the summit ridge. The snow-ice was hard, steep but safe. I moved up carefully until I found a place where I could get the axe shaft well into the surface. I ran the rope behind it, pulled in the slack and yawned.

"Come on," I shouted.

He came up grumbling, asking for a tight rope on the bulge. He went to pass me but I stopped him. It was *my* gully – and my finish.

There was a place where the cornice didn't overhang; it was merely vertical. I brought him up close and out to the side and watched critically as he belayed. This was potentially more dangerous than the crux. The cornice wasn't in ava-lanche condition but it couldn't be climbed as it was. I must have brought down at least a ton of snow ("Hell! You don't think anyone's coming up behind us?") then I had a steep trough floored with the old hard stuff. I kicked up this and over the top and suddenly there was nothing in front. Before there had been a white screen: of ice or snow, with palest shadows, but now, with the plateau covered and not a pebble to focus on, with thick cloud all around, for one dizzying moment you thought you were in limbo.

There was a lot of wind but we didn't mind. There was a pleasant descent of Number Four Gully with the lochan in the corrie below: black water under banks of snow, and an ice floe in the middle; the quiet happy wander down to the hut and the feel of rain in the air.

The days followed with all the caprices of a Highland spring. There were nights when we lay and listened to the rain lashing the roof, days when we read the log book with the blizzard raging and the stove red-hot among the steam-ing clothes. Climbers arrived; some stayed, others went away disgusted, but we waited and watched and worked out our forays from the only material available: observations and past experience, of the Ben and of snow.

Rain at the hut meant new snow on top. This would lie dangerous in the gullies but not, perhaps, in the steeper ones where it could run down to the bottom, leaving the ice pitches clean. High winds were good because they would whip new snow off the crests of the big ridges. On a face as vast as this one should find a route that was feasible, even after a night of storm.

Sometimes the mountain appeared to relent. One morning, after twenty-four hours of rain, we went out to find frost on the grass and the wind swung round to the north. There was a little mist about the summit but in places sunlight touched the buttresses – and we set out for Green Gully.

It was too cold. Although we worked in turns it took so long to climb the first fifteen feet that we retreated. We looked across the corrie and saw the buttress of Number Four Gully shining in the sun, but the wind was too strong: better to freeze in shelter than be blown off an arête, so we moved across to North Gully and found a pitch of over a hundred feet.

Spurred on by the memory of Gardyloo, annoyed by the retreat from Green, I determined to have the lead here: a short-sighted decision – with a bulge coming at the top of a long pitch, cutting holds all the way, and new snow on the ice.

I stopped after sixty feet, dug a stance and brought Johnnie up. I went on, rested but over-confident.

The bulge looked formidable, but I had the pitons. I hammered the long steel into the ice ("the bulge of the long pegs" I thought; why did quotations always come to me at critical moments?). There was something very satisfying about a running belay. There you were, miles above your second, and twice that distance to fall if you came off, but now you had this lovely safe pulley below the hard move. It was a little tricky effecting it while you stood on small holds; first there was the delicate work of detaching the peg from your waist-line, one-handed, the effort of stabbing it into a high hold cut in anticipation, and then the business of detaching the hammer from the slings. Then the solid, satisfying sound of the peg driven home in the watching silence, a carabiner through its eye, and the rope through the carabiner and, at last, the body relaxing — not much, just enough to forget about coming off and to concentrate on getting up.

I climbed the crux but I was tired. The angle relented and I drove in another peg. Inserting it into tough, viscous ice accounted for any energy that remained after the bulge. I rested there and the sweat dried and my muscles stiffened with cold and tension.

I climbed a little farther only to realise that this gully had a sting in its tail: another steepening above the crux just when you thought it was all over.

The retreat to the peg above the bulge was tricky and Johnnie was quite silent. There was no sound at all except for the whispered cracks of my frozen anorak as I stepped down, blessing my caution in placing the footholds close on the way up.

I drove in another peg above the crux and, belayed to two, brought Johnnie up. He passed me very quickly (he was cold) and was over the top in record time. Intent on getting warm, he didn't think about his holds and placed them in odd sequence.

"You've got two right legs," I grumbled, doing continuous mantelshelf moves up that last ten feet.

"You are a mug, Moffat; you'd done all the hard part."

"I know. I thought you should have a lead; even the rope was shivering."

We led alternately and fast to the plateau, into the wind and then out of it again as we came over the top. It was the middle of the afternoon and the Ben was in shadow, but down at the mouth of Loch Linnhe there were silver patches on the water where rays came through the clouds like inverted searchlights. To the south Ben More and Cruachan were luminous shapes, hinting that they were in the sunlight, but it was a stormy sky. To the north-west it was black.

We trotted along the edge, trying to strike a fine line between avoiding the fracture lines of the cornices and the rocks which would strain our crampons. Close to Carn Dearg, at the side of the great funnel that is the top of Number Five Gully, there was no cornice, and we came down easily, stopping occasionally to study the mountain from this angle.

Below us the glen of the Allt a' Mhuilinn was very dark and green, in strange contrast to this nearer world of white and black. Then the threatening snow clouds started to break and blue patches appeared. Above the hut the last sun lingered on the slopes of Carn Mor Dearg, then it was gone and the long grey clouds lay like fish with scarlet bellies over the western hills.

The poor weather continued. We did lesser climbs, and brought a fallen sailor down out of Number Two Gully. We saw ptarmigan in the Castle Corrie and Brigitte Bardot in Fort William. We wallowed in hot baths at the Grand Hotel, having worn the same clothes for over a week when washing had been cat licks in the icy burn.

We returned to the Ben on a bright bitter morning and were defeated immediately on the North-east Buttress. The wind rose and the clouds came up the glen, while spindrift flowed down the sides of the buttress in rivers. I didn't feel my feet for hours. We retreated and in the evening the cloud lifted to show every detail of the mountain clear below a milky sky. It rained for twelve hours, the snowline retreated to three thousand feet, then the temperature dropped and it was snowing at the hut.

We went up Ledge Route and wandered along the edge of the plateau identifying the tops of the gullies. Johnnie suggested we should descend Number Two Gully. This was a new technique to me: descending a gully with an unbroken cornice at the top, and this was the one where the naval party had fallen a few days before; you could still see the chutes where their bodies had swept the gully clean.

Going out to the edge of the cornice and flogging away at it until it sagged below my feet was like sitting on the branch of a high tree and sawing it off between yourself and the trunk. Johnnie pointed out that if I didn't go down first, I must come down last — with no rope from above. I came back from the edge and put on my crampons. The delay and my caution infuriated him but I paid no attention. He hadn't seen the cornice.

I went out to the edge again and started pecking at the snow. He made rude remarks. I looked back at him, noted the solid belay, the tight rope: I could fall only a few feet. I collapsed the cornice with savage hacks, descended the trough carefully, facing in, then found there was nowhere for a stance. There was a skin of new snow on ice, and the ice too hard to take the shaft of an axe. I started to dig a hole, hoping to find a layer that was more accommodating underneath. Johnnie was growing impatient, and here he was, appearing over the edge:

"I'm *frozen*! All you've got to do is cut a stance and belay me. You've been there five minutes and you call yourself a guide!"

He peered at the slope under the trough, at the trough itself, and started to twitter.

"I might fall backwards off this!"

"It would be better not to; I haven't got a belay."

"You haven't got a *stance*!"

"Go back and hold me then. I want a top rope."

He disappeared, muttering. Touch of indigestion, I thought, studying the slope while I waited for my rope to come taut again, mustn't have all these fried breakfasts.

Eventually I found a place where I could get the axe in to a safe distance. He joined me and hacked at the surface.

"It *is* hard, isn't it?"

.   .   .   .   .

We stood outside the hut that evening in our duvets, planning. Cloud was fretted in streamers towards the south-west and the moon was on the tops.

"One more day," he said, "and perhaps Green Gully will be in condition. We've done nothing for a week."

He meant nothing hard. After a week of watching and waiting, of long but strenuous minor routes up and down, now we were ready again, if only the weather would hold. The glass was high; we would give the mountain a day for the snow to consolidate.

Next morning we went straight up Carn Mor Dearg above the hut: two thousand feet of unremitting hard labour, in the shadow at first, panting to reach the sun, then full in that glorious golden glare, and goggles out for the first time this holiday.

It was a day for staring: at the mountain across the rift of the glen; for sitting quietly, idly watching Johnnie drunk with unaccustomed warmth and light, photographing the Ben in sections: Castle Ridge with its crest white against the pewter of Loch Eil, Carn Dearg and its black cliff with the great rock climbs; the funnel of Number Five Gully and the fierce buttresses of the Trident; Tower Ridge and Observatory Ridge and the North-east Buttress: great classic routes up crests, shadowed on one side, shining on the other — and then the lovely bowl of Coire Leis with all the pointed Mamores pushing for prominence through the haze.

We ate our lunch on the Carn Mor Dearg arête, then walked up the long shoulder to the summit of the Ben. At the top of Gardyloo my trough was still visible, but the cornice at the head of Tower Gully was unbroken, waiting to be descended.

I went down first again and the good snow-ice took the whole of the axe shaft. As I brought in his rope I could enjoy my surroundings. Below me the slope was steep and untracked; the gully walls were draped with icicles; some straight, others twisted by the wind into curving talons. The sky was deep and dark, sometimes overdrawn by a fine veil of mist when it paled to mauve: a good sky.

Until now every route we'd climbed had been virgin. It might have been climbed this season but fresh falls had wiped out old tracks. Few people came up the glen and fewer stayed. We were jealous of our privacy and our pristine routes. This day, as we came out of the foot of Observatory Gully, we paused and stared at the hut. The chimney was smoking: we had company.

CHAPTER 4

Company on the Ben

THE ATMOSPHERE of a climbing hut varies with its occupants and your attitude towards them. Sharing the place with one other person you can lead an ordered life, keeping your equipment neatly on empty bunks so that everything is to hand, cooking methodically or even with flair when you're not too tired, washing up in hot water. Then other visitors arrive and quiet organised living is disrupted. Within an hour your small neat world can become the epitome of squalor: a mountain slum. The table is covered with grease and crumbs, your food is handled by a man with a streaming cold who, in default of a handkerchief, blows his nose in his fingers; dirty dishes are set in the sooty pool of paraffin about the Primus stoves, and the dishes themselves, passed perfunctorily through cold water, are left with a revolting veneer of stew.

You try to block out your revulsion by reminding yourself that you are here to climb and nothing else matters, but the fact is that the simple decencies of living are the more essential here where you sleep and eat in one crowded room and where so much mental energy is expended during the day that there is little tolerance left for the night.

That evening as we paused to watch the smoke going up from the hut, I was full of these baleful thoughts and we came down the glen like wary animals wondering what had entered their cave. We were doubly apprehensive because we were no longer booked and had no right to beds.

The hut was crowded: a dozen men, I thought (there were nine). We introduced ourselves. It was a Cambridge University meet. Their president, Peter Mayo, was most courteous. We offered to go but expected and obtained protests. We insisted we should sleep on the floor. They allowed Johnnie's insistence but not mine. We were brought tea. I basked in an atmosphere of respect, of sincere and boyish enthusiasm, of good manners. The snag was their intentions. University clubs have a bad reputation among rescue teams, particularly at the Nevis hut. Cambridge always had good men, I remembered, but "good" could mean lucky gymnasts who got away with severe rock climbs in Snowdonia and came to the Ben to climb hard ice routes before they were proficient on easy snow.

Cambridge were not like this. They were so modest that we thought they were beginners on snow; it wasn't till much later that we learned Mayo had been to the Alps twice, had traversed the Obergabelhorn, and that a large South African called Spottiswoode had spent a season in Austria and the Valais. They asked Johnnie what he suggested for a first day. Far from feeling any resentment at the invasion I felt guilty that all the moderate gullies were sullied by our tracks. At least they should have had the cornices intact.

Next morning they breakfasted early and left the hut in meticulous order.

"It's not true what they say about university clubs," I remarked.

"You've only seen them in the hut."

"That's one of the things I go by."

"Just because they leave the table clean!"

"*And* get in water and coal, and put their food away, and none of them snores. They're too young, I suppose."

Cambridge lightened the atmosphere. Usually, in the evening, when you went outside for a last look at the Ben, you felt presumptuous to be planning a route up it for the next day. But last night, staring up at it, with the others having their first sight of this face in the moonlight – and the lilting tune of the Elizabethan Serenade coming from inside the hut – then the Ben lost some of its remoteness and became an adventure: hard, but like the young men, fun.

At eleven thirty we stood at the bottom of Green Gully dodging the icicles which came trickling down the runnel from the summit rocks.

"What a miserable vocation," I said, watching two figures prancing up Number Five Gully in the sun, "incarcerating ourselves in a north-facing gully on a day like this."

"We'll soon be in the sunlight," he said.

I looked at the third pitch (we could see three or four) and I said nothing. The third pitch was supposed to be the crux – if you didn't do the bottom one. Most people avoided this, but for Johnnie it was all the gully or nothing.

There were eighty feet of ice to start. I wasn't wearing my duvet, having hoped the first pitch would be climbed in the hour and that I would retain the heat which I'd engendered trudging up the corrie. I was wrong. The pitch took nearly two hours. It involved a false cast on the right wall before he found the true line, and the climbing was on ice under rotten snow. After an hour of this, when I'd reached the stage of controlled shivering to keep warm, I insisted on putting on my duvet. Johnnie, balanced on small holds, watched expressionlessly. Leaders keep warm and lose all sense of time. It needs recurrent spells of being second themselves to remind them what it's like to stand still in snow for long periods with the temperature below freezing and the wind in the north.

After the first pitch we struck a better system; he led the ice pitches, I led the relenting slopes between. This, I thought, scraping my way up what was now good solid snow-ice, is perfect – and I'd get to the foot of the next pitch, belay and turn and gulp. The gully was straight as an air shaft; below its foot a steep slope dropped into the corrie, so looking down was harrowing: the pitch I'd led, himself seemingly on the very lip, then the corrie a thousand feet below. I had thought after Gardyloo I might have the makings of an ice technician. Green Gully cut me down to size.

As we climbed, two figures appeared on top of one of the buttresses and stood in the sun watching. It was so still that when they spoke to us we could hear every word although they must have been half a mile away and several hundred feet higher. A little later they came glissading down Number Three Gully and out of sight, going back to the hut and tea. We had the face to ourselves now in a silence so profound that you were aware of the slightest noise: the rope rasping over ice, the light scrape of the adze, sharp pecking of the pick — and then the metallic ring of a piton hammered home.

The snow grew deeper in the upper part: deep but sound, and I could kick steps. It was still afternoon; we would finish this one in the daylight. We were moving fast now; we hadn't been extended on the middle pitches and we thought the difficulties were over. They were in a sense because the fifth pitch, although it bulged at the top, was not severe, but Johnnie — perhaps aware of exposure and fatigue — used two pitons on the crux, first a tubular peg, then an ice spike.

We were high now, at about four thousand feet, and no sun had touched the gully all day — all the season perhaps. I climbed happily to the tubular peg and it lifted out like a charm as I passed. I reached the ice piton which was driven in hard. Johnnie had the hammer.

"Bang it with the axe!"

I banged.

"Take both hands to it!"

"I'm on the bulge!"

"Hang on the rope then!"

It was no good — even though I grew so fierce every time I swung, my feet came off the holds. The peg had frozen in. It took me half an hour to dig it out with the pick and even then the tough ice held it to the last inch. I crawled up to him exhausted.

I panted past him, the angle steepening as I approached the

top. There was one last pitch, making six in all. Thirty feet above, the rocks were tawny in the late sun.

There was no cornice. I stepped out of the gully and saw the rim of the sun slip down behind a belt of haze.

We came down in the sunset: all peacock colours tonight – emerald and aquamarine with a hint of purple in the clouds, while almost overhead the moon was in its second quarter.

There was mist outside the hut next morning. Again we let Cambridge get away first, bound for the ridges: Tower, Observatory, the North-east Buttress. We followed gloomily but as we approached Coire Leis the clouds broke and figures appeared on the first platform several hundred feet above us and silhouetted against the sky.

With the sun on the flank of the North-east Buttress the traverse to the first platform was menaced by falling icicles. We led through and while I was belayed I remembered a perfect murder where the victim had been stabbed through the skull with an icicle. Balaclavas seemed scant protection.

It was bitterly cold. We had the advantage of tracks but we were only too quickly aware that Cambridge were following the summer route, not always the best in winter. They were tigers on rock, judging by the line they took, and often it would have been simpler to take an alternative way, but, faced with a choice between untrodden snow and steeper rock where the holds had been cleaned, we chose the latter, and Johnnie grunted and heaved while I froze on the stances, swearing that this buttress was the hardest, apart from the longest of the four. The North-east Buttress is less a snow and ice climb than a winter rock climb: a serious proposition, and near the top, when you're tired, comes the Man Trap.

For some time Johnnie had been asserting how hard, excruciatingly hard was the next pitch; that we were slow, we would be benighted. But as we were high now and there was neither sight nor sound of the others, I reasoned that they were over the difficulties and what they could climb, we could follow.

Johnnie belayed to a rock peg and brought me up to the Man Trap. We stood and looked at it. In summer the pitch is a ten-foot wall, Very Difficult in standard. Today its height was the same but the holds were glazed with ice. Johnnie wanted me to lead. I argued for a while, then I thought: it's only ten feet — and launched myself at it. I climbed until I could peer over the top and take stock. In summer this is a mantelshelf move but today the ledge had a thick covering of snow and ice which sloped towards me. A mantelshelf on the edge of that would mean abrupt precipitation backwards. I climbed down and pondered, looking for an alternative. There was none. I made another attempt at it; after all, a fall of ten feet: I could scarcely hurt myself, let alone do serious damage — and it was so humiliating and uncomfortable to be benighted.

It's astonishing how attitudes can change in ten feet. Looking up, I castigated myself for a coward; pawing at the icy ledge for a second time I chided myself for a fool. You could do considerable damage if you fell badly — even ten feet. I came down again to point out that the crucial move needed a long reach: I'd made two attempts, now it was his turn.

He untied his sack and pulled out the *étriers*. Well, I could have done it with a ladder. He left the axe and took the hammer. Festooned with ironmongery he climbed to my highest point. Reaching up, he inserted an ice peg and clipped an *étrier* to it. Another peg and a second *étrier* provided the solution and, climbing like pot-holers up ladders, we escaped the Trap.

The cloud came in again, which was beneficial for us. We were tired and tense: the moment when exposure makes itself felt suddenly, particularly at four thousand feet on this face. But in the mist, traversing the knife-edges, we could see nothing of the drops on either side and we had no more difficulty until we came under the summit rocks and found we must step into a curious bottomless chimney.

We moved along a ledge from the right and there was this corner with the chimney inset beyond it. The precarious part lay in rounding the corner. The ledge ended abruptly and too soon; below there was nothing but cloud.

I didn't see how Johnnie did it; I was belayed well back and his body hid the moves. When it came to my turn I saw I should lean into the chimney – across space – but the far wall was a long reach: I would be horizontal if I left my feet on the ledge and put my hands against the opposite side. I pondered the move and decided that if I jammed the spike of my axe on the icy wall I could use it as support in order to reach round and up with my right hand.

It was a nasty moment: wondering if the axe would shift with all my weight on it. At such moments you forget you're on a top rope and the maxim: the leader must not fall, becomes *one* must not fall. Too many seconds have whipped their leaders off the belay, too many axe shafts have broken. Now, on the Ben in winter, approaching darkness breathes at your back and you put your trust in reason (he *must* have a good belay; the spike will hold on that wrinkle . . .) and you climb, and the spike stays on the wrinkle and there's a good hold for the right hand.

Coming down he insisted that he was doing no more hard routes, he was stale (he had been climbing and walking for six weeks before this holiday). I said I would climb solo.

"On this face? You're mad."

"I'll take you up Moonlight tomorrow then."

He had to agree; the weather was too beautiful to do anything else but climb, and we had only two days left.

It was the name of Moonlight Gully that attracted me: the climb looked as if it rambled too much to be classic – but we'd see another section of the face. You needed a dozen holidays to know the Ben.

As we climbed next day a Cambridge party explored in

our vicinity, appearing and disappearing in unexpected places like curious rabbits. In contrast to the grim grey classic routes there was an aura of fun about Moonlight.

Halfway up the cliff I found a cave where someone had been before me, making a through-route behind a chockstone. The hole was small and the groove below was full of ice. Above the chockstone was a rotten chimney. As I studied this I felt that there was something familiar about the situation but I was too concerned with my own progress to identify it.

I pushed my rucksack through the hole and grovelled after it. The rock above came away in chunks which had to be thrown down. Startled cries wafted up to me.

"Do you have to bring the whole mountain down?"

He was peering out from an overhang, getting cross. He would be regretting that we weren't on a hard route.

I emerged at the top of the pitch to find the Cambridge men lounging in the sun on a ledge below, one demanding indignantly what I was doing in his cave.

I stared at them, suddenly aware of the identity of that feeling down below when I'd been annoyed because rotten rock was no longer cemented to the face by ice. They were sunbathing. Was this the thaw and the end of winter climbing for another year?

One more day and the thaw coming: Johnnie changed his mind and next morning, determined to shoot his bolt, led me up the corrie towards the hard ice gullies on the side of the North-east Buttress. The wind was blustery, inconsistent, backing. It dropped and the snow came: wet soft snow, and as we stood below Zero Gully and watched Cambridge working on the long second pitch, saw the icicles dripping down the bare rock, we knew that everyone must retreat. The winter was over.

Only a few months later we were to be shocked by the news that Mayo and Spottiswoode had been killed on the

Täschhorn, and that two others of the party with whom we'd shared the hut during that last week, had died on the Matterhorn. Cambridge lost four of its best climbers overnight – and I shall never see the Ben in the moonlight again without hearing young men sing.

Ben Nevis in winter

Johnnie at Edale

CHAPTER 5

Guiding Comeback

WHEN I FIRST knew Johnnie we had one thing in common which wasn't obvious – like the climbing. We never planned our lives. There seemed no need to do so in his case; he was happy in Mountain Rescue and had signed on for a long time, and for me it was impossible. To find work all the year round was so difficult that I never looked farther ahead than the bookings for next season. We took everything for granted and left our characters out of consideration completely.

At the time of our marriage Sheena's school closed down and she came home to attend school in the village. I stopped guiding because she was far too young to come home to an empty house in the afternoons and I could no longer go away on trips. And because of uncertain hours and possible emergencies to a large extent I stopped climbing for fun. I didn't deplore this; I accepted that now I should stay home and raise a large family, that there would be no more serious climbing until the children were grown up. For a year I wallowed in domesticity and the new and delightful affluence of an adequate house-keeping allowance. I considered buying a cow and hens. I didn't consider Johnnie. His attitude to women is fundamentally conventional: their place is in the home. At the same time, for him climbing is the most important thing in life. Where I was concerned he suffered no conflict in this respect; he made an exception of me.

We discussed this no more than we planned anything. For a year life seemed to run smoothly, but on the eve of his going to Cornwall to join a course with the Marine Commandos, and when I made some reference to the loneliness of Maen y Bardd in the autumn, he showed me the situation with considerable force and clarity.

He was profoundly disappointed in me. He had married a climber, a professional guide: independent and successful. To give up climbing voluntarily was to him a kind of sacrilege.

I was outraged and angry. I was also hurt, and because of this I knew I was in the wrong. No one can hurt you when you know you're right: you're invulnerable.

I had six weeks alone in which to think but it didn't take six weeks to work things out. Both Johnnie and I saw my position as immoral; he saw a guide being wasted, living on him; I saw a kept woman. If he used forceful arguments to rouse me from my lethargy, he used those which would succeed. The end justified the means. I started to organise my life.

Guiding was seasonal work so I could expect few engagements before Easter. My sales to journals and the B.B.C. had been increasing over the past few years and I reckoned that if I could write well enough to sell talks and articles, I might produce a full-length work. During the coming winter I would write a book.

If Sheena had been happy at Maen y Bardd and the village school I wouldn't have returned to full-time work, but she missed the company of other children in the evenings and at weekends. There was a small boarding school up on the Denbigh Moors. We would try this for a term and if she weren't happy there I would have to reconsider the situation.

When Johnnie returned from Cornwall I had made a start on *Space Below my Feet* and already I had bookings for the following summer. These last were no coincidence. Requests for guiding came in all the time but for a year I had turned them down.

Sheena started at her new school in January. She settled down quickly and I, trying to comfort myself with the thought that if she was happy nothing else mattered, suppressed the emptiness of Maen y Bardd and wrote and climbed – and looked forward to Easter, for during the holidays I could return to domesticity without guilt.

Guiding started with the summer term. Most clients knew that May was one of the best months for weather in the mountains and I went straight from household chores to rock climbing.

For long engagements, a week or more, I saved on petrol and time by going round to the Ogwen Valley and living in a climbing hut, but for day or weekend jobs I lived at home.

I got up early – and with no difficulty. A pair of redstarts nested above the back steps and every morning the cock was up with the dawn and fighting his reflection in the landing window. If it were an off-day and I wanted to sleep late, I had to pin sheets over the glass.

At six o'clock there was a mist lying up the river on good days and usually a cock pheasant with his harem of hens feeding over the garden wall. There were pheasants and hares later in the day too, but it was only in the early morning that they wandered unconcerned about the farm.

I fed the cat after I'd eaten and just before I left. This was to keep her occupied and to stop her following me down to the car. If she did that, she didn't go home but waited under a hedge until I returned in the evening. She was there, a little running shape in the dark, as soon as I cut the engine. If the weather turned cold and wet I preferred to think she was in her hay box in the dairy, rather than keeping vigil under a dripping hedge.

The run down the mountain was a delightful start to the day: plunging through the bog where the wetter parts were clumped with waxy kingcups, bursting through the wild hedge into the Pheasant Field (a sloping bank more than a field where anthills attracted the pheasants) and usually there was a woodpecker feeding on the ground and taking off in a blur of crimson and green, startling the jays as he swooped laughing through the woods.

It was twenty-six miles to Ogwen or Pen y Gwryd where I met my clients, and my old car did it in three-quarters of an hour. The trip never became monotonous. I thought of nine-to-five commuters in crowded trains. This was the way to commute: slowing for the first bridge and the magnolia which grew above it and covered the road with petals; curbing your impatience at a flock of sheep by a calculating appraisal of the lambs, coming through Trefriw and noticing as always how the forested hill was just like the Alps: the firs in shadow under a luminous sky.

One had to remember the hazards: that round this next bend the peacocks from the castle might be all over the road, that red squirrels and blackbirds were active at this time in the morning and could misjudge the speed of an approaching car.

The sun accentuated everything: colours and the scent of flowers, bluebells in the woods, drifts of wild garlic on the verges; even the birds sang more loudly on a fine morning. As I came through Capel Curig the Snowdon Horseshoe lay beyond the lakes, and if I turned right for Ogwen the road would be familiar and so empty that I could watch the black bulk of Gallt yr Ogof—not because that was interesting but because, in a moment, Tryfan would appear behind it, sudden and splendid, standing proud with all the east face shining in the sun.

After the life in the valleys, the busyness of the trip round from Maen y Bardd, the quietness of the cliffs was very marked. Now the only bird song was a wren among the rocks or the sharp clatter of a ring ouzel, and the only human sounds our calls through the distant rush of streams.

Mid-week was the best time for the classic climbs: then we had the cliffs to ourselves and the client saw the routes as they should be, empty and waiting for him, not strung with ropes and novices as they were at the weekend.

There were climbing jobs and walking ones, but the best were those where I had a client for a week or longer and he asked to work up to climbing. Walking, to the layman, is a deceptive term; to the mountaineer it's anything that isn't rock climbing – and it can be considerably more strenuous. I didn't take my clients' word for it that they were fit. We started on something simple like the north ridge of Tryfan: a scramble of two thousand feet where there were wild goats – and a promise of fun to come as I glanced down the top pitches of the east face routes. On the summit, when the more nimble clients had been photographed sitting on the monoliths of Adam and Eve, once I'd pointed out the peaks and they'd realised they were on the lowest of the three-thousand-footers, usually nothing would satisfy them but the turreted line of Bristly Ridge which would take us up on the Glyders. Clients usually wanted to know and see what lay beyond the next hill.

The length of the day and the standard of the route fluctuated with the competence of the weakest member of the party, always bearing in mind, if it was a long engagement, that if the client were pushed too hard he'd soon need a rest and after this the weather might break. He would be cross and I'd lose a day's pay. After five years as a guide I could sum people up pretty well now: how far they could go, when it was advisable to descend, whether it was fear of the unknown or fatigue that made them say in mist or wind: "I feel awfully sick; can't we get off this ridge somewhere?"

I didn't shorten the day with unfit people but took it more slowly; for them Tryfan on its own was as satisfying as the Snowdon Horseshoe for a more energetic person. We stayed out as late as we could, leaving time only for a bath before dinner at the hotel. I was adamant about giving the client his money's worth, so that even when he came down tired, if there was half an hour to spare, I could fill it up with nests or flowers or a detour to visit a waterfall.

From several climbs you could, by ingenious and tricky

negotiation of overgrown ledges, look down on ravens' nests (this was early in the year; young ravens are flown by May); there were at least two cliffs where we'd see peregrines, and there was a merlin up in the back of the Llanberis Pass. There were choughs on the Glyders and foxes everywhere.

On the big black cliffs, in the season, there were cushions of moss campion and purple saxifrage. These, like the ravens' nests, required roped traverses along exposed ledges; too many climbers and keen gardeners had cleared the routes, the gardeners taking the alpines for their rockeries, the climbers thinking a clean hold more valuable than its cover of saxifrage.

At first Johnnie had been amused by my interest in flowers, by my habit of associating them with a climb: a hard traverse identified and remembered by the spires of navelwort marking the start, the difficulty of a crucial move if you avoided trampling on a particularly fine rose-root. He was annoyed though when I pleaded with him to clean away only grass from vegetated climbs, to leave those plants which would die on the exposed scree below. But as he came to realise this was not an affectation he became interested himself and stopped giving me climbing equipment for presents but gave me New Naturalist books instead because he wanted to study them himself.

When a client had walked the hills for a day or two, particularly in good weather, he started to view the cliffs as more than background. He'd glance at nail marks as we came down Cwm Cneifion beside the Idwal Slabs.

"Does a climb go up there?"

"Yes; it's called Suicide Wall."

"What morbid minds you climbers have. Would you be taking me up there?"

"Not just yet. Come on down and look round the corner."

We come out on the level at the foot of the Slabs. Above us the rock sweeps up the mountain, glowing in the sun.

"That crack looks as if I might manage it. Could I?"

"Yes, but it's uninteresting. There's Hope, the one with the twin cracks, and that's Tennis Shoe on the edge."

He ponders and I calculate. Nearly ten days left. With a start on the Milestone Direct, within a week he could manage Tennis Shoe — if he doesn't mind exposure, if he can use his feet.

So it starts: with the next day on the Milestone and First Pinnacle Rib. If he is competent on the wrinkles of the Milestone traverse and the tiny striations of the Yellow Slab halfway up the east face of Tryfan, if he can look down and say: "now why did I find that hard?" instead of: "there's nothing harder above, is there?" the chances are we'll be doing Severes at the end of ten days.

With some clients I never progressed beyond easy climbs. With some I needed very large belays and good places to stand to hold a fall. Most people weighed more than me — one man, at sixteen stone, weighed twice as much. Johnnie said he never had to ask me how it was going; he could judge my clients' competence (and my ability to hold them) by the condition of my back. A running rope can leave a burn that scars for weeks.

Long engagements meant that Maen y Bardd was neglected. Occasionally I'd rush home in the evening to collect mail and give Jet a meal, not so much because she needed one (she stayed fat hunting the mice in the barns) but just to show her she wasn't abandoned.

It was the garden that suffered, and I needed its produce for the summer holidays and the autumn. As I came over the stile I was shocked by the height of the weeds, by the lettuces all crowded together and crying out to be thinned, by the length of the grass on the terrace. In the intervals between jobs I hoed and planted out and got the place into some semblance of order again. I welcomed an off-day not as a respite from work but as a chance to do a fortnight's gardening in twelve hours.

I could earn a decent living as a guide only if I were working every day, and now there were too many guides practising; there wasn't enough work to go round. In the gaps between engagements — if there were time to spare from the garden — I worked on the book.

I followed the sun round the house, naked, but with a dressing gown within reach in case the bailiff came. I started on the front doorstep in the morning and finished on the chopping block which caught the last of the sun before it dropped below the line of the mountain. There was one place in the garden below the wall Johnnie had rebuilt after a heifer crashed through one night, where the temperature was in the nineties in high summer and I had to write in pencil because ink ran on the sweat-soaked paper.

When the sun went down and the dew started to fall, I'd collect my cushions and the cat and go indoors to light the fire. Jet had to be collected because she spent the day sleeping on a shady bank — a little black ball curled up in the pansies — and by nightfall she was so dead to the world she'd be in a kind of torpor from which she had to be wakened, otherwise she'd come in soaked with dew and I'd worry about rheumatism.

On these days I wrote for over twelve hours and by bedtime I was deliciously exhausted but still wrapped in that other world, whatever it was at the moment: Ben Nevis in the snow, a storm on Mont Blanc. My actions: cooking, eating, lighting the lamp, were purely automatic — and productive of rude shocks.

One night I went to the dairy for water. My hand was outstretched in the darkness in case the door was closed. With the other hand I fumbled for the light switch on the door post. We had electricity here: about one candle-power, run off a torch battery. Simultaneously, as one hand clicked the switch (and nothing happened) the other hand encountered something hard and warm and hairy, at shoulder level.

I stood in the doorway, hopefully clicking the switch and trying to summon enough courage to do something else. After a while, from the other side of the room came a long rumbling belch.

I reached up for the battery above the lintel and found the wires.

The light came on to show me a large black cow standing diagonally across the dairy. On the highest shelf in the corner, squashed up among the tooth mugs and watching her with their eyes on stalks, were the two kittens of the moment: Pirbright and Cockroft.

There was no room for the cow to turn round. I had to crawl underneath and back her out.

Welsh summers, any mountain summers, are not, on the whole, a succession of hot lazy days on sun-drenched rock. You can have weeks in June when it might as well be winter, except for the absence of snow. You wear your winter complement of two jerseys and a woollen shirt, breeches and – with a howling wind coming through the tweed – even tights. Some clients are slow and it's cold on the stances. On these days you dream of Yosemite where the hazards of rock climbing are sunstroke and dehydration.

Just plain rain would have been easy to cope with; on wet days I climbed in nailed boots so slimy rock didn't worry me although I had to remember that the client, in rubber soles, would be sliding about like a penguin where my nails held. Rain was all right, it was wind that was so dangerous. With cloud driving over the summit and the clods flying I'd lower the standard until I felt I was over-cautious, and even then the gale would catch us on an exposed section of the climb and I realised that, higher, it could whip me off like dead grass. The only alternative was to abseil and find a climb on a sheltered cliff.

Lockwood's Chimney was the last resort on days when the gale precluded even walking. It starts low in the trees of Nant Gwynant and leads by pleasant little pitches to a black hole in the base of a cliff which, to the client, is fearsome: exposed, vertical and — at this height — naked to the gale.

You dive into the hole, climb up over the chockstone and take a stance above it. The second starts to climb, perhaps a little resentful of the anti-climax, a little bored with the weather and low standard of the climb, with the fact that the guide's attitude indicates this isn't a serious day. He gets stuck at the chockstone in gloom so deep he can't see any holds, and if they were visible his body, contorted in positions he would have thought anatomically impossible until this moment, hides them completely. Sometimes one gives clients the benefit of the doubt when no issues are at stake. It isn't inconceivable he may find a better way of getting up than yourself — but it's unlikely.

"I think you're facing the wrong way."

"I'm facing left."

"You're facing right; I saw your glasses flash."

"How do I face left?"

"What's stopping you?"

"Me."

It wasn't really a place for a bulky novice but we had some good clean fun.

There were days of walking through the lighter gales, half-strength ones, or mist where you steered by the compass, notably on the top of Carnedd Llewelyn where all the rocks looked the same and if you turned round once you were lost. The client, who had no compass and wouldn't have known how to use it if he had, panicked quietly as I consulted mine. This was disaster: the guide had to check — and now we would wander aimlessly till nightfall, then die of exposure and exhaustion. The clients knew of all the fatalities on the mountain of the day but they didn't know navigation. When

I brought them down out of the cloud, and the lake or the farm or the track appeared right where I'd said it would be, the expression of stark amazement on their faces (which at one time would have filled me with a sense of insult) became the expected climax to walking in cloud. Sometimes it didn't stop there; some would study the farm — or the lake or the track — and conclude that it wasn't the right one; we were in another valley. I kept quiet and plodded on. As we lost height and more landmarks came into view (finally putting paid to that tiny twinge of doubt which suggested you were not infallible and you really would look a mug if you *were* in the wrong valley) there would be a long silence, on one side surly, on the other expressionless but suggestive of supreme and unassailable confidence. Later, over dinner, most of all over liqueurs, would come the request, made with charming diffidence:

"If it's misty tomorrow, do you think you could show me how to navigate?"

On rare occasions low cloud had unexpected compensations. There was an October day when the weather had been dull and grey for weeks; according to the radio there were pile-ups in the fog on the motorways, and in the mountains the cloud ceiling stayed solid at a thousand feet.

On this Saturday I was climbing with a party on the east face of Tryfan, climbing in mist so thick even our shouts were muffled. As we neared the top I became aware that the atmosphere was lighter. On the summit we looked up and it seemed that the cloud was very thin. There was the slightest movement, a hint of blue.

We went up Bristly Ridge and on to Glyder Fach. As we started scrambling up the tumbled boulders I knew there was no cloud above, and suddenly we broke through into a clear blue world of light with the sun blazing across the top of the cloud sea.

I looked for the other peaks — and there they were: Y Wyddfa and Crib y Ddisgl, black and shapely points;

Glyder Fawr, a heap of rocks; and the two Carnedds like the backs of whales basking in the foam. There was nothing else: just the top few feet of six mountains.

Our summit filled up with people like insects crawling up a stick in a pond — until there was no room to stand and the firstcomers had to give way to new arrivals. I gave one last look at the other summits and guessed that each had its dense little throng of people lost in wonder while the rest of Britain laboured, unaware, under the fog.

I lost my wedding ring on the east face of Tryfan. I was with Millicent Bishop, a recruiting officer for the Women's Royal Army Corps. I liked climbing with her; she was active, amusing, intelligent. Nothing worried her: grease on holds, mist, the approach of darkness. Millicent at a loss was a contradiction in terms.

I was at the top of the first pitch of Terrace Wall Variant: a pleasant Very Difficult where one can become confused by the proximity of Long Chimney: a delicate Very Severe. I hadn't done our easy route for some time and, balanced on small holds sixty feet above Millicent, I looked up the rock and couldn't see the line of the route. The light was poor so I took out my spectacles case. In this, besides the glasses, I kept odd valuables: paper money, Johnnie's notes designating a rendezvous — always a map reference, my wedding ring. I didn't wear this climbing, the slightest catch when I made a delicate move might upset me. I pulled out my glasses and something tinkled on the rock. I turned and looked down. The tiny ringing sound faded. As it did so, Millicent's face, upturned in enquiry, assumed an expression of utter stupefaction.

"My ring!" I shouted.

"*What?*"

"My wedding ring; didn't you see it?"

"I heard an odd little noise coming towards me."

I descended and we searched the heather and the bilberries, recruiting the services of other climbers, but we never found it.

Sometimes I stayed at Ogwen at the end of engagements. Climbing for fun was a delightful change from professional mountaineering. I could do hard climbs with hard men: not the hardest routes but those which I couldn't lead. Johnnie insisted I had the technique to lead but he disregarded the fact that I didn't want to place myself in this position. Reason was no weapon against the fear of serious injury. I might reason that a climb was within my limit technically, that if I made a mistake a reliable second wearing gloves could hold me; even crippled I could write for a living. None of it made any difference. I knew what I could lead without being frightened and I stuck to it. So, seconding the harder climbs, I had the best of both worlds: climbing difficult rock on a top rope. It was years before I came to realise that intrinsically I incurred far more danger leading some novices up climbs of a low standard than by leading hard routes with a competent second.

In June of my second season's comeback I met Johnnie one night in Bethesda. I'd been to the Black Ladders and had a glorious day climbing Western Gully. It was just after the weekend and I'd gone there to escape the crowds which were starting to spill over into the week. Johnnie had been training all weekend.

"I'm sick of people," he said, "and it'll be worse in the Alps."

Our leave was very close. We'd talked idly of Zermatt and Chamonix, but these would be full of climbers.

"What about the Dauphiné?" I asked.

"Too early."

"No, they're little mountains. The ridges will have lost their snow. There are some great rock routes."

"What about the Weisshorn?"

"It won't go away. And what about that refuge above

Chamonix where the tourists had all the beds and we slept on the floor with our legs up the walls because there wasn't room to stretch out? I don't know though — some of the routes in the Dauphiné are supposed to be rather hard . . ."

"Well, I suppose we can get the guide-books as we go through London . . ."

CHAPTER 6

"The Little Mountains"

THE TRAIN WAS running through a desert of gorges and crumbling cliffs all bleached by the sun. It was eight in the morning and we were somewhere above the valley of the Rhône. I left Johnnie asleep in the couchette and went into the empty corridor. It seemed curious that no one else was interested in this strange new country, but then probably we were the only English people on the train, and only the insular English think that deserts begin in Asia. There were compensations in ignorance when you could be so pleasantly surprised.

The stony wastes gave place to swamps intermeshed with innumerable streams, very fast and shallow. Big bushes grew on silt spits and, but for the prevailing chalkiness which marked the water as glacial, you could imagine crocodiles in the bushes, big snakes and nameless things.

It had been grey at Dover and wet in Paris. When we left the train at Briançon the sudden heat came as a shock, but then it began to act like a partial anaesthetic. In England we had chafed at the hours we must waste in this place searching for a Monsieur Georges who would renew our membership of the French Alpine Club. It was Sunday and there was no bus to Bourg d'Oisans till Monday. The heat dulled our impatience. We wandered up into the town in a happy stupor, out again into an area of walled villas with sprinklers sparkling through gateways, heavy trees, bright flowers and the persistent hum of insects.

We found M. Georges watering the cacti in his garden. We

drank coffee and talked about mutual friends. He told us it was an early season: already in June much of the snow had gone; the rock climbs were bare. There would be much ice in the couloirs. He talked of the new refuges, now supplied by helicopter. I felt a pang for the old days and the mules plodding up to the huts with mouthfuls of flowers, but no regret for the simple lavatories where you perched hundreds of feet above the glaciers and paper wouldn't go down the hole in a high wind. M. Georges was very pround of the *eau courante*.

I bought boots and a piton hammer in the town, and we inspected the fort. The whole town was a fortress: a straggled city on several hills with great man-made walls and bastions and watch towers like cliffs. There was no ornament, no carving; this was a place that had known conflict more often than peace. Ponderous wooden doors hung in the narrow gateways. There were tiny barred openings at eye-level and dry moats where jackdaws nested among the hanging clumps of flowers. The streets and alleys inside the walls were steep and twisting. There must have been fighting at every corner.

There were few tourists about. When darkness came we dined on an empty terrace in a cobbled street where the odd street lamp shone on windows half-open to catch the breeze, and cats slipped through the shadows like shapes in a dream.

The weather broke overnight and as our bus ground up the long gorge to La Bérarde we saw that the cloud was down. Rain had filled the streams and the sides of the gorge dripped with waterfalls. The road was so narrow that traffic up was confined to the morning; if you wanted to go down you must wait till the afternoon. We wondered what happened to emergency services.

We went through hamlets, pushing past manure heaps, stopping in farmyards to deliver goods while goats and

The Dibona

Les Bans and the Pilatte Glacier

The south face of the Meije

lambs bleated from dark byres. There were no mountains visible, only the forested cliffs with occasionally the grey snout of a glacier peering over a lip like an ogre.

La Bérarde was little more than two hotels, a few houses and a church. The French Alpine Club's dormitory was not yet open so we took a room at one of the hotels: a bare white-washed room with an iron bedstead and an old candlewick quilt. There was strip lighting over the wash basin and the water came hot if you ran it for long enough. We never discovered a bathroom.

That afternoon we walked up the valley through a thin drizzle. We didn't know where anything was, although we knew the stream we followed came down from the Pilatte Glacier. There was still snow on the north-facing slopes, and spring flowers in the flattened earth below the melting drifts.

We crossed the torrent and returned through an alder wood. All the flowers were bigger and brighter than at home: a huge indigo columbine, a ranunculus larger than a globe flower, and then suddenly, our first gentians: an unbelievable blue in the sodden grass.

There was sun in the valley the following morning but the cloud was still low on the tops. The path to the Soreiller Refuge starts from a hamlet called Les Etages. The hut was not yet open but we met the guardian's wife who said she would go up, but slowly since she would take her daughter. The child was about ten, so we added some of their load to our own sacks.

The sides of the valley were so steep that the ascent started immediately you left the road. The hut was about three thousand feet above Les Etages and the first section of the path rose in sharp zigzags towards the mouth of a rocky ravine. This opening was the only breach in a tall band of rock. Springs came bubbling out below the cliff reminding us we hadn't bathed for days. We left the path and picked our way

E

through cream foxgloves and orange lilies until we found a pool warmed by the sun.

"But it's melt-water," Johnnie complained, soaking himself in two inches of pool. He looked like a slightly perverted Renaissance painting: all muscle and tan in a frame of magenta orchids.

The vegetation stopped when we entered the ravine: a cold dim place where we walked silently, watching the toes of our boots, and the path came so close to the torrent we moved in a bitter fringe of spray.

We emerged on a high upland in the cloud. As we followed the track the air grew lighter; there was a feeling of a break coming. Deep shadows appeared in the cloud, paled to grey and then we saw the shadow was too solid for cloud. Very high there was a shift in the veil, blue sky. Against it, in it, without a visible base, the tip of a grey spear showed. We waited, silent, and the cloud dropped gently until the Aiguille Dibona stood naked, all of it — from the crumbled screes to the top — and as we came up the long moraines the granite started to glow in the evening sun.

"Where's our route?"

"Straight up."

"What, *this* side?"

"You'll love it. Just your kind of climbing. You can lead."

We led through. We'd started late because there was no glacier and few stone falls — and the rock was warm on the south face. I came round a corner and there was the hut five hundred feet below with the little girl playing on the helicopter platform.

We traversed above the chimneys of the refuge, the holds a little too rounded for the climbing to be easy, but the rock rough and clean in compensation. There was a couloir with a steep crack at the top. I brought Johnnie up and he disappeared round a corner. After a while he came back and looked at the rock above me. This was the Stopfer variant, graded a little harder than the direct route.

I like to travel light in the Alps, preferring to forestall eventualities with speed. Johnnie anticipates eventualities by carrying everything he may need: a practice which has disadvantages for me on harder rock when he changes sacks. Following him up the Stopfer variant, with his loaded pack halfway down my back, was a kind of weight-lifting at every move. I had a tight rope all the way and the overhang at the top was a trial of strength with himself pulling, me clawing at the holds, and the rucksack hanging like a dead man from my shoulders.

We exchanged sacks in eloquent silence.

Easier pitches led to the summit. A thousand feet below, the screes fanned away from the base, but I glanced at them only once. After that I kept my eyes on the next few feet of rock until suddenly I was on the top and, to my astonishment, found I had room to sit down.

There was room for both of us, not ample – and a sudden move from one would elicit twitters of alarm from the other – but we were belayed. However, common sense failed before the prospect of being knocked off to dangle, paralysed by terror, above a thousand feet of air.

We had come to the Dauphiné primarily to get away from people and we had tended to think of these as little mountains, second-rate, but they were little only in comparison with the Pennine Alps. At Zermatt, the Mettelhorn – at eleven thousand feet – is a view-point for tourists, from which they can see the fifteen-thousand-foot giants. Somehow, sub-consciously, we had felt the Meije for instance was only another Mettelhorn. But when we studied it from our training climbs of the following days – with its stupendous southern face and the mile of spiky summit ridge – we knew our sense of proportion had slipped.

To compensate for their lack of height these mountains

are sharp and steep, and their glaciers, with nothing to compare in length and area with the big ones of the Valais, are riven and tortured by crevasses. The Pilatte Glacier looked like one great ice fall, with nowhere that you could relax your caution as you can on the level stretches of an extensive ice sheet.

We went up to the Pilatte Refuge hoping to climb a couloir on Les Bans, but M. Georges had been right about the early season. Through the guardian's powerful field-glasses we saw that all the snow had gone from the couloir; it was bare green ice for over a thousand feet.

We looked at the rest of the mountain. It was a series of graceful buttresses with the ordinary route running up the far skyline. One buttress was the left flank of our couloir. If we climbed either buttress or couloir we must traverse the summit ridge to descend by the ordinary way, and our experience warned us that the traverse might be long and arduous: a succession of gendarmes and clefts – and then possibly a descent of the complicated glacier in the dark.

A series of mistakes ensured that we should climb neither buttress nor couloir. We were called late, then, suspecting crevasses under the snow, we cut up bare ice on the glacier where, as it transpired later, the *névé* was safe and we could have walked up. The sun was high when we were still an hour from the foot of the couloir and although we were surprised to hear no stonefalls, we knew they must start coming down at any moment.

Johnnie was cross and resentful at the late start, besides, he – who is usually so adept at finding his way across strange glaciers – had met his match in the Pilatte. I suggested we should do the ordinary route. He looked at it sullenly. It would serve as a reconnaissance for tomorrow, I pointed out, and we'd know the glacier by then; it was a very complicated glacier, I added, putting him on his mettle.

We went on, weaving slowly in and out of the crevasses

which continued right to the top. The bergschrund was on the watershed.

There were two little snow knolls between us and the start of the ordinary route. We traversed them carefully, the snow softened now by the sun – and the bergschrund, with a nice sense of timing having divided itself into several gaping mouths, waited for a slip on one side, while a long lethal sweep of ice dropped away to the south.

We left our gear in the snow and with a sudden sense of security stepped on to the rock. It was beautiful climbing on rough red granite, but really we considered it only as a prelude for tomorrow, and from the summit we stared down at the glacier, determined to find the key to the maze. Certainly we hadn't found it on the ascent; we saw our tracks wandering backwards and forwards as if we'd been lost in mist. Now we could see what might be the correct way but there was an hiatus marked by avalanche debris.

"Perhaps people crossed the debris," I said, "and the light's wrong to see tracks on the other side."

We descended the rock ridge and traversed the knolls where we sank to our thighs. By the time we reached the avalanche debris we were suffering from glacier lassitude, and our physical torpor – combined with the compulsion for speed and caution – made us bad-tempered.

We moved fast across the debris only to find no tracks on the other side. Frustrated and pushing our luck we continued under a big rock face to a place where we could push it no longer: we were under a mass of tottering *séracs*.

Appalled and exhausted, we paused to catch our breath, realising in that moment that we stood in a zone of crevasses running in the same direction as our line of travel. I wanted to turn back but Johnnie wouldn't pass under that rock face again where the snow was peppered with fallen stones.

We had to move fast, but to move upright across those crevasses would be asking for trouble. They weren't open; there was merely a line, an indentation in the snow here and there to show their presence. To distribute the weight we sat and glissaded fast down the slope. My shirt parted company from my breeches and I was sodden with wet snow. We stood up, shook ourselves and hurried on until our way was barred by more and deeper crevasses and we knew we must retreat.

We were still below the great mass of *séracs* and if we had been frightened glissading fast away from them, toiling slowly up that two-hundred-foot slope towards them was so dangerous as to seem ridiculous. Mad, mad, mad, I thought savagely wincing as the ice cracked and the avalanches rumbled and roared in other places. I tried to comfort myself by picturing *séracs* which I'd avoided one season and next year they'd be in the same place — yet every *sérac* must fall some time. Gravity is an inescapable fact.

We stopped climbing and contoured the slope, moving in echelon because we were travelling with the crevasses again. Once I found myself walking along a big one: something invisible and menacing as a shark at night, a shark that touches your leg and goes away, and comes back. I floundered sideways, axe and feet going in at every step, feeling the blackness and the emptiness under me. Johnnie shouted unheeded advice, my face streamed sweat and I was blindingly angry.

We stopped below rocks to recover. Here we were safe from avalanches and the falling stones were small. We might dodge them; you couldn't dodge a hundred tons of snow.

We found our old tracks of the morning, and came to a path which was too well used to be any but the correct way. It followed a tortuous line, in one place passing under a leaning tower of ice so close we could touch it. We came out into the middle of the glacier and the danger was over — but our exhaustion was complete.

We spent the next day lying in the sun among the alpines and studying the glacier. I refused to acknowledge that we had lost our skill; we had merely underestimated the

Dauphiné. I was quite happy to make another attempt on the buttress of Les Bans, but after yesterday's fiasco Johnnie was eager for another mountain. Last evening we had stood on the terrace and looked past the Ailefroide, with the sun pink in its summit rocks, to the Meije with the little square glacier hanging in the top left corner and, all along the top, that great classic traverse: a ridge climb at thirteen thousand feet.

Lying on his back in the alpines, reviving in the sun, Johnnie suggested we should go down next morning and head for the Meije before the weather broke. I agreed but pointed out we might try something on the way down. From the refuge we could see a fine crenellated ridge: the east arête of the Pic du Says. We calculated that if we made an early start the following morning we could run down the track towards La Bérarde and stop *en route* to nip up this ridge — just to fill in an hour or two — reaching La Bérarde in time for lunch. We could go up to the Meije in the afternoon.

No one called us the next morning but I woke at five and we were away in half an hour. We had eaten most of our food and breakfast was crusts and butter.

We descended from the refuge until we met the glacier coming down from the Pic du Says. We left most of our gear on the moraine, including our duvets. At my insistence we took one torch. I sneaked my pullover into my sack while Johnnie was squinting at the ridge and wondering whether to take his anorak.

The guide-book time for the ridge was four hours to the summit but we hoped we could beat this, travelling light and fast. The descent was by way of a ridge that looked simple enough: *peu difficile* — an hour for this, we thought.

Our way lay across untracked moraines covered with yellow rock roses, and the ridge rose ahead with a long rocky couloir to reach its crest. I started up this and, about thirty feet from the ground, I heard an unmistakable animal snort.

Johnnie shouted and I looked down to see a chamois doe leaping across the screes with her kid. I paused long enough to impress on him that we mustn't tell the locals (who might shoot chamois) then I went back to the climbing.

The rock was loose but we didn't comment, both hoping it would improve. It was an intricate route to follow. There was much perusal of the guide-book, and traversing of easy ledges to niches on the skyline in order to find the crest of the ridge and then *not* to follow it but to climb below the arête, first on one side then on the other. We knew from the book and our previous glimpses of the ridge that there were a number of towers to be traversed, but we hadn't been prepared for these to multiply once we were climbing. Each tower masked a litter of progeny behind it, to be turned or traversed. These weren't mentioned in the guide-book, and Johnnie's criticism of the editor was scathing.

We muddled our way upwards, putting on our anoraks (because the granite was like sharkskin,) taking them off (because the sun was like a furnace). While Johnnie led I studied the glacier below, working out our descent, noting the crevasses, the fallen stones stippling the surface under the steep cliffs. The hot still morning was punctuated by the clatter of rocks, the thunder of avalanches, and under it all was the continuous roar of a torrent, rising to us in waves. Through and above these came the song of a bird somewhere on the cliffs below our feet.

I was happy leading. The rock remained loose but, with the sun hot on my back dispelling all sense of urgency, I was enjoying myself, even though every running belay was a loose flake cracked all the way round. Johnnie hated it.

We were on one of the big towers and I was leading its upper section. The angle was relenting and I was a hundred feet above him. Until then I had climbed the pitch fast but now I came to an overhanging wall – and I knew the finishing holds would be rotten. I paused to size up the problem but I didn't say anything. Now Johnnie delivers a running commentary all the time he is leading, but I am so lost in delight at the easy sections, so absorbed by concentration on the crux, that I climb in silence – and he is exasperated to the point of panic, not knowing what I'm doing:

"Why have you stopped, Moffat? . . . Is it hard? . . . What can you see? . . . Have you got enough slings? MOFFAT! What are you doing?"

I worked out my holds with great care and climbed the crux trying to do something that is almost impossible: to surmount an overhang without pulling hard on the handholds. Johnnie came up sweating and very angry. He said he'd been praying for me. (Sheena tells me now that her seconds do this too. Do we take it as evidence of their regard or an insult to our technique?)

In the middle of a false cast, trying to turn the ridge by a snow couloir with ice under the surface, I realised that bad weather was coming in from the south-west. The wind had backed and the air was sticky. The cloud level had dropped below the Meije.

We reached the north summit at six in the evening. We'd had nothing to eat since breakfast and hunger made us rather tired. The peak was in mist now and Johnnie was cold without a pullover. I began to think about being benighted. If the ascent had been so long and difficult, how many hours would we take on the descent? There was still the south summit to go over.

Johnnie, who must have been entertaining similar doubts about descending the *peu difficile* ridge in the dark, announced suddenly that there was a snow couloir debouching between the two summits: we could glissade down it in half an hour.

"Roped," I said firmly.

We went over another gendarme and below us was a dirty steep gully dropping into the gloom. A short cut to the main couloir, Johnnie said but I demurred: it would end above the couloir in a shattered wall – with nowhere for an abseil point

on this crumbling mountain. We must go on to the head of
the main couloir.

Another gendarme, and Johnnie, dehydrated, kept stopping to drink from the flask while I fumed with impatience,
watching the gathering night.

The main couloir held scarcely any snow; there was just a
very steep bed of scree with huge rocks resting on it, waiting
for a touch – or even a current of air to dislodge them.

We descended for about two hundred feet, then Johnnie
swore that we were in the wrong gully, so we toiled back to
the top and continued, only to find that a subsidiary ridge
came in on our left which was the one we'd meant to descend
originally, so we'd gone too far; the nasty scree gully had
been the right one after all. We went back.

We had agreed that so long as the climbing was simple it
was better to descend slowly in the dark rather than spend
the night shivering on some high ledge in inadequate clothing.
But when we talked about descending slowly we hadn't taken
the state of the gully into account. You spend as little time as
possible in a rubbish chute. Moreover, the gully was about a
thousand feet long and it twisted: the worst place to fall
in – we would be dashed to pieces against the walls. Boulders
would ricochet too, making it more difficult to dodge.

As I started down for the second time I felt that I was
descending into the jaws of hell. The ridge had been holding
the last of the light – now I went down into the Pit. As I
passed the poised boulders I felt them catch their breath, then
creep forward with a whisper of gravel . . . Clumsiness would
be fatal; we mustn't touch anything loose – but there was so
little that was solid. Just occasionally there were short pitches
where the bed-rock was exposed, seamed with grooves, and
here we could bridge down fast, facing out, but always with a
wary eye for any ledge at the side where we could hang for a
moment if a boulder came down from above.

About halfway down I was glissading on a hard tongue of
snow when I sensed it running out. I managed to fall on my

face and brake with the pick but I lost the skin off my knuckles. Fixing the belay in a cave I looked at my bleeding hands and reflected that a little blood and skin was a small price to pay for getting down this gully alive. The belay was as insecure as I felt. The rope was threaded through some rotten blocks which supported a huge capstone. I called up to Johnnie to stop carefully; if he overshot that cave and pulled me on to the belay, if those blocks moved and the cave collapsed, he'd be held all right, but it would be by a corpse under the capstone.

While I waited I wrote my obituary in my mind and wondered which papers would rate me one: the *Daily Worker* perhaps, and the *North Wales Weekly News*. I emerged from the cave in a mist of tears: sentiment and reaction, for he'd glissaded and stopped with great competence, and I followed meekly, thinking it couldn't be far now, surely that glow was starlight reflected off the glacier a few hundred feet below.

Then I heard it.

Something was moving far above us: clatter, then silence, then cracking thuds—approaching too fast for me to be afraid. There was no time to identify it: whether it was one rock or an avalanche of them, no time to climb the gully walls; indeed, one quick swing of the torch beam showed no ledges, only smooth rock, unclimbable.

We didn't shout to each other. I flattened myself against the wall, knowing he must be doing the same. I didn't look up: I wouldn't get it in the face; I stared in cold anger at the bed of the gully, my torch a pool of light on the wet gravel.

There was an ear-splitting crack just above us, something monstrous slid past my feet and was gone: big enough to have weighed half a ton. My boots were covered with gravel.

"All right, Johnnie?"

"Yes, come on; get a move on!"

The boulder had driven out all fear; we went on calmly, but still listening. We could never be so lucky a second time, not both of us—but next time there might be a ledge to jump for.

I wondered how the couloir would end: a vertical shaft of rotten ice or a tremendous overhang? Either would plunge straight into the bergschrund. How long would it take to abseil—and how many abseils? Would the mountain hold its fire that long?

The light of the torch didn't reach far. Sometimes, from the top of a pitch, I'd look down and think the bed of the gully miles away when perhaps it was only fifteen feet. But suddenly, unmistakably. there was nothing below: we had reached the bergschrund.

As we paused I felt that there was something beside us, over the retaining wall, but close. *Over* the wall, was it that low then? I turned my head, and the torch beam swung along gentle rocks to where a high bay of the glacier lapped up the mountain.

Johnnie took the light and left me in darkness. When the rope stopped moving through my hands I felt very much alone, perched like a skittle above the bergschrund. I could hear stones falling on the glacier but nothing moved in our gully.

He called to me and I started to climb. At first I moved by touch in the darkness, but the traverse was easy and as I came into the radius of the light there were glacier crowfoot growing on the ledges, more lovely that night than any flowers had been before.

We came down the glacier exactly as we'd plotted it from the ridge that morning, the *previous* morning, avoiding all the crevasses and the cliffs with their falling stones. Some of the rocks ran down the slope but the snow was soft and they slithered, so we had warning of their approach. It's when they bound that it's so difficult to dodge.

There were no crevasses on the lower glacier. Our caution left us; we relaxed and began to stagger like drunks. It was half past three and the first light showing when we reached our gear. It was bitterly cold. We pulled on our duvets and Johnnie lay on the moraine as he fell, looking so much like a corpse that it was unbearable. Besides, he was lost in sleep, but I was wide awake – and frozen.

I prodded him awake and drove him down to the valley, but when we reached the first grass he collapsed again. I walked on, thinking it safe to leave him, then I too dropped and slept.

I heard whistles – a sinister shrilling – through my dreams, and woke shaking. The sun had not yet reached the valley but the marmots were all awake, rearing up like stoats and peering at me over the herbage, summoning all the laggards with their piercing calls. I went back, got Johnnie up, and we continued to the first chalet where we were revived by a nice kind peasant with bowls and bowls of coffee: proper coffee – hot and sweet and black as sin.

CHAPTER 7

The Singing Axes

"THE NEXT ROUTE we do," he said savagely, "we're going to do properly."

"We did the Dibona and the Soreiller without any trouble," I pointed out, "and we did get through that glacier in the end —" (I had a sudden picture of our toiling up under those *séracs* — and blocked it out) "— and the guide-book did miss out an awful lot of towers on the Pic du Says. I think we've coped very well — in the circumstances."

"It's not worth coming if we don't do something good."

In fact I, too, approached the Meije with a kind of savage determination, but he didn't know this. If he thought I would commit myself he might push it too far. But mine was only a partial self-deception; although I might seem determined to get over the Meije at all costs, there was a limit to the risks involved. Deliberately I refused to consider this limit beforehand, but when the moment approached I would know where it lay. I sympathised with Johnnie over our past mistakes and I implied that the Meije would be a delightful climb without incident — when actually I felt that this one, the hardest of our climbs to date, would detonate the big guns. The Pilatte Glacier and the Pic du Says had been mere sniping.

We planned to go over the mountain and down the other side to La Grave, returning to La Bérarde by the Romanche Valley and an easy pass. There were two reasons for this: firstly, the usual route of return, the Bréche de la Meije,

was supposed to be impassable this season; secondly, returning by the Romanche Valley would mean seeing new country.

The Meije is a ridge with a north and a south face. The
latter looks down towards La Bérarde and is about three
thousand feet of rock. The north face is all high steep glaciers
lapping up the mountain, with rock and ice mixed at the
top, under the mile-long crest. The usual approach for the
traverse is from the south, by way of a subsidiary ridge at the
western extremity of the south face. Perched on this there is
an unguarded refuge. The climb starts from its door sill, goes
up the ridge, then a couloir to a fine steep wall under the
Glacier Carré. Above this is the summit ridge and the next
mile is simple. The top is followed eastward with no alternative: no spurs or secondary ridges, no way of turning obstacles;
the line goes straight along the crest to the Pic Central.
Beyond this a long abseil takes you across the bergschrund
on to the Tabuchet Glacier where there is another unguarded
refuge.

It seemed too simple so, by elimination, I arrived at what
must be the trickiest part: the wall below the Glacier Carré.
What were these rock pitches: the *Dalle Castelnau*, the
Dos d'Ane, the *Pas du Chat?* They were graded "3" which was
only Very Difficult but I had my suspicions of donkeys'
backs and cats' steps. If something is innocuous it isn't worth
identification. And then those teeth on the ridge: how many
more were there which the guide-book deemed unworthy of
mention? Then there was the general description: *Belle
course d'arête aérienne à très haute altitude* – I thought of abseils
on rotten rock over the three-thousand-foot drop of the south
face, and I gritted my teeth.

The expedition started well. We approached our peak by
easy stages. Still not completely recovered from our twenty-
four hours on the Pic du Says we took two days to reach the
Meije. We stayed overnight at the valley refuge of Chatelleret
en route, throwing casual glances at the steep little ridge of

the Pic Nord de Cavales, but always one's eyes were drawn back to the Meije and its splendid crest. It permitted dawdling but no concentration on minor peaks.

The next day we came to the Promontoire Refuge. It was reached by way of a rock climb with several exposed pitches. These were festooned with rusty sagging hawsers which came towards you when gripped, arousing doubts concerning their anchorage at the top. We didn't use them, but difficult rock — with the glacier hundreds of feet below, and a loaded rucksack swaying on your back at every move — is unpleasant solo. We climbed roped.

There was a French couple at the hut: Claudine and Daniel. They were young and hard: a type that climbs on guts rather than technique.

That afternoon we reconnoitred the first part of our route. We roped at the hut and, carrying nothing but slings, we climbed for an hour up beautiful rough granite until we came to the stony couloir which led to the final wall. We retreated at this point; the weather was deteriorating, and no sooner had we reached the hut when the storm broke.

A party of seven arrived with a guide. Rain lashed the roof and the atmosphere was gloomy.

I was too much involved to feel emotion. I would feel it later on the climb but a few hours beforehand I was completely detached. Rain on the roof aroused neither disappointment nor fear; it meant merely that if it were pouring in the morning, if the rocks were iced, we wouldn't go. If the rain stopped and it was a mild night, we would climb.

Daniel's alarm clock went off at two-thirty and the four of us were up immediately. We looked out and the rocks were dry. We gave the French couple ten minutes' start, and at three-thirty we closed the door behind us and started climbing.

Claudine and Daniel had missed the route so we caught them up and passed and now, taking advantage of our lights, they trod right at our heels and I felt the first twinge of annoyance.

Reaching the final wall was a dangerous business. The guided party of eight overtook us in the stony couloir and rocks started to rattle down from above. The gully crawled with people and the atmosphere was electric. At one point I saw Claudine clawing her way up slabs now ice-sheeted on finger-nails and knees while the air rang with cries of *"Attention! Pierres!"*

We reached the top of the couloir and sat down to stare morosely at the weather. A dirty haze hung in the south, and a ravure was stretched across the summit of Les Ecrins. To the west the lower part of the sky was black, supporting big white boilers. Where the sun touched a peak the granite glowed red and angry.

There were ten people ahead of us on the mountain; we couldn't pass them now. There was a bottleneck at a slab: the first pitch of the final wall. From our vantage point we watched the guide — in bright red socks like an oyster-catcher — taking his troop over this slab. With a drop below of over a thousand feet, no one was happy.

We gloomed at them and the weather; we winced at the stones clattering down the face, and we looked at each other.

"Let's go down," he said, "once you're on the ridge you're committed — if there's a storm. We can't retreat down this wall."

I thought we might; surely we could climb down rock of that standard — but we would be exposed to the storm. We started to retreat. After two or three rope-lengths we looked at the weather. It was no worse.

"Come on," he said, "they're well ahead now. Let's risk it."

Back we went at the double, over the steep slab and up the splendid wall. It was a zigzag line: a triumph of route-finding in the first instance. There was always a way if you looked for it, and never hard. We'd come to the top of a delightful slab

F

or an exciting little crack and there in the gravel would be the tracks of our predecessors, pointing the way along a ledge to the next pitch. All the same, as I came up the amusing overhang of the *Pas du Chat*, I was aware, almost subconsciously, that the haze was thickening and the cloud dropping fast.

The little square glacier was a nuisance with the snow so soft that we sank to our knees, and as we waded up the side of it stones were falling from the cliff above, landing in the snow with deep and sinister plops.

We came to the summit ridge and looked over and down to La Grave but the usual delight of topping your mountain was lost. There must have been new glaciers, and pine forests and a strange town in the bottom but I didn't see them; I saw only the grim sky in the north.

To our right, at the start of the traverse, rose the Grand Pic. We moved up this together until we came to a steep pitch below the summit. I belayed at the foot of a red slab and stood there, listening to explosions from the direction of the Lauteret Pass, and thinking how like home it was: climbing above Llanberis with all the quarries blasting.

Johnnie called to me and I started to climb. The rock was pleasant with good holds, but near the top I came to an overhang and sidled underneath it, looking for the easiest way.

"Don't hang about," he shouted urgently, "grab the rope and come straight up."

I froze. What was wrong?

"Keep the rope tight then," I said – and as I pulled up the overhang, hating him for making me climb in a hurry and badly, another peal exploded over the Lauteret, and I saw his face – and I knew it wasn't quarry blasting at all, it was thunder.

"We may beat it," I said after a moment, "or it may miss us."

But the storm was almost here – and we were on the

highest peak for miles around. We raced over the top, with startled glances at the stone Virgin standing – a little less than life-size – on the summit, then I saw something white below. It was paper; it pointed me down the slope to an old rusty piton from which we could abseil into the gap beyond.

Claudine and Daniel were just ahead of us now and we had noticed them having some difficulty with the pitches on the other side of the gap. This was the Brèche Zsigmondy; leaving it is considered the hardest part of the climb, mainly because the route now being on the north side of the crest, the rocks are often glazed with ice.*

The first pitch wasn't long. When it came to my turn I found that technically it was simple: the holds were there. What worried me was not so much the exposure over that sweep of fluted ice which was the north face, but the rucksack on my back. I was off-balance and hanging over the drop; it was too much to have the sack conspiring with gravity. One consolation was that there was no ice on the holds.

The second pitch of this diagonal traverse was much longer. I couldn't see Johnnie. A hundred feet of rope ran out and I watched the remainder anxiously. Thirty feet, twenty-five, twenty left. I shouted. There was no answer. The rope continued to run out. I kept shouting. There were ten feet of rope left on the stance. I turned and shouted across at the Grand Pic to try to bounce an echo off it, pitching my voice high. All the rope ran out and I felt a tug at my waist. If he were climbing, now he must retreat, unrope or fall.

For ten minutes I waited. Occasionally there was a tug, then a slackening of the rope – but not the three sharp tugs that mean "come on". He could have been flicking the rope, or pulling it to give him enough to reach a belay. If I took off my anchor to give him those extra feet, he might be on a

---

* Since then the Brèche Zsigmondy has disappeared in a rock fall. The route now traverses much lower on the north face and is considerably harder, involving very severe climbing and one artificial pitch (A.2.)
G.M.

critical move, still climbing — and suppose he fell then? All the contingencies went through my mind. I still shouted, my throat very painful, and in the hopeless pauses I saw, beyond La Grave, white pillars of rain marching across the hills.

In the end I took off my belay and started to climb. The slack rope was caught under flakes. I took up the coils as I moved and was pleased to see that the traverse was spiked with pegs, all of which he had used as runners.

He'd heard me all the time, he said when I reached him: communication had been one-way. I'd been right to wait ten minutes; he hadn't found a belay till just before I'd shouted I was starting to climb.

Between us and the Pic Central, now plainly visible jutting out over the south face, was a succession of pinnacles with people on them: the guided party and Claudine and Daniel. We were catching up fast.

Mist came up both faces to meet and swirl in agitation all along the crest. Fascinated, I watched the passage of the first snowflake.

My hair lifted and crawled about my head, and, as I followed Johnnie along the crest, I was aware that I, too, was being followed. There was a soft sweet singing behind me like a swarm of insects. I whirled round but it was still at my back. It was my axe, alive with electricity. We had put them in our sacks to have our hands free for the climbing.

The storm came closer, a silent sinister approach of which we were unaware until there was a sudden terrifying crash, simultaneous with the lightning and directly overhead. Rocks went plunging down the south face.

After the first crash I knew we were in the centre of it and fear gave place to a strange exhilaration. There was nothing we could do to escape it. We couldn't get off the ridge: there was nowhere to go. We couldn't leave our axes: we needed them for the descent of the glacier. We went on, our gentle, almost casual progress punctuated by those glorious explosions, and between the thunder, all the time, the axes sang in the charged stillness.

There was sleet and flurries of hail on the last peak. We went over it and scrambled down easy rocks to where, at their lowest extremity, we found Claudine and Daniel crouched by a piton and waiting for us.

We were in thick mist. They explained that the bergschrund was too far below for their rope to reach over it. We combined forces and knotted our ropes together.

The French went down first while I safeguarded them on a top rope. Through the cloud came cries of "*à droite, à droite*" and then: "*corde d'assurance libre*" which seemed unnecessarily verbose. It was very cold. Hauling back two hundred and fifty feet of safety line (we had knotted these together too) was warming but strenuous. My arms were feeling weak.

I went down third, having some difficulty with knots and a carabiner, feeling the ice glassy under my vibrams, feeling the others watching, trying to pierce the cloud.

The bergschrund loomed below with Daniel and Claudine on its lower lip.

"*À droite, à droite!*"

I peered and saw a most unstable snow bridge marked by tracks. I swung gently across the ice sheet and, still grasping the abseil rope, joined them, treading like Agag above the abyss. Urgent shouts floated down to us as Johnnie felt the ropes go limp.

Coming down the glacier we had no trouble following the tracks of the guided party for, whatever his faults, that oystercatcher guide knew his glacier. Soon we were out of the cloud and looking down bare ice – startlingly blue after hours of no colour – to the hut, perched on rocks above another glacier, more tortured than any we'd seen yet. Claudine and Daniel said they had skied down it.

The refuge was shuttered and barred. The storm (which rolled away after we left the ridge) now returned suddenly and the steel hawsers fastening the building down sizzled and spat like something in a frying-pan. No one was anxious to handle the metal bolts and, most unchivalrously, we watched Claudine struggle alone. Lightning flashed and, seeing she was still whole, not charred, we all rushed to help, before the next strike. The door burst open and we fell inside to end in a heap on the mattresses, while overhead the last great peal of thunder cracked and all the echoes went rolling round the cliffs.

I got up at nine next morning to a grey day with cloud about the top of the Meije. The French came out and explained the intricacies of the Glacier de l'Homme: the one they'd skied down. As I stared into those gaping maws, at the sharp white knives of ice between, I forgave them their imprudence in carrying ropes too short to pass the bergschrund on the Meije; whatever they lacked it wasn't nerve – and they must be most accomplished skiers.

By the time we got away from the hut the glacier had softened. Claudine and Daniel went gaily down the cliff to try to trace their ski route on foot (but they had to retreat and follow us). We decided on the Tabuchet Glacier, the continuation of yesterday's descent and the usual route to La Grave. Even this had its moments. Forced on to the gravelly moraines by ice falls, we picked our way carefully downwards until I saw that we were approaching the top of a cliff which barred any return to the ice. And there, just when we must retreat, we found an abseil peg. To have said: "well, we'll have no trouble with *this* descent," would have been tempting Fate. I kept quiet and wasn't at all surprised, once we'd abseiled and were back on the ice, to realise that another storm was approaching.

We were about to glissade a steep part of the glacier. Above us on the right moraines and a precipitous hillside of broken ground ran up to a rocky crest. There was thunder about; probably it had been there all the time; we had become so used to it we didn't hear it until it came close. It was close now, but another storm made no difference. It had been raining since we left the hut and we were soaked to the skin.

As we stood at the head of the slope, our axes in position for the glissade, lightning struck the ridge above and great rocks came bounding down the hillside. They would hit a ledge then leap into the air, some at least fifty feet. Johnnie swore that one, as big as a house, was a hundred feet up on one occasion. They were crossing the line of our descent and were about a hundred yards away.

We let them settle and then we started to move: glissading down the slope, edging on to the moraine to avoid some steeper ice, then back to the glacier. One belated straggler came down from the ridge and sent me running hell-for-leather down soft snow, not caring about crevasses, thinking I might stand a chance of climbing out of one, but never a chance with a hundred tons of boulder on my back.

At last we reached a place where it would be simpler to leave the glacier altogether and take to the moraine. The scree was fairly small and we could run down it. The rocky crest was still above us but the storm seemed to be retreating. All the same we ran — myself in front.

I heard shouts behind me.

"Come back, come back—"

'He cried in vain, across the stormy water—' I thought, a little hysterically:

"Why?"

"I've dropped my goggles."

"Leave them."

"Come back and help me find them!"

I made the appropriate comment. The goggles were free issue to Mountain Rescue, this was our last trip — and we were still under the crest.

He found them and we went on. Clumps of alpines appeared in the scree, then grass among the stones. A shower passed, licking us with its fringe, and as we came to the first high pastures the sun came out, and we walked softly on turf until we found an empty chalet with a hollowed log for a water trough and a stream. We stopped and stripped, hanging our clothes on our axes to dry. I peeled off my socks and paddled. The hot breeze sighed in the tops of the pines, the clouds had gone and the sun blazed in a sky blue as the spring-blue gentians.

Later, sitting on the hotel terrace in La Grave, we looked at the Meije, now shining and benign, and there were all our last two days in reverse: the roofs of the town stepping down to the river, the black pines climbing to the bare pastures, the grey moraines and the ridge that had been struck by lightning, then the glacier stretching back – on different levels so that it seemed a succession of ice falls – right back to the bergschrund etched below the north face, and then the main ridge and the peaks.

The storms hung about but they didn't bother us. Our holiday was over. That night I lay awake, not thinking, just being happy, listening to the thunder that walked like friendly mammoths round the fringe of our world.

CHAPTER 8

Triumphant Spring

I HAD FINISHED *Space Below my Feet* before we went to the Dauphiné. Jack Longland had written the foreword and during the autumn I was making minor alterations which he'd suggested, preparatory to sending it to a publisher. I didn't climb much. I felt strangely lethargic. At first I attributed this to reaction: relief that the book was finished, but as the weeks passed I realised that there was more to it than that. I tired quickly on climbs; at Maen y Bardd I had begun to detest the chores of carrying water and sawing wood; even going down the hill for mail had become an effort.

I was refusing engagements. I had a good excuse: my arm, damaged about a year ago, was weak. I couldn't pull up on it; I was afraid I couldn't hold the rope if my second fell.

It was my mother, at Maen y Bardd on her annual visit, who persuaded me to see my doctor. Since those unsuccessful operations six years ago I had never been really fit. The doctor sent me to a surgeon. Both doctor and surgeon were women, fond of fell-walking, sympathetic. I was told the condition had gone too far for the surgeon to operate but there was a specialist in London who might take the chance. The choice was mine.

To my mind I had no choice. For a long time now the thoughts of cancer and a colotomy had never been far away when the pain was bad. I'd tried to block them out. Now I couldn't climb any longer, not even for fun. I said I would go to London.

. . . . . .

My last engagement that winter was guiding Sandhurst cadets on manœuvres. I rested for a week, then, the day before the job, I drove round to Pen y Pass and ran up Glyder Fawr in good time. I was pleased. If I could charge my batteries with enough energy to last a few hours I'd be on top of the engagement. It was only a matter of going to the top of the Glyders.

It was a night exercise. I was to meet my men outside the Pen y Gwryd hotel before dawn. There were passwords I had to remember and an air of adolescent play. I wasn't amused.

The officer in charge drove me to the Pen y Gwryd in the dark and figures rose out of ditches to accost us. I looked at the black bulk of the Glyders and the large tough men and I felt like hell.

We started up the mountain, myself in front. They tramped on my heels and breathed down my neck. A good guide sets a slow pace and holds his clients back, but I was full of shame and anger at my weakness and this resulted in an over-whelming compulsion to beat them. I stepped up the pace – and they clung like shadows. I felt that I was flat out, but you felt like that on rescues and there were still reserves; there were always reserves until you dropped. I drove myself faster and, in the dawn, saw them starting to string out, but still the hardest of them breathed heavily right behind.

As I put everything into it and noticeably increased my stride a voice gasped:

"Miss, slow down a bit. They can't keep up this pace you know. Can't we have a little breather? We're not as fit as you."

"What happened at the top?" Johnnie asked, sprawled by the fire at Maen y Bardd.

"They shot at us."

"Who?"

"Territorials. You know that group of rocks west of Llyn

Caseg? I'd been told we'd be ambushed and it was the only place. I kept an eye on it while we stood on the edge. I was picking out the way through all those little ledges and drops that go down into Cwm Tryfan. I saw these chaps get up and level rifles at us. Then they opened fire."

"Blanks, of course?"

"No. That's what I said to the sergeant major, and he said: 'Blanks, Miss? We always use *live* ammunition!'"

"I bet you dropped!"

"Straight over, and they came after me. I jumped a bit here and there. But when I reached the bottom and looked back they were coming down like stones, just rolling over the drops. It was fantastic."

"It must have been live ammunition then."

"Either that or they thought my method was the correct way to go down fast."

Just before Christmas the book was returned to me. I wasn't surprised. Publishers are professionals; it was only my family and friends who thought I had a winner. I sent the book to the next firm on my list.

February came – and the summons to a London hospital. I stayed the first night at a little hotel in Russell Square where the proprietors were Welsh and friendly. They invited me into their living room to drink tea. I didn't say why I was in London; only my family knew. If I went back to guiding I didn't want the authorities to know I'd had these operations. They might doubt my ability.

The specialist was a little old man with clever eyes that looked through you and saw your defences as well as the dark things in your mind. He told me his first operation was unsuccessful and he asked me if I would risk another attempt. I had, he said, a fifty-fifty chance. I didn't need to think about it. I was in a ward of colotomies and ileostomies and women dying of cancer. Even if the growth were benign at the moment, I had no illusions that it would stay that way. In any event it was definitely malignant to me. If he operated again and succeeded I could climb; if I had a colotomy I might still climb, but if he did nothing, recent experience showed that any strenuous activity was beyond me. I didn't tell him that I had no choice, merely that I'd made it.

He was in the ward when I came round from the second operation. He smiled at me. I'd never seen him smile before.

"You're fine," he said.

"I haven't had a colotomy?"

"No. Just a piece out and that was that. Clean away. You'll be fit in a few weeks."

I spent six weeks in hospital. There was one normal moment in that bleak period between the two operations. The type-script of *Space* came back from the second publisher. A little Irish nurse opened the parcel for me.

"You've written a book! How clever."

"Yes. That's two publishers have sent it back."

"Don't you know any more?"

"There was another but I don't know the address."

"I'll wrap it up again and get the address from the phone book."

She could do what she liked. The book was part of that outside world in which I had no interest at the moment.

Two months after I left Maen y Bardd on a grey morning, I came back—on a golden afternoon. Larks rose singing out of the sedges, the hills dozed in the haze, and the sun shone on the closed windows of the cottage that waited like something animate to be opened up and loved again.

I stood on the terrace with the Hallelujah Chorus pouring out of the radio to join the larks. If I could ride now, I should have a wild colt to break; if I could ski, I could take the steepest hardest run. A great climb wouldn't have satisfied me; I wanted speed and glorious physical exertion, not the quiet delight of rock. I walked through the copse and touched the bark of the sycamores and I grew calmer. I knew I wanted nothing: I had it all.

The Easter holidays came. I climbed with Sheena and we rode with friends above the Machno Valley. My arm was X-rayed to reveal an unsuspected chip fracture. The muscles had atrophied. Within a fortnight, weight-lifting exercises had restored them to normal; once again I could do pull-ups – and cope with a horse. The excitement of that holiday was epitomised by splendid gallops with the thick hairy neck under your hands and the clods flying, the milling and prancing at a gate, holding them in while it was closed, and then away: the ponies lunging and plunging and the hunter leaping ahead: squelching out of the peat on to the green ride through the bracken, the hard drumming of hooves, the sheep scattering, and the kestrel sliding startled out of his hover.

Suddenly I remembered *Space*. I was almost detached about it. I was about to go to Skye and I didn't want the typescript following me round the country. I wrote to Hodder asking them to send it to my home address.

I stood at the mail box looking at the yellow envelope with all the wariness of people who send telegrams only in emergencies. It must be Sheena or Mother or Johnnie – and just at the last moment I knew it could be my clients cancelling the Skye visit.

It said: *Contract for world rights your fine book already posted. Space Below my Feet has full Hodder enthusiasm.*

There was no positive reaction. The impact of good news can be as stunning as shock. My immediate calm was conditioned, necessitated by close involvement with the violence which so often obtruded on our lives. As I walked up the mountain that morning I thought, with detachment, how unnaturally I was behaving. I felt nothing.

The second shock wave – the one that released me – came, but I never associated my resulting joy with the book or the last successful operation.

I arrived on Skye a few days later feeling that the island and the hills and all the sea were mine to play with – in a heat-wave. Life for a seemingly timeless sequence (but it was only a week) is a memory of rock and heat and gleaming fluid days separated by nights in an attic bedroom when I'd wake and see the skylight shine and remember that in Skye, in high summer, it never got dark.

My clients, a married couple, hadn't climbed before and I introduced them gently: Window Buttress, and the Cioch by some easy route I've forgotten – and then the delightful exposure of the Cioch Upper Buttress: looking down that awesome drop into Cioch Gully and wondering if your second could hold you if you fell, and laughing at the thought.

Our best days were on those classic scrambles which I'd always wanted to do and never had the chance. Bad weather had defeated me when I guided here six years ago, and when I climbed for fun on Skye there was always some desirable rock climb that took precedence over the Dubhs and the Pinnacle Ridge of Sgurr nan Gillean.

One morning we drove round early to Sligachan, at the other end of the seven-mile range, and approached Gillean by a path above a deep-cut burn. There were gorges and pools with saplings in young leaf. There was a multitude of birds – and ahead of us the great pinnacles growing higher and blacker and more exciting with every mile. Once or twice, despite the fact that I knew they were only moderate in standard, the aspect of these fierce towers made me wonder if the party could cope. But we had a rope and if I were careful with the route-finding they should be able to follow. In the event the traverse was nothing more than a stylish scramble and we used the rope only once: to remedy (as I'd anticipated) a mistake in my route-finding.

Although the Pinnacle Ridge was a good day, the traverse

of the Dubhs was longer, higher, more airy. The sea was calm that morning and there was only the slightest breeze over the water when MacDonald, the boatman, and husband of our landlady, took us round to Loch Coruisk. Eigg and Rhum and Canna floated on the surface, insubstantial in their own haze, dreams rather than geographical locations. It was hard to think that people lived on these shadowy shapes, bought soap powder and scoured the pans, pulled the chain and read Sunday papers ...

MacDonald, a large and attractive islandman of great charm, brought the launch in so close to the Skye shore that the basking seals bestirred themselves to watch. Blunt heads like Labradors' broke the surface and stared and submerged and I knew what it was like swimming free deep down in the cold green water.

The Dubh Ridge starts almost at sea level on the shore of Loch Coruisk and rises in rocky convex arcs for over two thousand feet. Below was the vast bowl of Coire Uisg: bare, dry and hot; not crudely and overwhelmingly impressive as it is on stormy days with the cloud tearing itself in masochistic fury along the serrated tops, but not friendly either. The rocks may be hot and dry and visibility perfect on the ridge, but if you look into the back of the great corrie where the gaunt cliffs are seamed by unclimbed unknown gullies something is there that heat and light can never neutralise.

On the climb there was nothing of this; the rock was hot to the hands but the heat wasn't oppressive as it would have been in the corrie. On the top the ridge was narrow enough that even without a breeze there was a tremendous feeling of light and space. Below and very far away the sea glittered beyond the heather moors where burns were marked by pale threads of gravel: pink in the Red Cuillin, grey in the gabbro hills. There was no white water anywhere; the burns were too low. Even Eas Mhor, the high fall above Glen Brittle

House, was only a few fine spider threads whispering down the drop.

At the end of the week my clients left to walk in Wester Ross — and the weather broke. I spent the last morning sitting in the MacRaes' kitchen at Glen Brittle Cottage.

The people of the Highlands and Islands have the most natural gift for story and gossip of any I have met. Hugh MacRae would have been a bard in an earlier age. He is a large loose-limbed old gentleman, slow-moving, slow-talking, speaking English with the Gaelic cadence: the first syllable emphasised and the ends of the words dying on the breath like the fall of the sea.

He told me about the Viking settlement — and the subsequent inhabitants of that strange isolated community away on the point above the Atlantic; of the lochan with the channel to the sea up which the Winged Hats brought their ships for shelter and repair. I listened and didn't take any notes. MacRae's memory, like mine — and my imagination — is visual, and once I have seen a situation in my mind notes are unnecessary.*

He told me about the gander that killed Mrs MacRae's hens and attacked the R.A.F. rescue team so that no one would go to the yard to draw water. But he was a devoted mate and when the fox caught the goose the gander disappeared. MacRae found the bird, unmarked, away out on the point, dead of a broken heart.

There were two local boys, he told me, working away, who returned to visit an aged relative at Drynoch. They were warned against going on the Cuillin but when the old man was at market they set out for the Viking village. They found a pot of paint left by a digging party in the ancient watch-

* In fact the point was inhabited long before the Vikings. In addition to the watch tower (a galleried "dun") there is a fine Neolithic chambered cairn, and there will have been dwellings in the vicinity since the Early Iron Age.   G.M.

tower and one daubed his name on the stones. I got the impression that MacRae considered this a kind of sacrilege, a factor in the man's fate, but a pointed question didn't produce an explicit answer, only a mysterious inference.

From the ruined village the men decided to walk right round the Cuillin, but before they'd gone far the weather deteriorated and they made the mistake of crossing a stream when it was unnecessary (it made a right-angled turn half a mile downstream, and they could have stayed on the near bank all the way). They separated about this point and one man came down to Sligachan alone. His companion arrived next morning: a corpse in the loch, washed down by the flooded burn.

MacRae had stories of lost climbers and great rescues, of hard frosts when the Ridge wore ice like armour and never a cloud in the sky; he talked about the deer — and you knew that people had talked like this since the islands were first inhabited, when they killed the deer for skins and there were wolves at Armadale.

Long before I sold *Space* I had planned my second book but doubts concerning my ability kept me marking time until the acceptance of the first resolved them. Had the heat-wave continued I would have stayed and climbed on the Cuillin but now, with the weather wet and windy, I decided to start collecting material for *Two Star Red*. This was to be the story of the R.A.F. Mountain Rescue Service and I was concentrating on the activities of two teams; Valley and Kinloss. It was with these that Johnnie had been associated longest (and I wanted it to be his story too) and they covered the areas I knew best.

I left Skye to go to Kinloss in Morayshire. I stayed at an hotel in Forres and worked on the R.A.F. records for three days, spending the evenings with members of the team.

As I progressed with my research I became aware of an extraordinary lack of information regarding accidents.

Rescues were recorded in detail but to my questions: why did the victim fall? Why did the survivor take so long to call assistance? — there was no answer, only speculation. Like judges overtly unconcerned with morals, the teams were concerned only with the result of the accident, not with the cause.

The whole truth could be discovered only through witnesses who, for the most part, were survivors. To interview them personally so long after the event would have been cruel, but they had made statements to the police — and while their memories were still fresh.

Without much hope that my request would be granted, and thinking that I must abandon the book if it weren't, I wrote to all the chief constables concerned. To my surprise those in whose areas I was most interested gave me permission to study their files. Inverness-shire, Ross and Cromarty, Gwynedd (which included Snowdonia) were courteous and helpful. Two constabularies referred me to newspaper reports: a significant comment on the regard they had for the local press.

I returned to Wales for Sheena's half term which we spent virtually on horseback. We had only a few days together but the wrench of saying goodbye was tempered by the excitement I'd felt on those rides when hot sun brought out the resin scents in the forests and rivers brawled like glacier torrents, unseen below the cliffs.

The day after I took her back to school, I left for the Alps.

CHAPTER 9

Alpine Diversions

MY ENTHUSIASM that summer, engendered as much by heat-waves as by the sale of *Space* and my physical recovery, had produced a kind of wry pessimism in Johnnie. He refused to go to the Alps with me; he said the routes I wanted to do were too hard for us. He arranged to go with three of his friends and, in a state of pique but confident that I would find someone to climb with, I arrived in Zermatt alone at the end of June.

I stayed at the Bahnhof, run by Bernard Biner and his sister Paula. I was welcomed with the warmth the old guide reserved for English climbers, and I installed myself in the cellar, in the women's dormitory. Bernard, besides being adviser and mentor to his tenants, acted as intermediary for those who came looking for a companion, so having dropped the word to him that I would be grateful to hear of someone who was competent and steady, I set out to get myself in training.

Sitting in a glade full of globe flowers high above Zermatt, I looked across the valley that first afternoon and saw the Unter Gabelhorn six thousand feet above the town. Bernard thought it suitable for a solo attempt; indeed, he said I would need neither rope nor ice axe. I thought this was putting rather too much trust in my ability. I decided to take my axe but compromised to the extent of borrowing a length of line from him to save carrying my heavier climbing rope. I had no idea how one safeguarded oneself with a rope when climbing alone, but I expected I would find out if necessary and, in any case, I would have felt naked without it – on an alpine peak.

I woke early the following morning and realised immediately the first disadvantage of climbing alpine routes on your own; there is no one to shame you into getting out of bed. An alpine start solo demands a formidable amount of self-discipline.

I lay in the cellar, listening to the other girls' breathing and trying to convince myself that outside the basement window it was raining. But the feel of the morning was wrong, and how could I face Bernard if I didn't go?

I left the hotel at seven o'clock and raced up the hill – to be pulled up short by a small swarthy Italian at the entrance to the Trift Gorge. He gesticulated a lot and barred my way, talking about *mines*. A Swiss couple arrived and explained that the path through the gorge was being blasted. There had been rock falls and the mules couldn't pass until the track was clear. I found it curious but pleasing that, although the Dauphiné should use helicopters, modern bustling Zermatt still relied on mules for provisioning the huts. I wondered if they still crossed the Gorner Glacier to the Monte Rosa hut. If they did, they wore crampons on their hooves. I had spent hours one afternoon years ago puzzling over a heap of dung in the middle of that ice sheet.

We waited at the gorge for one and a half hours. I fumed with impatience; the Unter Gabelhorn was a long way away and six thousand feet higher. I glared at a slim dapper Dutchman in white linen cap, carrying a knapsack and with a map in a leather case round his neck. We talked and he was appalled at my project.

When the way was cleared we all rushed up the gorge, the Dutchman, who was called Hugo, pacing me and earning my admiration. He left me at about nine thousand feet, saying he would call at the Bahnhof that evening to make sure I'd returned safely. Since I'd told Bernard not to worry until seven (but by stating a time at all implying he could start worrying then) there was a limit to my day, and with the check in the gorge I began to think I wouldn't reach my summit.

I passed the snowline. It was so hot that the sheep were lying on the drifts with outstretched heads, baring their throats to the snow.

Above me a ridge ran up the mountain to the summit. I climbed carefully. The route was easy but the rock was poor. There was a lot of scree on the ledges and the pitches had many loose holds. There was only one difficult section: a chimney just below the top. I emerged from this, scrambled a few feet, grinning with delight (my first alpine peak solo!) and stopped short.

Below me was a deep cleft: the *gabel*, and beyond, about half a mile away and six hundred feet higher: the top of the Unter Gabelhorn.

With a companion I would have been articulate. Alone, I stood silent and pondered.

The way down into the cleft looked harder than it should have been for a moderate route. I must have missed the way. Perhaps there was a traverse across the face from some point on the ridge which would lead into the bottom of the gap. The last six hundred feet to the summit looked feasible: harder than the route so far but within my limits. I looked at the time: 1.45 p.m. This was late in the circumstances. I turned and studied the weather.

The air was sticky and in the south thunderheads towered above the Col de Théodule. Already the big peaks were in the cloud. I wouldn't reach the summit that day. I might, but I wouldn't take the risk.

I retreated and found the suspected traverse which led me to the top of a snow-filled couloir. This was steep to begin with, steep enough to force me to face into the slope as I kicked steps down it. Then the angle eased and the surface hardened so that I could glissade until the snow ran out and left me at the top of a scree slope where, for a thousand feet, the stones were deep and undisturbed and small as road chippings. I came down so fast that, although the afternoon had grown sultry under the overcast, I cooled in my own slipstream.

The air struck heavy when I stopped. I found a ewe sheltering in a dark and dripping crevasse under a rock. Her lamb was beside her: black, with floppy ears like a cocker spaniel.

"What about sciatica?" I asked, "and rheumatism – and lumbago?"

They stared at me, comatose and uncaring.

A breeze sprang up and I saw the rest of the flock, lying on the drifts, get up and move back to the grass to graze.

I came back to Zermatt by a wandering route linking up the high paths. In one place I overtook an old man descending with considerable difficulty. He wasn't a tourist but a peasant with a frame that would have been powerful once; an old guide perhaps? His hair was cropped close, and his eyes were childlike in a dissipated face. "Grüss Gott" I said pleasantly and he mumbled something. How did he get there? He leaned heavily and painfully on his stick. I described him to Bernard. Yes, he said, he knew the man but he died ten years ago.

I had forgotten the Dutchman, Hugo. He arrived at the Bahnhof while I was taking a shower. Bernard came thumping on the cellar door.

"A gentleman for you!"

"Who?"

"A gentleman. He *says* he met you this morning."

Bernard's disapproval came through the door like something tangible. We were climbers: set apart. We had no truck with tourists. Besides, he was annoyed about the Unter Gabelhorn. I'd let the side down.

Hugo took me to Seiler's for dinner. It transpired that he was a journalist, wrote film scripts and was the Amsterdam agent for an American movie company. When he learned something of my background he relaxed. On the mountain I had been an enigma but now I was an author, above convention. I was accepted.

It rained for two days and I was absorbed into the social whirl of Zermatt. This consisted mainly of eating and drinking and even if the town did go to bed at ten, the trout and the *fondues*, the cream pastries and the rare cheeses, the raw Rhône wines and exotic liqueurs, all ensured that by ten you were fit only for bed anyway. Unfortunately two days of this kind of indulgence is bad for the training programme and on the Sunday, when the storms stopped and the forests steamed and columbines shone like blue stars in the wet grass, I resumed my hard walks with a full pack, coming slowly up through the pines to find that there was new snow right down to the summer pastures.

Across the valley my rock ridge on the Unter Gabelhorn was white.

I hoped that this would have melted by the time I reached it on my next attempt but I had second thoughts the following morning as I came through the empty streets at five o'clock and saw the Matterhorn pink above the dark valley, with scarcely a speck of rock showing.

My doubts were justified; the ridge was covered with unstable snow resting on ledges where scree lay like ball-bearings. I reached the false summit and looked across the *gabel* to the peak. The last six hundred feet were swept clear of snow but the descent into the gap was drifted deep.

I retreated and tried the traversing line but after a few steps along it the soft floury stuff was up to my waist. Under my feet I could feel the scree shifting. Great clods of snow cartwheeled down the face, increasing as they went. I thought of avalanches, turned round carefully in the pit I'd made and pulled myself back to the firm rocks.

I retreated all the way down the south ridge, then turned west, going round the foot of the mountain to the couloir which led to the *gabel*. I had left my snow goggles in Zermatt and my eyes were beginning to feel the glare. I wondered about going on without the goggles but I saw that the snow slope was hard enough that I could kick up it quickly and arrive on rock before my eyes had suffered any real damage.

While I stood considering the situation there was a thud and a clatter far above me and as I watched, fascinated, searching the face, I saw the rocks coming, landing after a long free fall halfway down the snow slope, then skidding and tumbling to the bottom.

That was that. I turned and started back to the pastures and the gentle delights of flowers and sleeping sheep. I'd had enough of objective dangers for the moment.

If the lower peaks weren't feasible under these conditions, there was a possibility that a high mountain could be climbed. The snow would freeze hard overnight and still be stable in the early morning. But for a big peak I needed a companion, and now I met Paul, a small fair American student on his first trip to the Alps.

The weather remained unsettled. We went up to the Fluhalp to traverse the Rimpfischhorn but by the time we reached the col below the summit rocks we were in mist and it was snowing hard.

We decided to retreat to the Täsch hut but I was against the obvious route by way of the Mellich Glacier. I had crossed this in good visibility and it was laced with crevasses. I had the feeling Paul hadn't been on a glacier before.

We dropped down from the col to the safe snow slopes only to find we had about three miles of moraines to cross. They were safe but exhausting, relieved occasionally by fine clumps of purple saxifrage among the stones.

There was a glorious dawn next day with the Weisshorn flaming above a smouldering cloud sea. Chamois skipped across the broken cliffs as we mounted the glacier, and we saw a hare so large I couldn't believe it was a hare at all.

We were heading for the Allalinhorn and the traverse of its

south-west ridge. The climbing wasn't difficult and most of the new snow had melted, but I was puzzled by Paul's technique.

We led through on the more difficult sections. When he was in the lead he belayed by passing the rope round a boulder and then pulling as hard as he could. Either he'd seen a lot of bad films or his experience of seconds had been confined to the most incompetent novices. But he'd seen me lead . . . it was all very curious.

We arrived at the top without serious incident and saw that there was bad weather over the Saas Valley. This worried Paul, still more when I suggested we should continue our traverse over the Feekopf. He said the ridge connecting the two mountains was long and hard and we would be caught by the storm. I suggested that the Allalinhorn on its own wasn't really a full day's expedition.

Traversing the Feekopf ridge he said,

"We have probably made the first ascent of this route this season."

"Of the Allalinhorn – possibly, but not this last bit."

"Why not?"

"Tracks."

"Those aren't tracks!"

"Chamois."

The animals were using the ridge as a route between pastures.

We came down the Alphubel Glacier. We stopped on some rocks and I looked down the ice and guessed from its angle that under its blanket of snow it held quite a number of crevasses.

Paul delivered a lecture on the technique of descending wet glaciers. I was to go in front and he would hold me if I fell in a hole. I was to watch for suspicious lines, even shadows, and test the ground when I saw them. Did I know how to test for holes? He told me anyway. I listened with approval. His delivery was good; even his material was sound – so far as it went. He wound all the rope round him except for twelve feet or so which he carried in coils himself. I wasn't to have any spare rope. Well, some alpinists thought only one in a party of two should have the spare rope, but twelve feet! I didn't say anything. Paul discouraged argument.

He gestured to me to proceed. I stepped off the rock and he followed immediately. Now this is too much, I thought, it is time I made a stand. I turned to protest, and he wasn't there.

The rope disappeared into the snow.

Automatically I plunged my axe in – but the rope was taught at my waist. Before I could get it round the shaft and belay him I had to retreat a step, retrieving the axe and plunging it into the snow again. I wondered if he'd dropped his coils and was dangling – but then I'd be in there too. He must have wedged. In that case he might struggle and drop further, and even belayed, I was far too near that crevasse for safety.

There was no answer to my shouts. I crouched over my axe and sweated with anger.

After a while two hands appeared on the edge of the hole and he came out blinking like a little blond mole.

He brushed himself down without a word. I told him we'd have a little more rope between us now and he unwound it to give us about thirty feet. I took half the coils and pointed out that we would keep a respectable distance between us.

I saw to it that there were no more comic turns. I went down that glacier like a dog after truffles, smelling out the crevasses. I was more exhausted afterwards than at the end of a twenty-four-hour expedition. We never climbed together again.

It is seldom that everything goes right in the Alps. Now people arrived to climb with but the weather became more unsettled. I went up to the Monte Rosa hut with another American: a very large man also in his first season, but a self-confessed novice who recognised that if conditions stopped us climbing any routes at least I could show him how they were done.

Foiled by storms from an attempt on the Cresta Rey of Monte Rosa we spent a rainy day in the ice fall of the Grenz Glacier. He had never cut a step before but he was ambidextrous and I was intrigued and awed to watch him cutting up *séracs* left-handed while the right hand turned white in the wet holds. He was a linesman for a telephone company and accustomed to working at the tops of poles without gloves in winter. I thought that he might go far – and he did. The next time I heard of him on ice he had made the first ascent of the south-east spur of Mount MacKinley in Alaska.

Dorothea Gravina arrived. I had last climbed with her when she came on one of my courses on Skye six years ago. She was a remarkable woman; middle-aged already when she started climbing, she had recently been on the all-women expedition to Cho Oyu in the Himalayas. We climbed the Breithorn by the ordinary route: an exhausting plod relieved only by the absurdity of one tiny crevasse, signposted and covered by a wooden grille. Perhaps not so absurd when you remembered that skiers came down this side. We traversed the Furggrat which was fun for its snowy views of the Matterhorn; its Swiss ridge had been climbed only once or twice this year when usually by the end of July its ascents are reckoned in hundreds.

Johnnie appeared with his party of four and, with a New Zealand guide whom I'd met, we joined forces for the Lyskamm. We arrived at the final slopes late and only to find a sheet of ice between us and the summit. We agreed that there wasn't time for us all to climb it, and Johnnie and Basil, the New Zealander, reached the top alone.

Basil and I made an attempt on the Matterhorn. I had watched him working on the Lyskamm ridge and thought I had never seen anyone move so fast with such economy of effort. He cut one-handed with graceful flicks of his short axe and the holds were always exactly where you needed them. He was slight but very strong. He had a sharp face like a nice brown rat and was never seen without a knitted teapot hat. He even wore it to bed.

We were alone at the Hörnli Refuge on the Matterhorn. We'd had an hilarious trip from the Monte Rosa hut, crossing glaciers, treading unfamiliar moraines, scrambling up huge rubbishy cliffs without paths and where often, on hard slopes like clay, we used the axe to cut steps. Basil was an excellent companion. He told me about New Zealand and its Alps, the guides — and the kias. These are a kind of cockatoo: thieves and vandals, slashing tyres with their beaks and stealing windscreen wipers. On one occasion the guides were buiding a new hut and blasting rock when the kias raided the magazine and flew above the camp in circles carrying detonators. The men were running round with shovels over their heads.

A few days after I left him Basil fell off the Ober Gabelhorn. He fell for nearly a thousand feet, shooting the bergschrund, and arrived at the bottom with a fractured ankle which infuriated him because he realised immediately (since he was still conscious) that there would be no ski-ing for him during the coming winter.

At the Hörnli hut we woke the day we should have climbed the Matterhorn to find it was broad daylight. We were in dense cloud and there was half an inch of new snow outside. That season's third and fourth ascents of the Swiss ridge were in progress. Four climbers had been on the mountain since yesterday morning. The warden suggested we should still make the attempt but my aircraft left tomorrow and I had to meet Sheena from school. We doubted if we could be up and down in one day; we would have to spend the night at the Solvay hut below the summit. The wind was so strong it had driven all the cloud over the Hörnli to mass on the east face, so that the whole of the ridge was clean and clear as far as we could see — but it was bitterly cold and the wind was rising. The powder snow was blowing away horizontally.

We packed and went down, stopping at the Hermitje, a chalet on an alp in the forests where you can sit in the sun and eat meringues that ooze with cream, and drink Valpolicella until you don't want to move and see no point in moving. You move in the end, remembering your ultimate consolation: that the Alps are not an isolated passion but a facet of it. Home is only another range of mountains.

CHAPTER 10
Climbing Writer

I STARTED *Two Star Red* after my trip to Zermatt. The research was not yet completed (I was to visit the Scottish constabularies during the following spring) but I had studied the police files on accidents in Snowdonia so I could start with the first chapters.

My visit to Police Headquarters at Caernarvon was an enlightening experience. Until then I had regarded the police as oppressive representatives of authority at the best, shadows of Fascism at the worst. This was a legacy of my time as a deserter. I no longer had to avoid the police when I walked through a town at night but I had similar feelings of uneasiness when I was driving and saw a patrol car.

I went to Caernarvon in a spirit of defiant righteousness: they couldn't do anything to me now; I was on my lawful occasions and I had a letter from the chief constable to prove it.

I was received by men with good manners and without helmets. I was provided with a room and a cleared desk, asked if I needed writing materials, shown the Ladies, assured of tea, beamed upon, waited on, respected. My previous contacts with the police had been limited almost exclusively to rescues where for the main part they were novices whom one was compelled to accept on the hill and must watch carefully to see that they came to no harm. But occasionally, as in the case of our local man at Ro Wen and some in the Highlands there would be those who could play their part in a sweep search in bad weather, and searches, if not as dangerous as carrying a casualty down a big cliff, are the most arduous part of any rescue. But mountain rescue is not typical police work and my experience of this was confined to the matter of a threatening letter. The attitude of the police at Conway had been sensible and reassuring – and, of more practical value, they gave me much information about psychopaths and anonymous letters. However, I thought of the Conway police and good men on rescues as exceptional. It wasn't till I visited Caernarvon that I realised they were typical.

Through that winter I worked on the book, not steadily, for there were pleasant surprises which merited lengthy interruptions. At the end of the previous summer Houghton Mifflin, the Boston publishers, had bought *Space* for an advance of a thousand dollars. The cheque came before Christmas and I ordered a new van. The "new" is important. I had owned two cars and both were over twenty years old when I bought them. They were eccentric and lovable but now the rat-race cast its shadow ahead with the need to cover long distances fast and safely and, with lectures and dinners and interviews, the old days of leaving a broken-down car on the grass verge and thumbing a lift were over. I relinquished my unpredictable ancients and took delivery of a smooth metal box that had everything but character.

Sheena and I spent Christmas in Austria ski-ing. This was not an unqualified success for Sölden, where we stayed, had not yet learned to cope with large numbers of skiers, but the sport was delightful – until halfway through the second week when Sheena, trying to turn in deep snow, wrenched her knee and had to be whisked down to the valley on the back of an instructor. The doctor's verdict was rest, and the following day, seeing her settled in the lounge, I went back to the slopes for an hour or two. Almost immediately I fell on a patch of ice and hobbled back to the village to go through the routine: X-ray, strapping, immobilisation. We came home chastened but, despite the edict of an orthopaedic surgeon that I mustn't climb for three months, I was already exercised with the problem of how to reconcile this new passion with snow climbing. One needed winters twice as long.

When Sheena returned to school in the New Year I left for my annual trip to Scotland but with the strapped knee and the fact that I took with me the American proofs of *Space* to correct, the old days of living in the Nevis hut were over. Fortunately the weather was on my side (but not on Johnnie's for he was training potential team leaders again) and while he and his men worked in cloud and gales, I sat in my cosy hotel room and read galleys. When the men weren't camping they came down to Fort William and I spent the evenings with them. There was an element of sadness about this course for Johnnie had resigned from the R.A.F.

Johnnie has an aunt who is a successful novelist, producing a new book annually. With *Space* being published in the summer, and *Two Star Red* half finished, with characteristic optimism Johnnie saw me as another successful author. My apparent financial security was a chance to escape from the restrictions of the Service: red tape, the fact that he was on call for twenty-four hours a day, the lack of home life. We didn't live at Maen y Bardd; I lived there and he visited. It was unnatural, he said in the face of my remonstrances, and anyway, it was no good my protesting, he'd resigned.

I pointed out that it had taken three years to produce *Space*, four from the start to publication. If the same applied to *Two Star Red* that was not one book a year, but one every four years. If I made a thousand pounds out of each the annual income would be only £250 a year. He reminded me that with journalism and guiding I was already supporting Sheena and myself. He didn't need high wages – and there were mountain schools springing up like mushrooms.

Once I'd come to accept my new financial responsibility I realised its advantages. Until now I had suppressed the feeling that I had only two books in me, had refused to think of what would happen after I'd finished *Two Star Red*. That bridge would be crossed when I came to it. Now I realised that some bridges you must build yourself, and the foundations have to be laid in advance.

A third book was rather too much of a challenge when my mind was blank and the only incentive was money. I shelved the problem and considered other lines. I contemplated full-time journalism, working either for women's magazines or newspapers. Fortunately I had no idea of the competition in this field. I did think it might be easier to find a post on the production or editorial side, but I felt it would be churlish to take a job in London or Manchester and come home only at weekends, probably loaded with work. So it had to be free-lancing where I could work at home and be free in the evenings and at weekends.

Lectures were another remunerative line. I had given illustrated talks to climbing clubs over the last few years but I was a poor speaker and I detested standing up in public. If I could overcome this lack of confidence I might put myself on Foyle's list of lecturers. With a view to practising I circulated the local Women's Institutes.

My first engagement was a great success. By coincidence it was in my own village. I knew the audience, they knew me, and for years we had been trying to explain climbing in the pub. Now I had Johnnie's colour slides and, with my audience behind me and three Tio Pepes inside me, I went to town. Afterwards a woman photographer came up to me. She had been sitting next to an elderly farmer who had been shocked at the slides. He had erupted at every picture of climbers in action, protesting that no one could stay on walls like that, it was impossible. Halfway through he solved the problem:

"The camera is tilted," he told his neighbour, "the rock is sloping, but the picture comes out vertical. *Jesi Mawr!* No one could climb that!"

The photographer told him to look at the clouds which were horizontal, at the rope hanging free instead of coming in to the rock as it would if the angle were gentle. I think the sequence in question was one of Johnnie leading Mur y Niwl: the sensational wall on Craig yr Ysfa. I showed shots of the wall *en face* alternating with himself in silhouette. They frightened even me. I saw what the farmer meant.

"Faked," he announced at the end, "all faked!"

It was after my debut as a lecturer that I went to Fort William. It was a poor winter season but there were some tolerable days when I was persuaded, despite my game leg, to go out with the course: walking the big ridges or climbing the icy buttresses of Buachaille Etive Mor in Glen Coe. These trips fulfilled the need to see this last course in progress, to watch Johnnie at work. The new book needed a personal note, I thought, and a postscript with a thread of nostalgia running through it. Diligently and consciously I searched for my atmosphere, for background, incidents, word pictures, but the harder I probed the more they eluded me, or appeared to do so for success came like an explosion: the true inspiration that you dream of as a novice. At midnight on the last night I stood on a bridge in Glen Coe and looked at the light in the climbing hut, at low cloud on the hills and I saw the end of the book clean and complete. I wept, not for that but for the knowledge that all those weeks of search had not been wasted – and for the awareness that it would happen again, many times.

The course broke up, Johnnie went south to Valley and I stayed behind to work with the police, the medical authorities and the Highland Museum in Fort William. I returned to Wales with the knowledge that my research was completed and I could spend the summer climbing.

Johnnie must have seen the writing on the wall, have realised that when you work as a civilian climber there is little time for fun. This summer he was determined to take advantage of every hour of leisure. Through May and June we travelled round Snowdonia discovering old but unpopular routes and exploring new ones.

He took me to the steep little Moelwyn cliffs above Ffestiniog where he wanted to climb every route because he was writing the guide-book to the area. We went to the Devil's Kitchen and climbed the unfrequented routes which had a reputation for looseness but which we found firm. Although we had to wait for a drought when these north-facing cliffs would be dry, and it was momentarily frustrating to leave the sun and enter those great shadowed gullies, the day held compensations: the delight of new climbs, new views of the Kitchen which we had known since we were introduced to rock, the pink and purple cushions of alpines and ledges lush with orchids.

I was introduced to serious mountain photography. Hodder had warned me the Press would soon be asking for pictures. Johnnie and his friend, Vic Bray, set out to provide them. I spent ages poised on tiny holds a long way above my second and there, with my legs aching and imagining my feet were starting to slip on a friction hold, I would be ordered to move up, down, left and right (often contradictory orders coming from sideways and below), orders which had no bearing on the line of the route and forced me on to unclimbed rock.

Film was developed and the results pronounced unsatisfactory. My feet didn't show on a tiny hold; I must go back and repeat the climb in tricounis: every nail would be silhouetted.

Tempers frayed and I escaped with relief to guiding and the equable temperament of clients who wanted nothing more than to see over the next hill.

Charles was one of these: an enthusiastic, middle-aged bachelor, the type that makes climbing not so much a professional engagement as days of fun, the type from whom it is embarrassing to accept a cheque at the end of a holiday. He wanted to progress from walking to climbing.

I employed my normal routine of a long walk which could be abandoned at one of many points if necessary, and we started with the north ridge of Tryfan on a clear hot lovely day when I, fit as a cat, thought gloomily that Charles must succumb too soon to heat and exhaustion.

I studied him carefully on top of Tryfan and he was unaffected. I pointed out Bristly Ridge with emphasis on the fact that we must drop three hundred feet to the col and rise six hundred to Glyder Fach. His eyes gleamed.

We traversed the Glyders from the top of Bristly to the Devil's Kitchen. A strenuous introduction, I was thinking, and not sorry it was all downhill now; I was parched for tea.

Above the Kitchen I showed him Y Garn towering eight hundred feet above us, pointed it out casually: background material. Charles was inflexible – he'd done three mountains and he wanted a fourth. I could have demurred: I was the guide and had the right to say when we should go down. The snag was he didn't need to go down; I must forgo my tea and gird my loins.

On the top of Y Garn I directed his attention carefully northwards, away from Elidir Fawr: the fifth mountain of the Glyder group, and with a sly reference to the exigencies of the Snowdon Horseshoe the following day I managed to manœuvre him towards the valley.

It was considerably hotter on Snowdon than it had been on the Glyders. Although Charles knew his place, to the rear of the guide, I was constantly aware, going up that jumbled scramble to the summit of Crib Goch, that if the man weren't slowed down soon, I'd have an inferiority complex that it would take a summer of hard rock climbing to eradicate.

We progressed to climbing – but the first day was broken by a lamb rescue. We spent the morning on easy routes on the Gribin Facet (seeing with satisfaction that this was one place where I had the edge on my client) and then we moved over to the Idwal Slabs when the sun had reached them. Here, above Continuation Wall, we came on a tiny lamb, alone and gasping in a grassy haven where the temperature must have approached a hundred degrees. (Brought up on Fahrenheit, I have never mastered Centigrade.)

Years of living in sheep country had taught me that, contrary to appearances, few lambs are abandoned, but this one was in great distress, and the ewe should come back and move it into the shade. But when we studied the place we realised that although the ewe had escaped (she could have jumped, landing with difficulty on a ledge above the drop) the lamb must have been unable to follow. There were signs that it had been born there.

I scouted around in widening circles searching for the mother. The nearest sheep was about a quarter of a mile away down in Cwm Cneifion, feeding quietly with another lamb about the same age as the first. It appeared that she had dropped one on the ledge, moved and had the second in a less inaccessible place. Then, because the first couldn't follow or because it was weakly, she'd abandoned it to the crows.

We waited a long time but she didn't come back and in the end I could stand the lamb's distress no longer. Charles assured me he would be quite happy to walk on his own; carefully we outlined his route to the top of Glyder Fawr and once there he knew the ground from our walk of two days ago.

I tucked the lamb under one arm and started to descend. As soon as I came into the shade of Introductory Gully it revived. Its eyes brightened and it started to struggle. I moistened the dry mouth with water and continued. It wasn't the first time I'd had to climb one-handed, the gully was well-furnished with holds and the lamb was astonishingly light. I carried him down to Blaenant Farm and, finding the people out, shut him in a stable and left a note on the front door. Then I rushed to find Charles, very conscious of my cardinal sin: I had split the party on difficult ground. But he was waiting at the rendezvous; his walk had been without incident and he was most sympathetic about my shortened day.

We had only four days and on the last, with the sun blazing again, we linked the Idwal Slabs with the upper cliff of Glyder Fawr to give us nearly two thousand feet of climbing.

I remember professional engagements mainly by weather and incidents related to it. So some jobs are a memory of high winds and a visual picture of the rope sweeping out in an arc above the crux; others are of rain and seconds disappearing under waterfalls, but those four days with Charles left an impression of still hot air and a mountainside all rock from the lake to the hazy skyline; rock dry and rough as sandpaper: an empty heat-soaked mountain waiting for two people and a rope.

Space was published at the beginning of July. Johnnie gave me a party in the local pub, inviting for the main part friends who had played a part in the book. George Dwyer and his wife Nell came. George, the senior Welsh guide, had been one of my referees when I applied for my guide's certificates. There was Dicky Morsley and Dave Thomas with whom I'd climbed as a novice, Bill Trench who'd always been around whenever I wanted transport or a pipe mended or a chimney swept. Vic Bray, the photographer, came too, and Ron James at whose mountain centre Johnnie was to work when he left the R.A.F. in the autumn. There were four Welsh guides in the inn that night. It was a good party.

I left for London next morning. There was to be a conference with Hodder and an interview for the Columbia Broadcasting System.

With Hodder's promotion manager and an American journalist I lingered late over dinner at Prunier's and when I was taken back to my respectable hotel, the night porter was putting out the lights. The interview wasn't taped yet and had to go to the States the following day. The journalist said he would interview me in my room. The porter called the manager.

Reason prevailed. We found ourselves sitting on my bed with the tape-recorder and a bottle of whisky between us – and the door open. I found that my interviewer's engaging personality masked a very competent professionalism. Despite the fact that we laughed so much the manager came to ask us to close the door after all, I heard subsequently that the interview was highly successful.

On the first Sunday after publication I was with my family in Hove.

"Only three reviews," I said gloomily as I came back from the paper shop. My sister Jeanne said:

"Don't tell me you've made the *News of the World* at last!"

"With a picture!"

"They're running true to form: 'spirits either soar above the snow line or they swim miserably in the dark black depths of the crevasses . . . a remarkable biography.' Is this a good review?"

"I don't know," I said, "it sounds a bit sensational."

Mother said:

"I'm afraid the picture's smaller in the *Sunday Times*. Who is Edna O'Brien? She's picked out that nice description of the rhododendrons."

The third review was *Reynolds News,* monopolised by a quotation from the book.

During the following week the *Daily Express* gave me four paragraphs, and on the second Sunday *The Observer* started its review with the sentence that Hodder were to use afterwards on the jacket of *Two Star Red*: "As a story of climbing and of compulsive love of the mountains . . . *Space Below my Feet* is magnificent."

My reaction was one of continuous astonishment. After all, *Space* had originally been rejected by two publishers. But the book stayed on the best seller list for four weeks and shortly I was told that it had been selected by the Quality Book Club.

I returned to Wales and a flurry of Press and B.B.C. interviews. The first wave passed but then the book came out in the States and I was recalled to London for more interviews. Gradually the excitement died down, leaving me with a formidable list of lecture engagements and invitations to speak at dinners. Success had gone to my head in that I thought I could cope with these fringe benefits.

"All good publicity," Johnnie crowed exultantly, spurring me on to accept more and more engagements. It was years before I learned more sense.

Johnnie left the R.A.F. and after working for a time with Ron James he accepted a post as junior instructor at the Outward Bound School at Ullswater in the Lake District. The salary was half that which he'd been receiving in the R.A.F. and during his weeks as a civilian climber he'd found that vacancies in mountain schools were rare and when a post did fall vacant there was considerable competition for it. He'd found too, that a university degree usually counted for more than his own extensive experience.

His services to rescue were recognised in the New Year Honours list with the British Empire Medal – which made him observe wryly that you couldn't eat medals. Collectively the family was starting to feel the financial squeeze, but I was optimistic that eventually his experience would be recognised. Meanwhile the only work available was these chance jobs at mountain centres. That he should have to work as a junior instructor under men who were less experienced as mountaineers was a situation that rankled bitterly. He could never compromise. If a man were an incompetent climber he was beyond the pale even if he excelled in other fields of youth work. The fact that he must accept conditions in order to retain his job ensured that the next three years were to be the most miserable and frustrating period of his life.

He had bought a powerful motor cycle and although I saw him occasionally he had so little free time that the infrequency of these visits became another factor which increased his dissatisfaction with civilian life. He failed to find a home for us in the Lakes so, after spending the winter writing and lecturing, and the Easter holidays with Sheena, I went north in May to look for a house.

A few miles from the Outward Bound School, on a hill above Ullswater, I found an empty three-roomed cottage and rented it for a pound a week.

CHAPTER II

Men and Mountains

THE MOVE FROM Maen y Bardd was a disturbing upheaval, not only materially but emotionally as well. I had never placed a limit on my time there, never thought of moving; I was unaware of how much I had grown into the house until the time came to go. There I had been secure: financially, physically, emotionally. Johnnie was away for weeks and months at a time and I stayed on the mountain, not waiting but just being there. Over the next few years he was constantly regretting that we didn't buy the place and stay.

Although he grumbled about the inconveniences: the gates he must open if he came up alone in the Land Rover, all those niggling chores associated with life in an old house, these were minor annoyances; when we left he looked back on Maen y Bardd with nostalgia, like a person remembering holidays as a child.

Leaving Wales was tearing up my roots, and although I didn't realise it at the time, it was to be my last taste of security for years. But I knew that first morning when I woke in the cottage above Ullswater and, noting that there were three doors in the living room, made some observation about draughts. Johnnie said not to worry: we wouldn't be at Ullswater in a year's time.

"A month of packing," I said, "two days of supervising the move" (a tractor and trailer had taken everything down to the pantechnicon which couldn't come beyond the village) "with seventeen tea-chests to unpack and half the furniture in the yard to be broken up; no work done for a month, and landing here after a night drive with every bloody cat screaming and the engine boiling on Kirkstone and I've blocked it all out and made myself accept a situation where I just follow you around — and you tell me we'll be on the move again within a year! And don't pick that cat up; she's been spayed."

Jet tried to get under cupboards when there was trouble. She wasn't frightened, just prudent. He picked her up, she screamed and I threw a cup at him. He walked out, leaving me to reflect not so much on my position as a second-class citizen as on the stupidity of unpacking the expensive cups first. I should have known the first day in Ann's Cottage would be trying.

Jet's operation had been forced on me. I was like the woman in *The Pumpkin Eater* who wouldn't stop having children. I liked to have these recurrent families of kittens. But kittens are difficult to place and I had reached saturation point in Snowdonia. Putting them down was literally sickening (Johnnie refused to do it) but the task of finding homes was so exhausting that the last time Jet was pregnant I had decided that thirty-seven kittens was enough. She should have this litter and then be spayed.

So, after the latest kittens were weaned, Jet went to the veterinary surgeon and I suffered agonies of remorse when I took her out of the basket and she collapsed with her hind-quarters still immobilised from the anaesthetic. I discovered afterwards that many vets keep a spayed cat overnight to allow time for observation.

Jet and I recovered quickly from this experience and by the time we moved to the Lakes she was fit — except that she objected to being picked up.

In order to facilitate the transport of four healthy cats I took the van to Maen y Bardd on the last morning by way of the coalman's route: up the mountain and down from the Roman road to the cottage. The kittens had no objection to the cat basket and Jet climbed in the van and started a tour of inspection, but as soon as the engine started she set up a yell, and that yelling continued to Kendal: one hundred and forty miles. The kittens screamed in sympathy.

In sheer desperation, after a few miles I let the kittens out of the basket. They didn't, as I'd anticipated, get under the foot controls, and somewhere during the journey I succeeded in developing some kind of resistance to the noise which, since it never stopped, had a certain consistency.

We arrived in Kendal after dark and, driving up the main street, I was aware of something different, something lacking. It took a few moments for my battered brain to tell me that the noise had stopped. I glanced sideways. Four heads showed above the back of the passenger seat. They were watching the coloured lights, entranced and quite silent.

When the engine boiled on Kirkstone and I waited on the top of the pass for it to cool, the only sound was the snipe drumming and little exhausted snores from the back of the van. It had been a hard journey.

Our landlady at Ann's Cottage, in whose garden the house stood, was a vegetarian and very old. She had a gardener who came to the door a few days after we moved in to announce ghoulishly that he'd had orders to shoot the cats. We had told the landlady that we had one (which was true at the time) but she was appalled to find that we had four on arrival.

I locked the family in the house and rushed to Penrith and a solicitor. Telephone calls followed. I was assured *my* cats weren't to be shot, only "wild" ones. On the way home I called at the school. I wasn't staying at Ann's Cottage; Johnnie must find another house. By coincidence an instructor was about to vacate a bungalow in the grounds and we were offered this on the spot.

I returned to the cottage, to be paid a formal call by the old lady. She was really a charming person and I did sympathise with her practice of eating her vegetables raw. I'd once been vegetarian for a long time. She pointed out that the family was using her herb garden as a lavatory, and although I knew that this wasn't so – they were using a heap of builders' sand, I reflected that this might be unseemly too, so I kept quiet and said they would be encouraged to use grass. The following day a consignment of wire netting arrived to fence the herbs. I tried to retract the decision to move into the bungalow but Johnnie pointed out that the road to the cottage, being at a thousand feet, would be blocked by snow in winter.

Six weeks after we left Maen y Bardd we moved from Ann's Cottage to a pre-fabricated bungalow with all modern conveniences, a glorious panorama of Helvellyn from the living room window – and the main road a few yards away.

Almost immediately Jet was run over.

I was returning from placing the last two kittens in Derby and Northampton when I came in the door and heard Mother whisper to Johnnie:

"Don't tell her!"

"Don't tell me what?"

I rushed into the living room to find Jet on a chair, filthy, paralysed, nearly dead. She had been found by the Bursar's wife in the hedge that morning.

We had two excellent vets in partnership in Penrith: competent and compassionate. Jet, I was told, had suffered a heavy blow near the base of the spine. This had injured the nerve and a full bladder was causing further suffering. Too far gone for protest, she was given a catheter. After a cortisone injection she was allowed home.

The following day she returned for treatment but on the third day, iron-willed and felinely modest, she staggered into the garden and, with me in support, managed without the catheter.

She recovered almost completely although she would always limp. She still brings rabbits home but I've never seen her catch them. How she manages to spring from those weakened hindquarters is a mystery.

I thought I had practically finished *Two Star Red* before I left Wales but when I came to re-read it at Ann's Cottage I destroyed several chapters and re-wrote them. I was still lacking a final chapter, an introduction and a postscript. I knew what I wanted: a chapter on women and survival, Johnnie in action for the introduction, and, in the postscript, the pattern I had seen that last night of the last course in Glen Coe.

I couldn't recover the serenity I had known at Maen y Bardd when I could sit and write all day, often all night, and with no distractions. At Ullswater there was a plethora of interruptions: "Mr Lees says will you find his lightweight boots ... Mr Lees says he'll be home at five and will you have his tea ready sharp?" I hated Mr Lees who couldn't anticipate that he might want his lightweight boots and couldn't make his own tea.

He contracted water on the knee; a painful disease, but equally obnoxious was his frustration, when the fluid was drained away periodically, and feeling that there was nothing wrong fundamentally, he was confined to bed. He wasn't allowed to work for four months.

I had not yet learned to divide my life into compartments. I tried to combine the roles of nurse and author. Every month we were sinking deeper into debt and to me, who would never entertain the thought of even a hire-purchase agreement, the continued requests to my mother and the bank to tide us over until the book was published were humiliating. I couldn't shelve the book while Johnnie was ill but the compulsion to break off just as it might be going well, to make tea or administer medicine or to respond to a request to keep him company, these made me seethe with frustration. I knew he was right when he said that, writing a book, I was hell to live with.

Once he was a walking patient he spent his days at the school and left me free, but the rot had gone too far and I found work on the book impossible.

Jack Longland wrote asking after my progress. I told him. I had no illusions. I thought, as one critic had pointed out, that *Space* could have been a flash in the pan. *Two Star Red* might fail — and I couldn't even finish it.

Jack suggested I go away and climb. He said he would read what I'd written; he'd tell me if it was any good. He'd been right before, hadn't he? I agreed that every prophecy he had made concerning *Space* had been correct.

One afternoon in November I left Ullswater for the north-west of Scotland. In the van I had all my climbing gear but I also took my typewriter, my record files and the unfinished typescript. I hadn't much hope of recovering my sense of proportion. I was now certain I was a failure. Since that time, long before I feel this sick depression I admit that I'm stale and friends and family break down my obstinacy and my misplaced, mistimed sense of duty, and drag or drive me out to the hills: climbing, ski-ing, walking. And always, alone for a moment, as I walk away from the last pitch of the climb, or pause at the top of a ski run after a hard day, I become aware of the hills and of the fact that here, on my own territory, I have an advantage which is more than the recovery of my sense of proportion.

Such awareness comes slowly over a period of days. As I drove up the shores of Loch Ness the morning after I left Ullswater and looked at the yellow birches against a sky the colour of a dunnock's egg, I knew it was beautiful but the beauty — and my memory of other happier autumns — only underlined my sense of inadequacy.

I stayed in Scotland for three weeks. A sudden cold snap moved down from the Arctic preceded by gales. A hoped-for traverse of Liathach became an exhausting dash for the summit and a race down with Jack, who had been in his prime on Everest thirty years ago, always in the lead. Then, one morning after the snowfall, we started up from Dundonnel to traverse An Teallach, a massive mountain of several tops with a black loch lying below the long north face. The traverse was snowy, rugged and magnificent, and by the time we reached the penultimate top we were tired. We found a gully to descend where the snow was compacted and there was no fear of avalanches. After a few feet we were able to coil the rope and glissade.

The last long plod across the moor and along the weary road was done in darkness, squelching through the bogs, seeing pale rocks shine in the torchlight, moving automatically at the end, bumping into each other as we weaved along the tarmac and not bothering to apologise.

I was taken to visit the old explorer, Tom Longstaff and his wife Charmian in Coigach. By now Jack had read the typescript, and the combination of his favourable verdict and the climbing had dissipated my depression. Until Charmian asked me about progress I had forgotten those sterile weeks at Ullswater. Embarrassed, because I felt it betrayed a lack of self-discipline, I explained the difficulties of finishing the book.

They told me I must finish it there at Coigach. I could have a room where I could work all day, uninterrupted except for coffee and sandwiches, on condition that at five o'clock I came down to tea and spent the evening with them.

Another person who helped was Tom Patey, doing locum for an Ullapool doctor. He was already a legend with his ascent of the Muztagh Tower and, in Scotland, the new hard climbs which he had been putting up solo in Applecross. He was a solid chunky man, dark and attractive; subsequently television was to seize on him as a member of filmed climbing performances. He was a man of strange moods: playing his accordian in a crowded ski lodge one weekend, climbing alone on the great black western cliffs the next.

It was a wet day when we went to climb the Cioch of Sgurr a'Chaorachain: the rock, a smooth black sandstone was deficient in holds and covered with slime. I was astonished to see Patey use knees and elbows without embarrassment. Following him I realised the advantages of such clumsy and heretical technique: the more friction you had on this stuff the better.

We came out on top in the dusk and saw above us an eagle circling the summit cairn against the evening sky. Back at the car, changing into decent clothes behind a rock, I heard music. Patey was playing his accordion on the empty pass.

I stood in the heather and watched the lights in the croft houses reflected in the water of Loch Carron. It was my last climb in the north-west for the moment; tomorrow I was bound for Coigach and work. Patey had a fine sense of timing.

Charmian gave me a room looking out on the Summer Isles. Her "interruptions" with coffee and sandwiches fitted perfectly. I thanked her with one part of my mind and she went away. She had practice as well as understanding. She had helped Tom with his book: *This My Voyage.*

She was a gay attractive woman possessing those qualities needed by the wife of a big landowner in a small house. In summer they were seldom without guests and in winter there could be the chance bird of passage like me. Charmian entertained or succoured everyone but she wasn't tied to her kitchen. She walked the hills, painted in the studio Tom had built for her, and fished. She was an expert fisherman of sea trout: "so much more exciting than salmon." She was that enviable mixture, a woman who could be solitary or gregarious as the occasion demanded and enjoy both states equally. Tom adored her. Many years her senior he was still a vigorous old man – in the sense that he was full of life. His conversation, his intense interest in people and mountains gave you the impression that he was an active octogenarian although in fact, he suffered with his

I

chest and while I was there that bleak autumn week he seldom moved beyond his chair in the sitting room. In the same manner, while he sat, talking in his fine cultured voice, with his great hooked nose and his white beard, you didn't notice his physique and it was a shock to realise when he rose how very small and frail he was. He loved to talk about his explorations in parts that were then unknown and unmapped. I told them of the activities of mutual friends and they recounted local *causes célèbres*. The western seaboard is long but it possesses a form of sea telegraph and you can do nothing at one end that within a few days isn't known in every ludicrous and intimate detail at the other. Charmian told me I must come here and write a novel; they would let me have a croft.

I left Coigach with regret. It is a wild fairy country where, north of the big mountains, the little peaks rise sudden out of a sea of moorland: An Stac, a red and castellated fortress; Suilven, a bloated phallic symbol above the bustle of Lochinver harbour. It is a country I cannot think of, cannot visualise, without smiling. Johnnie, when he came to work here, felt the other-worldliness of the north-west but he found it repellent: claustrophobic and sinister. One's feeling for a country depends on the attitude of mind. Discovering a new confidence in the north-west I was happy and loved it.

I returned to Ullswater and those glorious months which went down in local history as "the bad winter." The snow came, quietly but in great quantities, and then the helm got up and blocked the roads. The helm is a local phenomenon centred on Cross Fell, the highest hill of the Pennines. It is sometimes called the fifth wind. Cold air comes driving up the gentle eastern slopes of the hills and, meeting the warm air over the Eden Valley, sets up a terrific aerial turmoil above the steep escarpment. The wind blows down trees and telegraph poles, damages power lines and sends not only the roof slabs flying but sometimes the roofs themselves. Lastly, it lifts the snow off the fields and hills and deposits it on the roads.

That year the high road over Hartside was blocked for more than sixty days and, ski-ing along the Ullswater road for provisions, I went over the top of a van. I didn't discover it until I returned, when taking a different line I caught a glimpse of green metal in the snow, and there were my tracks going over the roof.

For six weeks I skied every day in the field behind the bungalow. I met Eric Arnison, a Penrith solicitor and mountaineer who introduced me to the local ski club and the high white slopes of the hill called Raise. I was still a raw novice and my descent of the mountain, down the steep side of Keppel Cove, consisted of diagonal traverses. I would watch the others stemming competently at the corners but as soon as I had one ski pointing downhill I was away and Keppel Cove, a thousand feet below, was coming up to meet me with the speed of an express train – and with similar foreseeable consequences. These descents taught me two things: kick turns and how to fall.

From Keppel Cove a track runs down to Greenside lead mines where we left the cars. Catstye Cam and Helvellyn are up on the right with Red Tarn held in their horseshoe. One Sunday evening we were descending the track – which was drifted in the curious way of many tracks in winter, particularly those which you are required to ski down in the dark, drifted longitudinally, and it had odd kinks where it crossed the becks. Its descent was harrowing – with the drifts and the channels keeping you straight and never a place to do a turn and the snow too icy to edge your skis.

I was cursing and panting in the rear when suddenly I ran into the rest of the party who had halted and were conferring with a walker who had approached from the direction of Red Tarn. He had been descending late with a companion when they'd heard cries coming from the lake shore. A lone climber had fallen down one of the Helvellyn gullies and

appeared to have fractured his skull. One walker stayed with
the casualty while the other came down for help.

The skiers — the proper ones — started fast for Greenside and
the stretcher that was kept there. I considered abandoning
my skis and running but I knew I could go faster on them,
and the luck which safeguards drunks and the occasional
madman saw me to the lead mines safely despite the fact
that for most of the way I was out of control.

Perhaps it was the frosty evening that kept us going fast
after our tiring day, perhaps the knowledge that a man with
a fractured skull was waiting in that cold, but we had
almost reached the casualty with the stretcher by the time
the rescue team overtook us. I have cursed many young men
on rescues who, by their example, have forced me to keep
going hard, but Eric is the only man whom, considerably my
senior, I have cursed for the same reason.

The fallen climber recovered but he had fantastic luck.
The walkers who had heard his shouts were the last people
on the mountain and he regained consciousness at the
precise moment when they were in a position to hear him
calling. But for these coincidences he would have died of his
injuries and exposure, for those winter nights of '63 were
bitter. This was the time that Ullswater was frozen for much of
its length.

Some time after Christmas, when *Two Star Red* was with
Hodder and the advance had wiped out the debts and paid
the bills, I thought that something must be done about my
ski-ing. To improve at this most demanding of sports you
must have instruction and competition. Competition is one
of the things I like about ski-ing. Unlike climbing where
it is considered a sin, although often indulged covertly, in
ski-ing you know that the best way of improving yourself
is by executing your turns more competently than the next
man. I decided to attend a ski school in the Grampians.
Unlike the start of my autumnal trip to the north-west,

that two weeks' holiday was fun from the moment I left Ulls-water. Johnnie was now fit and ranging the hills with his camera and his boys so he could be left without a qualm, and I was full of delighted speculation, not knowing what lay ahead.

The roads were clear at first, so clear that somewhere in the Southern Uplands, as I grew tired of driving through the night, I had no hesitation in pulling off the main road to find a place to sleep. All I needed was a lay-by or, failing that, a gateway. I should have remembered that snow ploughs, keeping the trunk roads clear, would have no time for the by-ways. My road hadn't been touched, except by tractors which had left deep ruts, now frozen hard. I drove some distance with my wheels spinning on every uphill gradient and I knew that soon I would be stopped. I came to a junction and tried to turn but it was only impetus that had kept me going until now and suddenly I found myself stuck fast in a drift.

I got out and pondered the position. There was room to drive round me, the night was bitterly cold and the place was as good as anywhere to stop. I crawled into my sleeping bags in the back of the van and went to sleep. During the night I was wakened by steps on the crusted snow. I peered out and there was a big dog fox investigating the van in the starlight.

I dug myself out in the morning. I carry basic equipment for winter journeys: the coal shovel, chains, sleeping bags. With these I reckon I can either get myself out of trouble or, in the comfort of the bags, wait till the snow-plough reaches me if a blizzard precludes my going to find a tow. But having to be rescued by plough or tractor could be as embarrassing as being brought down off the hill by a rescue team, and the chains and shovel reduce such a risk to the minimum.

At Blairgowrie a notice said that the road over the Devil's Elbow was blocked. This pleased me immensely as the Glen-shee Hotel where I was bound was just this side of the Elbow and I knew there'd be plenty of snow.

As I approached Glenshee I was consumed by a kind of awed delight. The drifts beside the road were so high that they reached the tops of the telegraph poles, and round every hamlet and village the slopes were marked by ski tracks with not a patch of grass visible, only hay spread for the sheep.

I passed a postman putting chains on his van.

"You'll not get through," he told me, "they've been cut off for days."

"Are you going there?"

"I'll try, but I doubt it—and ye've got no chains."

I went back to the van and put them on. The postman watched gloomily then drove away.

Vehicles had got through to the hotel, but only Land Rovers and tractors. The road was rutted so deep I had to send the van hard up every rise and it rolled and bucked like a bronco and I knew that any moment a wing mirror could be shorn off against the shining walls of the drifts which looked as hard as concrete, it was so long since a plough had been here. Tendrils of broken telephone wires trailed across the road and whispered along the roof. I daren't stop and could only hope that one wouldn't catch on a wheel or the prop shaft. The sun was dazzling.

I arrived at the hotel as the classes were leaving, was enrolled on the spot and chivvied away to the nursery slopes to be scrutinised and allocated my class. One was back in childhood, first day at school, but there was an element of the market too, although the glint in the instructor's eye as he inspected his predominantly female class wasn't that of the pasha purchasing houris but the dealer contemplating horse-flesh. One's leg action might be admired but only in conjunction with a smooth turn.

The wind got up in the night sweeping new snow off the hills. Next day we went up the mountain behind the hotel. I was the only one with skins for my skis and I was most unpopular. First, I made light work of the ascent and then, when we got to the top, the others shivered in the bitter wind while I struggled to get the things off my skis and my hands stuck to the metal bindings with the cold.

Coming down was ski-mountaineering of a high order, at least for the intermediate class. Patches of ice would appear suddenly as the man in front changed course, and you went shooting forward to overrun Derek, the instructor, himself swerving in slow motion down the hill in the happy belief that his class was following in a long, slow, curving line. As you shot past you could hear him intoning:

"Turn — and bring the upper ski in — and traverse ... weight on the lower ski ... stem out — and — *where the hell do you think you're going?*"

Derek was a Cockney and given to temperament. A lot of this seemed reserved for me. I was unique in that, having lived for years in a dangerous world, I was captivated by this one where, if a broken leg could result from a clumsy turn, this was the worst that could happen. Fractured skulls and multiple injuries had no place here; death from exposure was highly unlikely when we went on the hills in a small flock. My reaction to the safety of it all resulted in over-confidence equalled only by my lack of technique.

It was *different* — that was part of the joy. In climbing there is only yourself to control; in ski-ing there are these two planks, not a pair of them but two individual objects, each going in a different direction while you are bent on another.

I watched the experts coming down the face below the ski lift. Would I ever do that? Would I do it with parallel turns, with parallels as lovely as that?

Ski-ing was a challenge, technically a greater one than rock had ever been, and when you could come swaying down a steep white slope, with turns so controlled and yet so quick that the detail couldn't be followed, wouldn't the run be as beautiful as a rock climb?

"That's right Gwen — nice-ly — round — to-gether — *together*! Get-your-weight-on-the-lower-ski! TOGETHER! Oh my Gawd!

Fill the hole up. Look, don't any of you ever listen to *anything* I say?"

He decided we needed rhythm. Right, we would exercise to music. So he bawled Strauss at us and the Ball of Kirriemuir with long pointed pauses as, rigid with concentration, we performed our turns while still trying to catch the words. We went up the chair lift and he gave a demonstration on the frozen lochan, skimming over the ice to the Skaters' Waltz while we watched and wilted in despair.

We were taught odd things which one needs to know in Scottish mountains perhaps more than elsewhere. There was a long slope with horizontal drifts across it. One look at the lie of the land and I had it sized up. I remembered the ski manual: straighten on the uphill, flex on the downward slope – or was it the other way round? I moved gingerly, aware of my audience. In a way I was the star; I could always be relied on for effects.

The first drifts were shallow and I picked up speed. I went over a top and the next hollow came up and hit me, shooting me out like a catapult and for one glorious moment I was airborne and curving gently and there was a curious familiarity about the huts away at the bottom of the lift with a little crowd of people gathered. Of course, I thought, picking myself up, it's the view from the top of the ski jump at the Olympics.

The second time I went down the drifts splendidly with my legs going like pistons – and went straight into some machine at the bottom. Derek peeled to a halt beside me.

"You haven't damaged it, have you?" he asked, peering anxiously at the paint.

Then there was the Bank. A burn ran through a shallow ravine, the sides of which were heavily corniced. The idea was to shoot off the cornice at an angle and drop with the snow to the lower level, then skim away across the burn which was covered with thin ice but with a snow bridge at the salient point. Derek could take the cornice where the bank was six feet high, dropping with the snow and hitting the bridge right in the middle. At first all the class chose the lowest part of the bank, then the bolder ones tried to emulate Derek – who reminded me of Johnnie in his desire to push our limit to the utmost; Derek telling us to follow him was like Johnnie telling me to lead a route from which he'd just retreated.

It was possible to aim your skis at the highest point of the cornice and to peel away at the last moment if your nerve failed. It was more likely that having shot down the hill at high speed you peeled away too late and, lying under your own avalanche, you screamed in panic, not because of the danger of being smothered but because you knew the enthusiasm of the course and suspected that they'd start using their sticks as probes.

Derek spent his evenings with us and we exchanged funny stories. I couldn't cap his best one. He was ski-ing on Meall a' Bhuiridh in Glen Coe and had decided to descend a formidable gully called the Fly Paper:

"It's narrow and very steep, particularly at one point, and there was this chap – a *climber* – cutting his way up it with an ice axe!"

"Were you surprised?"

"Wouldn't you be? He was too. I just caught a glimpse of his face as I went by."

The other skiers didn't appreciate it so much but I, with memories of all the steep gullies I'd climbed, was enchanted.

CHAPTER 12

The Healing Summer

BEFORE WE CAME to the Outward Bound school I had placed one of Jet's kittens with the warden's wife in the belief that it was a tom. Within a few weeks Jaspar turned out to be not only a queen but pregnant. She produced several kittens and was allowed to keep one. When we moved to the bungalow she came back to me with her kitten, Boy Fred. She was renamed Jessicat. She was long and lithe, black and white with golden eyes. She was neurotic about the Boy, boxing his ears for no reason then, in an agony of guilt, seizing him in both paws and washing his face until he squirmed in agony. With us she was aloof at first, never appearing to want affection, sitting on the hearth or curled in one chair, always the same one, with her head buried in her huge black tail.

When Boy Fred was weaned I took his mother to be spayed. A few nights later I was due for a function at the school and waiting anxiously for her to come home. She had been missing all afternoon and I didn't want her prowling in the dark so soon after her operation. There were foxes in the woods.

She came home at the last minute, jumping straight into a half-empty packing case, so it wasn't until next morning that I saw the suppurating wounds in her side.

"You'll have to help me," the vet said, "I've no assistants today."

He put her on the operating table.

"Get yourself some gloves; she could rip you badly."

I said I didn't want gloves.

I held her gently by the throat as he worked on her side.
"Dog got her," he said, "look, here are the teeth marks.
Missed the scar though."

She'd twisted her head so that she could look at me. She
held me with her great gold eyes. The vet clipped and
swabbed and cut. Jessicat lay still and I tried to relax my face
so that she couldn't see my clenched teeth.

"See she doesn't nibble those stitches," the vet said as he
put her in the basket.

All animals nibble their stitches unless you distract
their attention. I put her in my workroom to sleep and she
jumped on the bed. I was afraid to spend the night beside her
in case I rolled, so I slept on the floor. She had a good night; I
knew because I woke each time she moved and waited for
her to settle again.

Like Jet after her accident, Jessicat recovered rapidly, and
once her fur had grown again she was as beautiful as before.
She never walked anywhere, she ran as if on springs. Boy
Fred found a home but his mother stayed with us. I couldn't
part with her now. In the evenings, when Johnnie was home,
Jet was on his lap, Jessicat on mine. Sometimes, when I put
out the bedside lamp and Johnnie was still working in the
living room, I'd look out and see her dancing in the light on
the lawn, playing with the moths.

There were occasions, coming home from shopping, when
I'd find her waiting for me beside the road. I'd bring her in,
but the cats had their freedom and the road was too close.

Sheena was home that Good Friday when the warden's
son came to the door and asked if we had a black and white
cat.

"You know we have, Glyn," I said.

"There's one on the road."

She was lying as she'd been hit, frozen in a running position.
I picked her up and walked back with the stiff body light in
my arms. There was hardly a mark on her: a trickle of red at
her mouth, a smear of dirt on the white throat – but the

golden eyes were dead. One side of the head was a little out of alignment; she wouldn't have known anything.

I looked at the daffodils and I was overwhelmed to think that she wouldn't see the spring. I wished that I had never been capable of love.

Then I had to tell Sheena, calmly, sensibly, stressing the lack of pain, the short life of an animal compared with ours.

In the afternoon Sheena went visiting and I dug a hole, but after I'd lifted the first sods I had to go and look at her. I went to see if she were really dead. She hadn't moved. I fetched the blanket from her basket and wrapped her in it against the crows.

Johnnie came and finished digging the hole. I laid her in the bottom but as he went to shovel in the earth I stopped him. I had to make sure once more that she hadn't moved.

When Sheena returned to school Johnnie applied for leave and we went to Skye.

The island was swept by gales that spring. We slept in the tent and cooked and ate in the van. I was very ill. I'd get up and cook breakfast, unable to eat myself, then I'd be sick, and I'd lie in the tent all morning with an aching head and a terrible lassitude which might clear at midday and we'd go out and climb in the rain, but I was weak and clumsy and very frightened. Surely, I thought, lying in the tent, this can't be grief still? I had been looking forward to Skye.

After a week of this I told Johnnie I couldn't cook his breakfast any more, he must do it himself. He didn't; he ate bread and butter and we drove to Portree for a change of scene. On the way I realised I hadn't been sick, I didn't feel sick, I had no pain and no headache.

"I told you it was all psychological," he said.

But my head had cleared completely and I could be objective again.

"It wasn't," I said, "it was that bloody petrol stove."

I had never cooked on petrol before. For a week, while

Johnnie sat in the passenger seat by the open window, I had inhaled carbon monoxide as I crouched over the stove in the back of the van each morning.

My mother, who had always wanted to travel, came to it late in life. From the time I joined the Army she visited me all over the country, her holidays growing perhaps a little more amusing, rather more comfortable as I learned to know the country myself and acquired cars. When Johnnie and I returned from that stupid week on Skye, and Mother was due for a visit, I knew that to take her to new country would be not only a holiday for her, but seeing it through her eyes I might find compensation for the Skye trip. So we would go up the north-west seaboard of Scotland as far as the north coast, not climbing, just looking.

We drove out of Glasgow one hot June morning with all the windows down to catch the breeze. To salve my conscience (I was broke again) I had said that this would be a working holiday. We were to stay at hotels but I would need only one B.B.C. script to break even.

We drove through the birch woods and the bluebells on Loch Lomondside, crossed Rannoch Moor all shimmering in the heat and came slowly down the long rift of Glen Coe. We stopped at Fort Augustus and crossed next day to Skye. In Glen Brittle we stayed with the MacDonalds where I'd stayed in the heat-wave three years ago. It was just as hot now and the Cuillin pearl-grey in the haze. There were black-throated divers on the loch, and out to sea in the evening, the solon geese circled and dropped, while from the rocks the cuckoo called until the short night came and all the birds were silent except for snipe drumming above the flats.

We drove to the north of the island, running into a great dank belt of sea-fog which thinned a little as we turned east, then south, and saw the shattered pinnacles of the Quirang lean like petrified monsters out of the gloom.

We left the car and walked to what I thought was the top of the Kilt Rock and suddenly the mist parted at our feet and there was the sea hundreds of feet below, the waves advancing leisurely, marked by white snail trails of foam.

We spent a night in a croft house at Elgol and in the still grey evening walked to the top of another cliff from where we could look across the water straight into the dark bowl of Coruisk. Above the corrie the Ridge was black against the cloud. It was so still we could hear every squeak of the rowlocks in a boat below the cliff, and then the first thunder drops began to fall on the butterbur leaves and we came slowly back to the croft.

Next morning was clear and hot again. Under Blaven I found a level stretch of turf and Mother sat there trying to solve the problem of whether she should face the mountains or the loch while I went up the ravine looking for the herons I had seen when I traversed Blaven several years ago. They were there: a solitary pair with a nest in the top of a tree and five big green eggs.

We went back to the mainland, crossing by the Glenelg ferry, with the inn on the shore where the drovers, returning to the island after selling their cattle, were robbed and their bodies thrown into the Sound of Sleat.

We came up the long pass of Ratagan and suddenly the pines parted and all the mountains of Kintail lay before us beyond the glittering loch. Above Strome Ferry we saw buzzards hunting through a shower that was shot with rainbows. Round every bend of the road, on every hillside there was some new delight. There were heron by all the lochs, standing like grey posts in the reeds, and as we crossed the water shag dived off-shore and the glens and mountains opened out and wheeled as the ferry turned so that you stood at the centre of a world that pulsated with light and colour and the songs of birds.

We didn't intrude on the birds, only by accident, and then we did our best to remedy matters. There was the family of grouse which scattered in front of the bonnet as I came round a bend in Wester Ross. The cock and hen ran to one side, and chicks to the other. They might decide to cross just as another vehicle came speeding round the bend, and to increase our anxiety, one chick had gone belting up the road and was now a speck disappearing in the direction of Lochinver.

I left the van blocking the road and tore after him. As I shooed him back, Mother came to help and together by careful shepherding we succeeded in reuniting the family. One of the chicks had a mother-fixation on the van and, as we drove away, came out of the heather and started tearing after us, but the hen managed to catch him and hauled him back to the heather.

At Smoo Cave, way up on the north coast, we found cliffs thronged with kittiwakes, accessible cliffs in the sense that we could sit opposite on turf and watch the birds preening unconcerned. Starlings and sparrows shared the ledges like a kind of kittiwakes' domestic pet. On top of the cliff we found a man enjoying the sun in the garden of his cottage. We addressed him politely with observations on the wonderful weather and congratulations that he should have a colony of kittiwakes in his back garden. He replied in purest Cockney and told us they were fulmars.

We had been warned not to take the road to Altnaharra. For twenty miles, we were told, there wasn't a passing place and if we met anything we would have to reverse. So we took the road to Altnaharra and had no trouble except that I spent a hot wet hour stalking an unidentified drake on a lochan below Ben Hope and Mother, who had seen the bird get up when I stumbled in a bog at the start, was afraid to call from the car because she thought I'd seen something else.

We had passed through Coigach in one of the few spells of bad weather but, in the early evening at Altnaharra, we could just see, far to the west, those sudden jutting shapes above the moors. So we went west again to see An Stac and

Suilven, to take the twisting one-track roads that go by lochans strewn with water lilies and gentle curves through birches down to bays of silver sand and wet rock smelling of seaweed and the sea.

I made a profit on the trip and not only financially. When I broadcast about it a few weeks later the studio faded as I talked and I was back there with the curlews lilting above long moors and pools glistening in the peat, a place where the day held no bigger problem than the choice of which lochan, which flowery patch of turf to stay and idle in the sun.

In August we returned to the sea. Johnnie persuaded me that Cornwall was just the place for a quiet family holiday. Sheena was now thirteen; there were, he said, climbs of every standard at Land's End, and if she didn't want to climb she could swim. To me Cornwall smacked of the north-west gone wrong, of the Riviera. We were going at August Bank Holiday: the rocks would swarm with trippers. There would be transistors at the bottom, stones coming down from the top. The sand would be covered by tar. But Johnnie was determined and we went.

We travelled by night with Sheena sleeping in the back of the van. The roads were clear then but by the time we reached Dartmoor the next morning every lay-by was crowded and the moor sprouted a crop of summer frocks and brilliant shirts. Not exactly a quiet family holiday, I thought, as Sheena petted the ponies and Johnnie prowled with the camera, but definitely conventional: the Lees-Moffat *ménage* on the way to the seaside.

As we approached Land's End the roads became more crowded, the fumes more pungent until we turned aside to an old mine-building now a Climbers' Club hut – and we left convention behind.

Beyond the hut fog was rolling in from the Atlantic. We came to the top of what must be a cliff, below which there were noises: gulls, and water heaving and muttering to itself.

For a week we climbed surrounded by movement and the sound of water. In mountains the background remains still and reassuring; on sea cliffs half your world is in continuous motion. I had always imagined there was no danger in climbing above the sea; you could fall with impunity and swim away. But that first afternoon, listening to the unseen water smacking its lips in the cove below, I remembered that rocks are covered with barnacles and that only in the calmest weather can you land undamaged from them, while in a swell you might not land at all. I remembered swimming recently in Sussex with my sister Jeanne, and the danger flag flying and our saying how much more fun it was when rough. It was she who pulled me out, grabbing an arm as I was washed back down the shingle towards the next concave wall of breaking wave, pulled me up the beach too weak to swear I'd never do it again. And what had I let myself in for now: on a rocky coastline – and with Sheena?

She revelled in it. On Bosigran Face that first day in the mist, we roped up to descend steep turf cushioned with thrift, then suddenly we realised there was rock above us: climbers' rock, vertical but covered with shaggy green moss like whiskers. That was the start of the cliff; as we traversed below it the whiskers stopped and the rock was clean pink granite like a peak in Chamonix, and suddenly we were all avid to be up there climbing into the fog, exploring strange rock which, ambiguously, was friendly and familiar because it *was* rock and fundamentally the same as every other cliff we had ever climbed on, gritstone or granite or the burred gabbro of Skye; there were holds and there would be a drop; there was a start and a finish and an unknown quantity between.

We started with a Hard Severe and, seeing Sheena sil-houetted above (with the sea so far below) I was frightened, then angry with myself, because – with Johnnie ahead and me below – she was safe, so I tried to repress my fear and failed dismally. They seemed so careless on the stances: Sheena sitting on the outside of every ledge swinging her boots over nothing. Fighting my way up overhangs, working round exposed corners, I'd hear them chattering and I'd swear under my breath and erupt:

"*Will* you stop talking and take in my rope?"

"Sorry Mummy, but we think there's a nest just above."

Once I'd got used to it I enjoyed it too. Every day after that first afternoon the sun blazed on the cliffs and Sheena and I climbed in bikinis. It was a lazy delightful cheat to leave rucksacks at the top of the cliff and descend, without map or compass, torch or food, by abseils or by moderate routes to the foot of the climb.

Once we left the car we never saw a tourist; they kept to the beaches and the bays.

The animals were curiously tame; perhaps in a stupor from the heat. Here in a world where reflected light shimmered in the shadows, a world of lustrous blues and greens, the gulls stood solemnly on ledges a few yards away and watched our progress, cocking their heads like dogs as we called.

Seals drifted into view asleep on the surface, eyes closed and noses twitching in their dreams.

"Look," Sheena pointed out, "what long whiskers they have."

And rocking gently with the swell the bell buoys tolled their warning on the breeze – with a note that spoke of storms and winter and those ancient shocking nights when wreckers lurked beside their cherished lamps.

The cliffs were brown: every shade of brown from pale biscuit to deep chocolate with sometimes an intrusion of pink or pearly grey. Some of the inlets (called *zawns* down here) were very deep and when the tide receded you could look down through ten or fifteen feet of water, past the fronds of oarweed to sand the colour of jade.

We found the ice plant *mysenbryanthemum*: unconventional

in this vertical habitat where it hung over the top of the cliff to mask the overhangs with drapes of rose and cream.

Once I left the others playing on some new route and wandered round a corner to find a line stretched across a ledge. At the end was a lobster pot about four feet below the surface. The water was absolutely still. In the pot were spider crabs and a piece of bait. More crabs were approaching like science fiction monsters across the sand and suddenly, out of the tail of my eye, I saw a long and sinister shape moving through the weed. Slipping like a shark through the water the conger eel circled the pot and I rushed to fetch the others.

We all had a good glimpse of him: quite a nice face really, not at all like a shark, and delicate fins like wings behind the head.

One of the crabs climbed the lobster pot and we were aware that there might be a conflict of interests. There was. They met at the mouth of the pot and whether the crab pinched the eel or the latter got his head stuck in the opening we couldn't tell, because the great tail broke the surface and thrashed until we were drenched with spray. Then the conger broke away and slid to sulk in the oarweed.

Although the weather stayed hot, somewhere out in the ocean there must have been a storm and the rough seas became a very real hazard when we approached our climbs with the tide coming in. We had to run the gauntlet of the waves and there was always the chance that if you fell in the backwash the barnacles would flay the skin off you, and the next wave trap you in its curve and pound you like a pile-driver. So we roped up and leapt the filling inlets with one eye on the breakers, the other watching for a slip. We ran like goats along the knife-edged ridges where the sea boiled and slapped below – and the only one to fall in was Johnnie.

I was usually third man: the one left behind on the first stance of the climb, tied like Prometheus to my rock, and Sheena saying as she left me with the spray breaking over my head:

"Never mind, Mummy, you can't be pulled off."

And all the time the sun beat down but no one suffered from headaches. For all the noise and urgency and the pounding of the sea you never felt battered, but part of it all—as in the thunderstorm on the Meije.

The last morning was the hottest of all—in the cove; there was a wind like a knife on top. At breakfast time someone had come in and said there'd be no swimming today and we had held our superior silence. It was an off-shore wind; the sea would be like a mill-pond.

Sure enough, as we left the hut we saw the water flat and untroubled clear to the horizon, and not a cat's paw in sight. Why then, as we approached the top of the easy gully, was there a sound of thunder at the foot of the cliff, why the glimpse of white off the end of the island, and a streak of foam out to sea from the cove? We looked beyond the foam and the sea wasn't flat at all; long shadowed bars stretched parallel to our line of sight, marching landwards.

In the gully we scarcely noticed the absence of wind and the presence of heat, we were concentrating so hard on that heavy rhythm below.

As we descended we saw the water with its long backwards dragging wash sucked down the shelves as if by a monstrous pump, and then the slow majestic gathering, the towering pile-up, and the thunderous explosion that sent the spray halfway up the cliff. In the vacuum that followed you could hear all that broken water fall back on the creaming sea.

We climbed in a kind of glory; not distracted but exhilarated, sure that when the swell struck, the rock shook under the impact—and after the strike the spray was cool on hot bare flesh.

Lying in bed that night I watched the lighthouse beam sweep the room and listened to the sound of the dying swell in the cove below. Thinking back, the summer seemed all holiday, after the sad spring. I had seen Mother delight in the north-west and Sheena in Cornwall. Because of Sheena this holiday had carried an aura of childhood for me, of Hans Andersen: congers with kind dog-faces and wings for fins, of forests of seaweed and sunken ships, and of the moon reaching down through pale green water to paler sand where all the shells are made of mother of pearl.

CHAPTER 13

Border Country

CONTRARY TO Johnnie's expectations we stayed at Ullswater for two years, the reason being that he was unwilling to
subject me to another move, another bout of house-hunting
so soon after leaving Maen y Bardd and Ann's Cottage. In the
end I convinced him that I would prefer to live in a tent and
store the furniture rather than continue living in material
comfort with himself so unhappy. I was wholly in sympathy
with him, not to the extent of agreeing with all his theories on
the running of mountain schools but in seeing that, for him,
being junior to men who were less experienced mountaineers
than he, was an impossible position. When he handed in his
resignation in the spring of 1964 I was relieved and started
house-hunting with a new enthusiasm.

I went to Wales and on horseback by day, in convoys of
cars in the evenings, I searched Snowdonia with a bevy of
friends and Mabel and Mary, the two sisters who had the
ponies and with whom we had ridden so much in the year
before we moved north. We roamed the forests and the
moors, penetrated up hidden combes and emerged on high
alps; we looked at forestry bungalows, crumbling cottages,
houses with leaking roofs and gardens full of stinging nettles;
solid houses, condemned houses; some by trout streams, others
halfway up mountains, but none that was not occupied in
summer, already taken, or where the Forestry Commission
would only let to its own employees – and I couldn't see
Johnnie working with trees. I went south to Merioneth and

inspected remote cottages which looked out towards the nuclear power station at Trawsfynydd – and I went to Shrewsbury to try to inveigle the Forestry Commission into making an exception of us (as Welsh guides) and to let us have one of their good empty houses in Snowdonia.

Johnnie hadn't wanted to return to Wales, the idea had been mine because I thought he would find work there as a guide; he had wanted to live on the Northern Pennines. When in Criccieth one day I saw an advertisement in an estate agent's office for a house near Kirkby Lonsdale, of all places, I cut my Welsh losses and returned to the Lakes.

I visited the house near Kirkby Lonsdale and found it running with moisture. Then I put myself on the lists of twenty-three house agents in the six northern counties and received the usual replies: from hovels for sale to mansions for rent. But among these was one which we followed up – and on a lovely afternoon in May we drove down a sunken lane on the Pennines, a lane where the banks were friezed with cowslips, and at the end of a long track, hidden behind its sheltering barns, we found Bloan.

It was a big house with seven rooms. It was neither L-shaped nor T-shaped but something of both, all jutting corners outside, and inside a long passage on each floor. When we returned to Ullswater that evening, having decided on the way home that this was the house, I couldn't draw a plan, couldn't remember to which point of the compass the rooms faced, could only recall that the two windows of the big bedroom looked out on the garden wall covered with yellow stonecrop and house leek, on a wide shallow beck, on sycamores bright with spring foliage and one lone pine on top of a knoll. Beyond the knoll lay the hills. In this room the whole of one wall, including the door, was panelled in oak.

It was the situation as much as the house which appealed to me. Bloan might have existed anywhere: an old house (seventeenth century) which had been modernised with a

bathroom and indoor lavatory, electric light and the telephone. That was surprisingly good, six hundred feet up and
in the backwoods, but it was its surroundings that intrigued
me.

This was country where there had been centuries of fighting. From Penrith eastwards the castles stand across the
north of England: Brougham, Appleby, Brough, Bowes. This
was the land of Border raids, of violence and murder, great
loyalties and shameful betrayals. And long before Edward
built his castles the Romans came through on their way to
Hadrian's Wall. After the battles and the raids the land was
settled and farmed and the people had a greater enemy: the
elements.

Even on that first visit we learned a lot about winter on the
Pennines. The farm manager who showed us round was kind:
he didn't want us to think that country life was idyllic just
because the sun was shining and the birds sang. But already
we'd guessed that winter up here could be equalled only
by winter on the Cairngorms – with the difference that no
one lived on the Cairngorms. That afternoon I looked at the
hills harmless under the sun and listened to Jack Bell telling
us that the farm had once been cut off for ten weeks,
that the thermometer could show twenty degrees of frost for
days at a time. I thought of people dying who couldn't
be buried till the drifts melted, of babies being born with
no doctor and no midwife and the helm howling in the
chimney.

I fell in love with the cowslipped lane before I saw the
house, but I was too old for frivolities; it was the land and the
wildness and the people that drew me to Bloan. Mountains I
knew and in them I felt secure; they were an old lover,
potentially dangerous but I knew all the dangers. This
country was hostile; I wasn't deceived by the dancing beck
and the flowers, least of all by the house, asking to be lived in
again. Here was a challenge like the challenge of getting to
know a wild and powerful animal. I wanted to know the

bones of the country, its heart and its history, not the history that's picked up in parish records or from the local archaeologist, but the feeling you have in the middle of the night, alone in an old house, when you know it isn't empty. People who have lived long in a house leave their mark on it. Sometimes, in the night, in that panelled bedroom, I'd wake and hear the voices talking in the stream, and I'd remember all the other women who had lain there and heard the same voices: women in love and women in labour, women waiting or fulfilled, torn with suffering, dying.

And sometimes, walking by the river in the moonlight, there would come a clank of metal that could have been armour, and a gleam in the hedge that wasn't a fox's eyes. If you stared hard enough at the hills — after a long day, drunk with work and music — you could see the watch fires burning, smell like an animal the scent of conflict and tremendous triumph, and was this only because you knew that what you had written that night was good?

We moved into Bloan at the end of May. On the first evening, after the pantechnicon had gone and we had eaten, we leaned on the yard gate and watched hares as big as spaniels feeding by the beck. Martins and swallows swooped and dipped above the water. Trout jumped in the pool above an old dam. Downstream a dipper made busy journeys to and from its nest in the roots of a sycamore above the sheep pens.

Next morning I was wakened by the pre-dawn chorus. There were more birds at Bloan than at any of my houses. First there were the song birds and when you'd got used to those and dropped off to sleep again, you were wakened by the sun on the bed and more birds, but this time the song was laced with the calls of curlew, lapwings, redshank, pigeons — and always the cuckoo bubbling in the distance. Near at hand a sandpiper fluted on the roof of the barn at the end of the garden and, on subsequent mornings, swallows dived past the window, mocking the cats which sat on the garden gate and shouted for breakfast.

One of the stipulations when we were looking for a house was that it must be well away from a road. There was no fear of Jet being run over at Bloan: we were a good half mile across the fields from the nearest by-road. However, her joy in the new country and the exciting interiors of the barns was tempered by the presence of a wild blue queen whom I christened immediately Pushkin. They fought with such ferocity that I had to part them for Jet, with her weak hind-quarters, was no match for a young cat. But these screaming, fur-flying battles ended when Pushkin had kittens. When she came back into circulation they limited their hostility to flattened ears and threatening growls.

After we moved Johnnie went back to the Lakes to find work as a guide. With his friend Vic Bray he had hopes of finding a client and making a film on rock climbing which they could sell to a television company. I had no book in mind. *Two Star Red*, with the foreword by Lord Tedder, had been published in March and serialised in the *Scottish Daily Express* and the *Liverpool Daily Post*. We were no longer in debt but after we had paid a quarter's rent in advance and settled the bill for removals we had two pounds left. We divided this equally and now I settled to work full-time at newspaper and magazine articles with the occasional short story thrown in for fun.

The days, even these long summer days, were never long enough. I was normally a light sleeper but at Bloan I slept too much: waking with the birds and going to sleep for a few more hours. To compensate I worked late at night. It didn't matter how I organised my day; I had no one else to consider. The postman called but when he couldn't get big letters through the slot he opened the door and put them inside.

The days were similar to those at Maen y Bardd: feed the

cats first, then make coffee, then out into the garden to see what was coming through and suffer paroxysms of rage at the night's ravaging by the slugs. Why did they go for sunflowers when there were only a dozen seeds in the packet? Why couldn't they attack lettuces which always needed thinning?

Jack Bell had helped me dig the garden before I moved in. I had been embarrassed by his offer, undecided as to whether he was suggesting his services as a gardener. I said so and was met with surprise. Jack, despite the fact that he had a garden of his own, was helping for nothing.

Digging was hard work. During the winter and when the ground was very wet, cows had come in through the open gate and puddled the soil until now it was like cement. The effort of breaking up these compacted clods was more tiring than any digging.

It was a big garden and needed a lot of attention. I didn't begrudge this knowing that, properly handled, it could provide me with vegetables till next spring. Until it was producing I lived on stinging nettles and grated cheese, with bread and margarine. To save petrol (the nearest town: Kirkby Stephen, was five miles away and the first mile had to be done in bottom gear) I shopped only occasionally. A piece of cheese could last me a fortnight and I baked my own bread from wholewheat flour. By the end of June I was thinning the lettuces which was just as well because the stinging nettles were getting tough.

I ate one meal a day and kept very fit. I didn't smoke and my only luxury was coffee. My diet would have been improved had I cut the coffee. Occasionally I fasted for a couple of days. Your past experience proves that you will come to no harm from such a diet; you must remember to eat (which is difficult when your day is very full) and you must break a fast carefully and slowly. The only time I felt ill was when someone took me out for a good meal. The theory of eating a lot so that I could live on my fat didn't work, and I was consumed by a sense of ingratitude as my host watched me push the lobster aside.

I shared the fresh milk with Jet. I had discovered an excellent full-cream dried milk which was half as cheap as fresh but it gave Jet diarrhoea. I was very firm with the cats and gave them only a handful of houndmeal in the mornings, but I watched their condition carefully to make sure they were catching plenty of mice and getting their protein.

The days would have been long enough at Bloan had I not been so captivated by my surroundings. There would have been time for hoeing and planting, time for eight hours writing, if I hadn't explored so much. The River Belah, one of the headwaters of the Eden, was two fields away. There was a high sandy bank where sand-martins nested, and below this a shingle shore where the oystercatchers had their chicks. There were families of wild duck on both the river and the beck, and herons fishing – there was always something to watch.

I walked to the village for the newspapers and the milk. The cows at Bloan were suckling calves; I had to buy milk from the next farm.

The village was merely a group of houses and an inn run by two Geordies: Muriel and Arthur Drummond. Going up for the paper meant a lengthy circuit of over two miles: following the river to the road, then a coffee or a beer with the Drummonds – paid for later when I took them seedlings and produce, but never fully paid for – and then the slow saunter down the sunken lane where redstarts and yellowhammers nested and where, by June, the cowslips had given place to bluebells and stitchwort and the crushed pink and brown of water avens.

There was an old mill halfway down the lane, built in Edward I's reign. It was reputed to be haunted but I went up there on two nights and nothing stirred except the owls. What was interesting about the mill was that beside it grew the finest purple orchids I had ever seen. And when all the early flowers had died and you thought there would be nothing now until next spring except wild parsley and harebells, suddenly you were astonished by the appearance of the giant bellflower. Never having lived in limestone country before I couldn't believe it. I thought it was a Canterbury Bell gone wild.

After the morning's walk I cooked my meal and then I wrote, only to remember in the evening that I had a horse to exercise.

Our landlord's daughter had a pony called Toby. Sheena was determined to find a mount for the summer holidays and I had offered to exercise Toby in the hope that she could ride him when she came home.

The days were too hot for a pony to work but the evenings were cool and mellow, evocative of that atmosphere which lay everywhere under the surface. On these evenings walking the pony quietly by the river, I was part of that atmosphere: the centurion bringing reinforcements up for the Wall, tired, not concentrating, staring at his horse's ears, with the marching feet behind (they wouldn't be marching at the end of the day, but they should be, I thought, pushing Toby away from a rabbit hole, straining my ears to catch that irregular beat in the rear). And then Toby, turning up the hedge, would trot or rather run with such a short stride you felt silly if you kept with him, and were jolted to pieces if you didn't, but you couldn't canter up hedges because of rabbit holes and now you had to live in the present for Toby became skittish at night and blackbirds shooting out of thorns would make him swerve into the field, spoiling the silage and my seat.

We came up the bank on to the long track which ran to the farm and I turned him for home, letting him think he had his head, and in the gallop his hooves beat on the packed earth and you felt the hard little body working and forgot the soreness of your thighs, and there were other ponies with you galloping through the dusk and cattle running and lowing and a clear run to the Border if we got away. Then poor Toby was turned away from home to walk quietly back along the track to cool him slowly while the shadows thickened round the mill and the old heron got up with an angry croak from where we'd disturbed him at his fishing.

There was nothing to hurry for. After rubbing the pony down and turning him out I'd lean on the gate in the twilight and watch him roll in the lush grass, watch not because there was nothing better to do but because everything was worth doing, even watching a pony roll.

By the end of July my financial position had deteriorated to such an extent that I applied for a job as cleaner in a local hotel, only to find that all hotels were adequately staffed. I considered domestic work in a private house but knew that the pay wouldn't equal what I was earning from my writing The trouble was that although I was selling my work there was often a long period between its acceptance and receipt of the cheques. During the last two months I had seen very little hard cash and in order to meet the more pressing bills I was forced to borrow.

Johnnie had found no work in the Lakes; he and Vic had made a film (but not sold it) and the situation was desperate when I telephoned him one night to tell him Sheena was home from school with a throat infection and the doctor had prescribed invalid foods.

He came home immediately – with no money but the news that he had been offered a job at a mountain centre in the north of Scotland. Next day Sheena was better and a large cheque came in the mail. The luck seemed to be running our way again.

Mother and Father came to spend a holiday at Bloan. Father is a sea angler but he brought his best rods to try for the trout. He would disappear after breakfast but a reconnaissance would discover him eventually, casting solemnly in the middle of a field, surrounded by an attentive circle of cows. One lunchtime he came in very excited:

"You've got a *bull* with those cows!"

"That's Harry. He's all right; he can't run, he's got sore feet."

Harry suffered from middle age as well as sore feet. He spent a lot of time staring at the young and exciting heifers which ran with a younger bull in the next field. Harry couldn't chase an old cow, let alone a human being, but he had his uses. Because we were so far from the road strangers telephoned before they arrived. If I didn't want to see them I told them there were two bulls and warned them to be quick opening and shutting gates down the track. If the herd were close they must sit in their cars until the cattle moved away. I would not be responsible, I said. I had few visitors at Bloan.

In September I was alone again, looking at the house and my bank balance with a calculating eye. This is what it is like for a writer: yesterday stinging nettles and margarine; tomorrow, redecorating the house. We had leased the place for three years and much of it needed paint and whitewash. I decided that the sitting room and three of the bedrooms I would leave alone; the money might just run to doing over the whole house, but my energy and enthusiasm wouldn't. Besides, to paint and whitewash three rooms, the downstairs passage, the high stair well and the bathroom was going to take a long time and I had promised Johnnie and Sheena I would have it finished before the Christmas holidays.

The floors of the kitchen and living room were sandstone flags. These I covered with rush matting: the cheapest, strongest floor covering, and the ideal decoration for Bloan. Anticipating wicked winters I bought two powerful heaters; at least if I ran out of coal, I could have a good electric fire.

It took me two months to do my redecorating and I loved it. Like anything else, a country, an animal, a person, you come to know them best working in or with them. I did our

bedroom last, finishing with the oak panelling. I spent two
evenings with linseed oil and rag, gently smoothing the oak,
and it was only now, with the house finished, that I really felt
at home. In the first few months the place had been merely a
shelter; I had given it nothing. Now I had given it something
of myself. You couldn't caress those panels without loving
them.

CHAPTER 14

The Mountain Commuter

JOHNNIE HAD BEEN in Scotland only a few weeks when he telephoned to say he had a few days' leave, he could borrow a van and would I meet him in Borrowdale?

We met early one evening and climbed above Derwentwater until it was too dark to see the holds and all the jackdaws were scolding us for keeping them from their roosts.

We stayed at a climbing hut in Rosthwaite. It was the middle of the week and we had the place to ourselves.

"What's it like?" I asked, meaning the new job.

He didn't like it, he didn't want to stay – but the money was good.

"All that lovely country," I said, wistful.

The country was all right, except that there was no one to climb with – and then the staff lived in a communal bungalow; there was no privacy. There was an empty house in the grounds; we could have it if I would move north.

"A *tied* house!" I exclaimed in astonishment, remembering Ullswater.

Everything would be all right if I were there, he said; he would have a home, we could climb – except on Sundays: staff weren't allowed to climb on the Sabbath.

"*What!*"

"We could go away and climb."

"With Sgurr a' Chaorachain and Beinn Bhan on the doorstep you'd have to go to the Cairngorms so you wouldn't be caught! You only have Sundays off and you're not *allowed* to climb!"

The school had a Christian outlook, he explained primly, prayers every morning . . ."

"Good God!"

I was deeply hurt to think of all those splendid routes with only Patey to climb on them—but I must push Johnnie's problems to the back of my mind. We had three days now for climbing; the problems that mattered were overhangs, and delicate traverses with a boot nail missing.

Next day we went up Langstrath. It was a glorious October. There had been enough frost to turn the leaves but no wind as yet to carry them away. From high up the russet fellside the beck was marked by a wide, wavering line of yellows and golds, while here and there a rowan bloomed like a poppy on some grey crag.

The gully we climbed on Sergeant Crag was long, wet and interesting. The holds were covered either by cushions of moss or a veneer of slime. Moss was all right, when you scraped it away the hold underneath would be gritty, but slime was different, fingers slipped and could get no purchase. Water ran over the lips of the pitches and flowed up our sleeves and down our necks. While Johnnie climbed I sat in pools with my hood up, staring past the bones of long-dead animals to the floor of the dale where a man was shepherding: pale, pin-head sheep scattering like lice before the black speck of the dog. High up, the gully suddenly looked like one on Nevis, and we remembered the day in Gardyloo with the walls invisible under sheets of ice, and the crux running up into a huge cornice. But now instead of a cornice there was a rowan on top, and black water in the peat hags, and the only snow a sprinkling on Helvellyn and the Dodds.

We rounded off the day with an easy ascent of Heron Crag and we came down when the sun had just set and the clouds were reflecting and intensifying the light. Some of the oaks were glossy green with yellow splashes. The green went darker in the afterglow and the yellow came up; the birches dripped like golden fireworks but they were all only foils for the rowans that were neither orange nor gold but the colour of fire.

The furnace glow was too good. Next morning we plodded up the side of High Scawdel trying to raise the aggressive spirit as we heard the wind smashing over the pass above. We reflected that the day held one consolation: we were doing it for fun; there was no hard and dedicated client to whip us up the overhangs.

We emerged on top into the teeth of the gale. We looked for Miners' Crag and saw it only dimly as we were tossed about in the gusts. There was rain in the air.

"Where is the tarn? Shall we go and look at it — if it isn't blown away?" Prolonging the evil moment, hoping it would be pouring by the time we reached the crag.

It wasn't — and we climbed in short pitches because communication was impossible after fifty feet.

When the worst gusts came I lay flat against the rock — if one can lie when rock approaches the vertical. He laughed and told me to use my feet and I growled and cursed and fought, getting up not by technique but by adrenalin. And even then, with the cloud dropping fast and the rain arrived, he had to suggest another climb and I had to agree, although when we got to the top of that one there was a mutual move to untie knots and neither of us lagged on the descent to Rosthwaite, running until we steamed, and fresh rain came trickling down our backs.

Borrowdale, determined to show us all her moods, changed yet again for the last day and we climbed above Honister Pass on rock that was bone-dry, in sunshine so brilliant that it was painful to climb against the light. But the wind remained, shifted to the north-west and bitterly cold.

Honister Wall is a classic climb. Hard, steep, very airy but with big adequate holds except at a bulge not far above the screes. I climbed to the bulge, cast about, froze — and climbed down. I stood on the ground, warming my hands in my pockets, staring at the rock. Today it had to be the Enemy, it and the wind because you'd never get up anything without fighting.

"Climbing!" I shouted and stepped forward quickly, before my hands should go numb again (I'd been touched by frostbite years ago on Monte Rosa and again on Snowdon and my hands had never regained their old resistance to cold). I went up the bulge snarling, and now I could relax, drop my mood of contrived anger, for the rest of the climb was pure delight – but we had to do the top pitches in gloves, and with the wind (and sun like an arc light) headaches were starting, so we fled down to the valley and finished as we'd begun: on Shepherd's Crag above the lake.

I came off the first pitch of Slings for the rock and my boots were greasy, and I dropped and swung and all the protruding bones made contact with the rock and I was lowered. I had been trying to climb neatly but at the second attempt I went up like a furious elephant, and up all the rest of the steep strenuous rock hating it and loving it, and we came out laughing on the top.

We went down to the road and the cars.

"Where shall we meet in November?" he asked.

"Ben Nevis, Glen Coe?"

"In November?"

Yes, I remembered days and days of rain in past autumns.

"Come to Applecross, Moffat, and we'll find a house away from the school, a place like Maen y Bardd."

I was thoughtful as I drove home up the Vale of Eden. The ban on Sunday climbing was intolerable and ridiculous. It was Sheena and Johnnie himself who were the deciding factors. When we went to Ullswater Sheena had changed schools and was now in Cumberland. She would be taking her General Certificate of Education soon and, even discounting the fact that she was happy at Seascale, I didn't want to interrupt her schooling yet again and at this point. Besides, we had leased Bloan for three years and I had a suspicion we would not be able to break that contract. And how long would Johnnie stay at Applecross?

People turn to different things when they're troubled: drinks, drugs, religion. I started a book. I had several chapters written when Johnnie telephoned in November to say that the school was closing for the winter; he had two months' leave – with pay.

"When will you be coming?" he asked.

I told him about the book.

"Excellent," he said, "when are you coming?"

I was working, I said, couldn't he fill in time till I arrived? He was astonished. I'd promised to come, I was letting him down – and he'd found a house, several houses, under private ownership. He wanted me to see them; we could move in by February.

So much for thinking you can hide your head in the sand by writing, I thought, as I put down the receiver; once you were into a book you forgot the motive and it became an end in itself. To stop it would be like having an abortion. I continued writing for a week and Johnnie telephoned me a lot, becoming more angry, more insistent until a remark of his reminded me of a time I was living in a closed community myself, forced to stay there to earn money but hating it – and a friend didn't turn up to climb with me one weekend . . . I put the book away, packed the van, asked Jack Bell to feed the cats, and left for Scotland.

There was fog going north on Beattock Summit but when I telephoned Johnnie from Glasgow I was still confident I'd sleep on Rannoch Moor that night. He was impatient and cross; yesterday I'd told him I'd be at Applecross before dark.

I sat in the van in that suburban street wondering whether I should turn round and go back to the book. But if I did, Johnnie would be at Bloan in a few days and I would be unable to write anyway. I drove on, reflecting on conflicts of loyalties, wondering if I would ever reach a stage where I could reconcile them.

At Balloch the lights ended — at least, all the street lamps: the neon strips, the traffic signals — and there was only one orange light ahead flashing so intermittently I took no notice. I wasn't thinking about driving, but that there were three hundred mountains between me and the north coast (I always remember this at Balloch), and I started to sing as the swinging bends on Loch Lomondside began, and suddenly the van drifted on a curve and I slowed down, thinking this would be just the place to have a puncture. But the van continued straight and steady and I started to sing again, taking the corners a little more slowly, until I came to Luss where the orange light was stationary and I saw men beside a Council lorry waving me on. I acknowledged them automatically with my horn and continued, absent-minded, dreaming of snow climbs. But the surface of the road was different: it was shinier. It hadn't been shiny behind the lorry. They had been *gritting*.

I stopped the car, got out and fell flat on my back on the ice. Oh, Moffat, I thought, as I crawled back behind the wheel, you'll come to a bad end.

I crept up Glen Falloch at twenty miles an hour but as I came to the T-junction at Crianlarich two fish lorries hurtled past towards Oban doing fifty and I felt I was being over-cautious. I overtook one, but he didn't like it and moved up to box me in, then suddenly I saw my turning and I slid round the bend, leaving them to speed on to Oban with indignant blasts from their horns.

Ahead of me lay the long pull up the Blackmount, always the first place to be blocked by snow on this road, and now I thought it best to get over and down the other side. I didn't want to be stuck in a drift and rammed by a snow plough in the morning. So I kept going, tired but careful. Sheeps' eyes glistened on the right and there was movement on the left. They seemed tall for sheep. Pale quarters gleamed, there was a glimpse of foxy flanks, uplifted heads with huge ears — and a bunch of hinds melted into the moor.

A white hare ran into the light and crouched. *I mustn't touch the brakes.* I altered course slightly and she stayed still, unharmed.

There was the familiar rowan tree growing out of the cracked rock. I glanced at it fondly, and when I looked back to the road the first snowflakes were here: increasing fast as I came to the level and picked up speed on the long straight at the end of Rannoch Moor. The snow came faster, flying down the headlights and dividing in long parabolic streaks. The deer were everywhere: stags now, tossing their heavy heads and moving casually away from the light.

I came carefully down Glen Coe between the rock walls of the gorge thinking (as I always think on wild nights in this place) of the women and children running from the soldiers on the morning of the Massacre. Thinking not so much of the morning but of the night that followed (it was February) and of people trying to get out of the high corries: strung out on the rock faces, climbing the gullies with babies in their arms.

I eased the van gently on to the turf under the peak of the Chancellor and stopped the engine. Rain drummed on the roof all night and I puzzled over static layers of cloud across the mountainside. But with dawn these resolved themselves into snow-covered banks between rock walls, and there were rabbits playing on the turf and, with much noise and unaccustomed speed, a snow-plough came rushing past, furiously important about clearing the Blackmount. I saw I'd been wise not to risk being stuck up there in a drift.

Wind shook the van and I didn't leave it. I dressed, combed my hair and sponged my face without opening a door. I drove down the unfrequented back road to Glencoe village and came on a cluster of dustbins outside the youth hostel with a very large buzzard like a rather tatty eagle sitting on one of them. There was also a green woodpecker which emerged from under the canted lid of one bin and flew away into the woods laughing hysterically.

In travelling the first part of my trip in the dark, I made sure that I'd have the wildest scenery in the daylight. Perhaps because I hadn't seen the Highlands in winter for a long time, perhaps because I saw so many mountains under snow this day, I had never known them so lovely. And how could I have forgotten that they were so ragged and so high?

There was that glimpse of Ben Nevis through the gap in the hills at Three Mile Water: the walkers' side, but still imposing, and then *our* side on the way to Spean: the ridges snow-plastered and the rock walls showing through. I thought of Johnnie with affection: we were still the only guides to the Ben.

The new road between Glen Garry and Cluanie was snowy but beaten down. I'd had ice or snow, or both, now for well over a hundred miles and it would get worse. I began to concentrate on reaching the last pass before nightfall; I knew the main difficulty would be there.

I ate my emergency rations of apples and hard-boiled eggs as I drove. Now I was passing stranded vehicles, canted at odd angles, and above Strome Ferry there was a tar lorry dropped sideways off the road, its load hanging in extra-ordinary obscene drips from the tailboard to the heather. I slid past it like a crab, and the only time I touched the brakes was where the road ran straight into Loch Carron and the next stretch was by ferry.

The sun was going down when I came to the foot of Bealach na Bà and wondered grimly what was waiting for me on top two thousand feet higher. I sighed and yawned and put the van at the hill but on the first bend a lorry was coming down and the driver stopped and said he'd broken his chains trying to get over to Applecross.

I turned back and telephoned the school from the Loch Carron Hotel. I was told Johnnie was in Inverness and given the name of the garage where he'd be calling for the van. I rang the garage, delivered a message, left the van where he couldn't miss it as he passed, then I went inside and ordered as large a high tea as the place could produce.

He arrived to find me full of tea and sherry and ensconced in the bar with small nimble gentlemen who were giving me invaluable information on poaching. It was late when we went to bed.

"Moffat," he said as he closed the door, "you've no idea how glad I am to see you."

At that moment I responded to his happiness but I lay awake a long time thinking about the problem of book or Johnnie, work or family — and remembering that often work was for the family when it paid the bills. And I reflected with some amusement that had I been guiding Johnnie would have insisted I finish the engagement — or he would have hitched home. My problem was as old as the hills — or, at least, as man — but it had a twist. Why did he never resent my *climbing* for a living?

Next morning we took the school van and drove up that twisting road which I had walked down with Patey four years ago, and we came to a place in the high black defile where the vehicle refused to go any farther. We pulled out the chains and fought to get them on. There was a gale blowing and we were shrivelled with the cold. After half an hour we decided that the chains didn't fit so we went back to Loch Carron and took my chains which did, and we came over the top of the pass to leave the drifts and the gale and the cloud behind and drop down the seaward side to a dull grey bay fringed by dolls' houses: a tiny community on the edge of the ocean.

He drove me round that afternoon. It was low flat country with odd little outcrops of rock among the heather and the dwarf birch. He said there were sea cliffs where the boys were taught to climb, and there were seals.

"But it's lovely," I said.

"I always think of it as an island," he said gloomily, "it's claustrophobic."

He showed me the houses he had found. I liked one by a lochan. There would be water-lilies there in summer, and divers. But I knew we both looked at them objectively; they weren't for us.

He had reached a point where he was obsessed with small grievances: the fact that he couldn't get a *Guardian*, that he must drive the staff to dances, that he must go out to a telephone kiosk to find privacy to speak to me. The root of the matter was that he was bored. He was trapped in great climbing country with no one to climb with.

Next morning he packed his gear while I walked round the bay to the opposite headland. It was a wild grey day with snow showers driving down the glen, blotting out the hills and the long brown strand. I was full of melancholy for Johnnie; I saw what he meant about being shut in.

Birds were busy at the edge of the tide. I could hear duck talking in the distance and as I walked along the shore little birds ran ahead of me, converging into a flock which I drove like sheep along the edge of the water until they rose in a harlequin scatter of wings to reveal themselves as turnstones.

At one o'clock heavy snow and gales were forecast by the B.B.C. We left at four with the sky lowering and the first snow beating down with the wind.

"You'll never get out," the landlord of the hotel said dismally, and the warden of the school, who was to take us to Loch Carron, packed an overnight bag, just in case.

Johnnie took the wheel for the pass. At about a thousand feet, with a strange lurid light in the air as the unseen sun went down, we rounded a bend and came full on three stags, huge and antlered like ancient gods.

It was drifting deep on the pass and we switched on the headlights to make some shadows. We came to the top and looked down to Loch Carron and it was appalling to think that we had to go down *there*. I never saw an alpine pass so sensational as this: with the black buttresses of Meall Gorm dropping to the sloping corrie, and the burn a thin thread in the bottom. But the Land Rover moved down like a mountain animal, and we even turned round below the top hairpin and drove back, beating down the drifts for the warden on the return journey.

He got back all right, but only just. We waited at Loch Carron until he telephoned and then we stayed the night because it was too late to push on.

We spent two days then in Torridon looking in vain for pine marten in the wet forests above Loch Maree, and when the cloud lifted a little and the wind dropped, we trotted happily along the ridges of Beinn Eighe, glorying in this loneliness of mid-winter when the only tracks on top were those of a fox, and the only living things we saw were ptarmigan and a golden eagle. Then there were more gale warnings and we decided to go home.

The Cairngorms looked wicked from Strathspey, looming through a shadowless grey band of something that wasn't snow or rain but sheer dirty weather.

"I wonder how sailors feel on a night like this," he mused.

"Safer," I said, thinking of the rescuers setting out on the Cairngorms on such an afternoon. I'd rather set out at night and not see what was ahead of me.

There was a blizzard at Drumochter Pass and when we came south into Lanarkshire the floods started at Abington. It was difficult to hold the wheel. I'd overtake a lorry on the dual carriageway and run straight into water inches deep. I'd come out of that breathing hard and listening to the engine, thinking that this time I must have drowned the distributor, and then a gust of wind would hit me.

"What happened?" Johnnie'd mutter, waking up.

"I hit a flood and a hundred-mile-an-hour gust hit me."

"Well, there's no need to wake me up to tell me."

There were fish swimming down the high street in Appleby (it said so in the local paper) but the most dramatic part came when we arrived home and the beck was over its banks and pouring across the paddock. I couldn't see the track but I knew where it was and it had a hard surface so I drove straight through. It was hazardous putting the van away because Johnnie had to fight the gale and the barn doors but we daren't leave it out because the slates were flying off the roofs.

At three o'clock in the morning the drips started in the attics and we had to raid the dustbin for tin cans to catch the water before it came through the ceilings. No one, I thought, lying in bed, listening to him crawling about the roof, waiting for him to slip off a joist and come through into the bedroom, no one could call our lives monotonous.

CHAPTER 15

Blizzard Country

THE WET GALES continued. At Bloan we discussed the future. Johnnie decided that if he stayed at Applecross until the spring in the next few months he might be able to obtain enough engagements to start guiding in the coming season. What he needed, I said, was a publicity campaign; an article in the national Press was a multi-columned advertisement for which the paper paid you. He started to run over my contacts.

"What's wrong with me?" I asked.

In a café in Upper Teesdale I was leafing through old copies of *Weekend* when I saw a two-page spread on the wartime exploits of a naval officer. That was the way to do it: a big feature on one of Johnnie's mountain rescues; the response should bring enough work for both of us; it would set us up for the summer. Johnnie's optimism was infectious.

On Boxing Day I shut myself in my room and wrote the article in a couple of hours. For four afternoons I wrote an article daily and then I stopped. That was enough for the present. Sheena was home; there was ski-ing and climbing and walking; I would go back to writing when I was alone again.

Johnnie and I were agreed that Bloan would be inconvenient as a base for professional climbing. During the rest of the winter I was to try to find a house in the Lakes. Although I would regret leaving Bloan (and the time I'd spent on decorating) I knew I would soon get over this in Cumberland where I would be near Sheena and there would be climbing every day. It would be another upheaval, but justified this time when Johnnie was so definite about what he wanted to do. One night, after a week of gales, I said:

"You're quite sure about the guiding? You'd have to go out all the time – and there'd be rescues. Wouldn't a wet season be pretty miserable?"

"I could climb every day for a year," he said, "and never be tired of it."

I had lived with him for thirteen years but I didn't realise until then what he really meant when he said he only lived for climbing.

In the New Year a summons came from Applecross. He was to return a month before time to prepare for the February course. I took him up to the main road to start hitching north.

"Shall I go, Moffat," he asked, standing by the open window, "or shall I stay?"

"I can't make your decisions," I said, "you decide and I'll back you up –"

"I'm fed up with it all," he raged, "why the hell can't we have a life like other people?"

Because we weren't other people, I thought, driving back to the farm alone – but it would all come right in the end.

The next few months were busy. I forgot the book I had started in the autumn. I had to find another house, write the guiding features and accumulate money to tide us over if the engagements didn't materialise.

The house problem was surprisingly easy. I'd started taking the local papers and soon found an empty farmhouse near Keswick. I wrote to the owner who was only too willing to let it (which was suspicious) and at the same time I visited friends in the Lakes to spread the word that we were looking for a base there. Writing the articles was easy too; the four I had written at Christmas all sold, netting me a hundred pounds, or rather, the promise of it in the summer when they were printed. Now I realised our mistake; the publicity campaign was too late. Only *Weekend* came out in March with my two-page spread on Johnnie (glamorised and, I was thankful to see, not over my name) and even from that there was only one response: a former pupil of his who sent Johnnie the cutting but didn't mention guiding.

I didn't sit back and wait for results. As soon as I realised my mistake in timing I concentrated exclusively on making money, and now I felt was the time to kill two birds with one stone and get to know the hill folk. In February, with the hills snow-covered and the possibility of fresh falls cutting off the farms, I visited the women to find out how they lived in the winter months.

Their situation was not like mine. I didn't have to worry about the children coming home from school, about my husband up on the top getting the sheep down in the face of the threatening storm. Two years ago two shepherds had died in a blizzard and only a short distance from home.

"I'm a bit feared," one wife told me when I asked her how she felt alone in the house with the drifts piling up and the men away, "not feared for mesel' mind, but when men's up t'fell. Anything could happen up there, couldn't it?"

In the hard winter of '63 many of the Pennine farmsteads were cut off for weeks at a time. The R.A.F. rescue team took women to hospital to have their babies, dragging them over the snow on sledge stretchers. It was the R.A.F. too, who flew hay in to the hungry beasts, meal for the dogs, groceries for the people:

"An' I looked round and there was no helicopter and no kids; they'd gone up for a joy ride. Nice chaps they were; we didn't want groceries, I had ten stone o' flour as usual, and we'd killed t'pig, but dogs was gitting hungry and we needed t'hay bad."

"But how do you feel after weeks of it?" I pressed, "when you look out of the window and see there's more snow coming? Doesn't it get you down?"

She was an elderly woman, clean and spry; she had shown

me over her house (she did all the decorating) and fed me with her home baking.

"Ah well," she said, trying to remember what she did think, "you've got to accept it, haven't you? After all, we can last longer, can't we?"

The most remote farm in the area was Birkdale in Upper Teesdale. Nelson Robinson, with whom we played darts in the local, was cousin to Mary Bainbridge of Birkdale. He insisted I go to visit her – if I could get there. The roads in the valleys and even over the passes were clear but Birkdale was in a world of its own.

"You'll have to walk the last few miles," he warned me, "go in daylight and come back before sunset."

He was right about the walking. As soon as I turned off the Teesdale road the snow was feet deep in places, rutted by tractors. I stopped and put the chains on. I was wearing a sheepskin coat and tights under my trousers. The sun shone brilliantly but the wind was bitter.

There was a shed, a parked van and a fork in the track. Brian Bainbridge was loading sacks on to a sledge drawn by a horse. Yes, he said, this was as far as you could get in winter; from here it was two and a half miles to the farm. Mary was expecting me, would I tell her he'd be along soon; he'd got to shift an engine.

Near-by, men were working on drilling rigs, surveying for the site of the dam that it was proposed to build here. It was a controversial project because there were rare flowers growing where the reservoir would be. I thought it was poetic justice that their engine should have to be shifted by a horse, and that, a mile away, a Land Rover should be bogged to the axles and eight men trying unsuccessfully to move it. The hills were on top here, not the incomers for all their powerful machinery.

There were marks where a snow-plough had tried to get through and failed. In the distance there was a tree or two, a cluster of buildings. Drifts stretched across my path like

Bloan

Wrenside, below Stainmore – taken from
the R.A.F. helicopter delivering supplies

extended arms. Somewhere underneath these there was a summer track but now there were only the footsteps of a man and a horse and the lines of the sledge runners.

Birkdale was a tiny world isolated under the great white fells with the ice shining in the sun along their crests. In the farmyard the snow was beaten and brown. Geese, ducks and hens talked absently; there was a warm stable smell and a shaggy heifer blocked my way.

There were hyacinths flowering in a window, firelight flickering and children's voices.

Mary came to the door. I'd been expecting a big strong woman, a typical farmer's wife, but she was so slight she couldn't have weighed more than seven stones. She had huge dark eyes and clouds of black hair.

We sat by the fire and she told me about her fifteen years at Birkdale. When they first came it was February and she had a baby three months old. The furniture was brought in relays, on horse-drawn sledges. All the village helped. She hadn't seen the house until then and her first job had been to clear up after the rats and sheep which had come in because the front door was off its hinges.

She had four children now: three girls and a boy. The eldest girl boarded in Appleby and attended the grammar school there. The others went to school in Teesdale. In winter they were absent for weeks, sometimes months at a time. A year or two back the blizzard had started on Boxing Day and it was the middle of April before they could get out. The R.A.F. helicopter had brought food for the animals and themselves – and diesel oil for their generator:

"The helicopters weren't supposed to carry diesel, but the village knew we'd be short and someone shoved it in like, without the pilot seeing."

During wartime she'd been in the Land Army but then she joined the Women's Royal Naval Service thinking it would be more exciting and there would be travel, "but every time I saw a cow I wanted to milk it". Somehow she got her discharge, came back to Teesdale and married Brian.

She was unusual among hill women in that she liked to walk on the fells, so did her eldest girl, Jacqueline, but only Brian went out when the cloud was down. Except for last year when he was in bed with a broken leg and she'd been worried about some sheep. Brian said to leave them, she'd never find them in the mist, but she'd gone up with Jacqueline and brought the flock down. Jacqueline had known where they were, but she hadn't a clue.

If the children were ill they had to be wrapped up and taken thirteen miles to the doctor. No one had been ill in winter yet. They'd been fortunate.

She came to the gate with me when I left.

"It's so white," I said, "don't you ever get tired of it?"

"Aye, I love to see it black."

"The fells?"

"No, the sky. Black and the rain coming. When the rain starts after this the children run outside laughing. But we lose the sheep; they get under the drifts on the banks, the becks rise quickly and they're drowned."

I came away slowly, looking back often at the house with its chimney smoking. In all the white and windswept waste nothing moved but that soft grey plume.

They were in the papers later that winter. Brian, coming home in the dark, missed the track in the blizzard, stuck his stick in the ground and walked round it all night to keep alive. He reached home at eight o'clock. I could imagine Mary telling him she'd milked the cows and fed the calves, and how many eggs did he want for breakfast?

Then there was Mrs Donald who lived alone on the common above Bloan with a black cat called Betty. She had one outside water tap which froze in winter and must be thawed with kettlefuls of boiled snow, no lavatory, no electricity, and a coal and stick shed reached by way of a path usually lethal with ice. She was in her mid-eighties, ailing but indomitable.

I visited her daily in bad weather and carried coal and water. We regarded each other's way of life with mutual amazement.

Sheena's half term was at the end of February. On the Sunday we walked the hills above Buttermere. I was astonished at the absence of snow on these western hills but the Lakes too were to have their share. All day a grey murk out to sea intensified and as we returned to the car along the shore of the lake the first flakes began to fall, heavily out of a leaden sky.

On my way home the engine started to falter somewhere in the wilds of west Cumberland. I came to a halt south of Cockermouth and sat staring at the snow in the headlights. I was tired and acquiescent. Leaving the sidelights burning, hoping they wouldn't be drifted up, I got in the back and went to sleep.

I thought there was a blizzard raging next morning but it turned out to be the wind whipping the night's snowfall off the fields. I put on all my climbing clothes with windproofs on top, a scarf round my face, then a balaclava and ski goggles, and set out to find a telephone. The wires were down. I walked three miles before I found one that was operational.

A young man came out from Cockermouth with a breakdown wagon. The fault was snow dust in the distributor.

"Do you mean to say," I asked, "that all I had to do was dry it with a handkerchief?"

"Haven't you had this trouble before?"

"With floods, not snow."

He stared at me with amused contempt.

I left Cockermouth after breakfast and arrived home after dark. The distance was fifty-five miles by the shortest route but over a hundred by the way I had to take. At Appleby all traffic was halted while the ploughs tried to clear the road to Brough. I was ten miles from home. I did some shopping, laying in a fortnight's supply of food then, when the policeman was engaged in conversation with a lorry driver, I slipped past and headed for Brough.

At first the road was clear and the sun shone, but a few miles out from Appleby the helm was sweeping off the Pennines and the whole white landscape smoked. I ran into a world of swirling snow and drifts halfway across the road. I drew in behind a long line of vehicles and switched off the engine. In front of me was a bus, empty except for the driver and conductor. I sat with them and they told me I wouldn't reach home that night; as soon as the ploughs cleared a way, an articulated lorry would skid and block it. A breakdown wagon would be summoned and while they waited for it the road drifted up again. I thought of my cats, I thought of doing it on skis, and then I wondered if the road from Kendal home was clear. It was worth a try.

I went back to Penrith and over Shap Fell to Kendal. Then I turned north and came home, rushing the drifts, reaching the Bells' farmhouse in the village at dusk. Jack told me that the lane was impassable: the drifts three feet deep; I would have to leave the van in the village.

The wind had dropped now. I filled a rucksack with food, strapped on my skis and skied home across the fields.

For five days the temperature never rose above freezing. Bloan was a curiously silent place with the beck frozen. It appeared completely abandoned, unnatural in the daytime with all the barn doors shut and nothing stirring. Then I'd open a door and stand in the warm pungent dark listening to the cattle munching. They were very reassuring.

Jack or his son Leslie came down once a day to feed the beasts and I went up to the village to collect the milk and mail and visit Mrs Donald. It was a time of frozen pipes — which were thawed out by blowlamps; effective but dangerous. One morning I was talking to Jack in his yard when Leslie suddenly shot out of a loft shouting, "Fire, fire!"

Smoke started to ooze out of cracks. I skidded across the icy cobbles and into Mrs Bell's living room to the telephone.

Then because the horse trough was frozen, we dashed through the house with buckets from the kitchen tap. The carpets were a sodden mess of mud and water and straw.

While the cows bawled and the dogs howled Leslie threw the blazing bales down from the loft and Jack and I hauled them into the yard. I didn't know how the fire was going and I was nearly as frantic about the animals as they were themselves.

We heard the siren wailing in Kirkby and shortly afterwards the fire engine came belting along the main road, the chains rattling on the hard-packed snow and all the firemen trying to dress as it rocked round the bends. We heard afterwards that the barber left a customer half shaved. Since we'd got the fire under control by then, it was all highly amusing. It was an anti-climax that when they came pounding into the yard they had to ask where the fire was.

Two ancients, well-muffled by their wives, strolled up from the village. They stopped and looked at the fire engine, at the whiffs of smoke coming from the charred bales and then at us. I felt like someone who's called the Murder Squad for a bad smell in a locked cupboard and discovered an aged Camembert.

One of the occupational hazards of living at Bloan was associated with the sandstone flags that roofed the house. These were massive and old with wide chinks, and when the helm blew, the snow drove up under the slabs and filled the lofts. It wouldn't have been so bad had there been one loft but there were three, not connected, and each approached by a tiny trap-door. Before the snow melted and brought the ceilings down the lofts must be cleared, a job made far more frustrating by the fact that every builder had left all his rubble and rubbish behind so that for every full bucket you took down, seven-eighths was rubble and only one eighth snow. When the helm had blown itself out I reckoned it took three days to clear the lofts. At first I stood on a chair, threw the empty buckets ahead of me through the trap-door, then muscled up after them. I lowered the full buckets to the landing on a rope. Jack came to my rescue with an aluminium ladder and now I could clear the snow in one day instead of three.

The snow that year didn't last long but I knew what it would be like if one were cut off for months. The worst time of day was the middle of the afternoon. I might be fit, I might have a well-stocked food cupboard downstairs and a dry bed upstairs but reason was no weapon against that twinge of primitive fear when it grew dark at three and I knew there was more snow coming. But the fear was only temporary. After all, I reminded myself, we could last longer.

CHAPTER 16

Pair Territory

THE THAW CAME, first in the sun and then in the shadow. The beck was still frozen on its margin but there were snow-drops on the banks. The eaves dripped in the daytime and I kept well clear of the walls. I had once narrowly missed an avalanche from the roof of Maen y Bardd.

The wind was in the south one soft night and I heard the oystercatchers go over on their way to the shingle spit by the river. The first lambs were born and there were curlews nesting on the common. I found a primrose in the lane and then, the following day, it was as if the spring suddenly tired of this slow wakening and the sun came blazing out. A month before I had been fighting the helm in windproof clothes, now I sat in the garden for six hours, writing.

Mother and Sheena arrived for Easter, followed shortly by Johnnie who had left Applecross for good. The only work he had was a fortnight's engagement in Langdale in May, but he had over two hundred pounds — and plans for the summer. We would have a long holiday, he said, we would climb till the money was gone. It was typical; he'd give me a fur coat or three months' holiday and never think about food or electricity bills. But I was worn out; I had worked sixteen hours a day for six weeks; for a time, just one short summer, wouldn't it be lovely to be irresponsible?

Johnnie said I must come and help him with his engage-ment; I should climb with the wife, he with the husband. I pointed out that guiding wasn't a holiday.

"It's *climbing*! The important thing is to get you on rock again."

He thought he was helping me. He didn't understand the mental and physical exhaustion that came after a prolonged period of writing. All I wanted to do was to lie in the sun and sleep.

The engagement wasn't a success. I had no confidence and no strength. In the past two months I had lost two stones in weight. I could afford to lose the fat but not the muscle. Johnnie was ashamed that I should appear so incompetent in front of clients, who, he told me, had been led to expect something very different. The climax came when I retreated from Gillercombe Buttress: a Severe which, technically, was well within my limit. I crept home to Bloan to lick my wounds.

After a few days Johnnie asked me to go back. His engagement was finished, he said on the telephone, now we could have fun. On condition that he would start on easy routes I agreed to return.

Gillercombe Buttress obsessed us. It epitomised my weakness and his vicarious shame. He explained to me that he wanted me to be perfect, that when I fell short of this he was bitterly disappointed. We went back to Gillercombe on the tacit understanding that he should take me up it, then we would repeat it with me in the lead. Traversing the screes below the cliff I felt very forlorn. Suppose I couldn't get up it *second*?

We came to the foot of the buttress and I looked up at the rock. The cliff waited like a god, leaving it all to me. I uncoiled the rope, ran it through and tied on.

"You've tied on the top," he pointed out, "change ends."

"No," I said, "I'm leading."

There wasn't anything to be frightened of. What I had thought was terror of a hard move had been self-consciousness: the clients watching, the feeling of physical weakness, the fear of letting Johnnie down. The last was the most important and now I saw his peculiar pride in me as ridiculous.

Rock wasn't an arena nor an opponent. I wouldn't be set against it by anyone. The climb was there to be enjoyed.

At the top of the cliff I untied and walked away.

"Where are you going?" he called.

"I shan't be long."

He let me go. I went a little way and sat on a rock. All around me the ranges lay, rank behind shining rank. On paper, legally, all belonged to some great landowner, but mine was the true pride of possession. Almost every hill I could see I knew from its combes and its secret streams to the bare wild windswept tops. This was my world. I walked back to the top of the cliff and we went down the side to make a start on the hard routes.

I find it curious but delightful that I cannot envisage a different season from that which I'm experiencing at the moment. In summer you know that trees are bare skeletons in winter, that views are more extensive when the leaves have gone, but you forget little things, some, not all, so that each season becomes a joy of recognition. I knew that May in Langdale was colourful but I had forgotten the visual impact: of rhododendrons, crimson and pink and mauve, of acres of bluebells below Chapel Stile that made a mist of sapphire in the back of the woods, and how, after a shower, the earth steamed and all the colours came up new-washed like wet stained glass.

It was a time of long lazy days, of lying in bed in the morning drinking tea and idly discussing whether it should be Pavey or Gimmer or White Ghyll: all facing the sun, all steep. We climbed, sometimes till sunset, sometimes coming down early through the sprouting bracken to dinner at one of the Dungeon Ghylls. We never thought about money or time, nor, indeed, about work.

When the weather broke we came home to Bloan and took Sheena's canoe, *Osprey*, on the river, where the water ran high and stained with peat and the rocky drops were a turmoil of cataracts. I had done little canoeing in white water and never in floods like these. One moment you'd be sliding swiftly down the smooth brown stream, then you'd be round a bend and see waves breaking ahead. We would have reconnoitred the route beforehand but now the passage seemed to have contracted and the waves were higher. But as soon as you passed the point of no return and you were among the rocks and the tossing water, *Osprey* made her own way through the passage and you floated out at the end, out of the glare and the roar and the crashing movement into a back eddy, and clung to the bank, drenched with spray and too weak to laugh. Johnnie approached winding the camera.

"Your face! You should have seen your face!"

We had no crash helmets and no life-jackets. It seemed madly dangerous and I loved it.

We went to Buckbarrow Crag in Longsleddale and, deceived by a hot morning, I started up Dandle Slabs in a bikini; the sun went in and for the duration of the climb an icy wind played with my back. For days I was racked by pain. Johnnie said I'd got an ulcer.

"An ulcer — in my shoulders! It's rheumatism."

The B.B.C. were due to transmit Woman's Hour from Carlisle for the first time. It was to open with a discussion on the proposal to widen Lake District roads. I was to be the opposition.

Johnnie drove me to Carlisle but in the car park I refused to co-operate. I walked through back streets on my own, my shoulders twisted. The pain was excruciating. I was aware of someone beside me, an arm round my shoulders.

"Come on," he said, "we're going to the hotel."

As one of the workers I should have been at the reception half an hour ago. They would think I was doing a prima donna act, I protested, but we arrived at the same time as the Mayor and slipped in behind the skirts of his entourage. We stayed in a corner with the sherry and the hors d'œuvre and were pounced on by Jake Kelly from the Newcastle studios:

"You're late. Put that down; the photographers want you with the Mayor."

The man *for* widening the roads, an A.A. official sitting at a telephone in London, didn't stand a chance. The item was introduced with tape-recordings made by Jake and the motorists:

". . . and what are you getting out of the scenery? Are you enjoying it, sitting behind the wheel, reading the Sunday paper?"

It wasn't only the studio that I had behind me but the bluebells on the verges, geum in ditches, a thousand ancient beeches.

"You were splendid," Johnnie said, "the chap couldn't get a word in edgeways."

In the afternoon we went to see Sophia Loren in *Marriage, Italian Style*. I came away raving about her beauty, her superlative acting (I still think this was her best film). I wanted to write film scripts, to be a director; to make a story with people, not with words.

"How's your back?" he asked.

"My *back*? Oh, my back. It stopped hurting ages ago."

The money was dwindling fast and on my birthday at the start of July we had a few pounds left. He said he would take me to dinner at the Old Dungeon Ghyll.

We went to the Lakes on a dull wet morning but as we drove westwards the sun came out and there were rainbows on the hills. We stopped in St John's Vale and walked up through the trees to Castle Rock of Triermain. The sun was hot, the air scented with thyme, and under the cliff wild strawberries shone like garnets in the grass. Another shower moved south from Skiddaw and drenched us on the rock.

"What a shame," he remarked as he coiled the rope, "on your birthday!"

"It's a lovely birthday," I assured him through a mouthful of strawberries.

Over dinner I contemplated him with approval. He had looked tired and old at the start of the summer and he'd put on a lot of weight; now he was hard and brown again.

"I'm going to start work on Monday," I said, "I've got that series to do and we must have a new car."

I had been commissioned to write a series for a magazine and the van was five years old.

Johnnie made no comment on my decision to return to work, but the following week he took the van and drove away without telling me where he was going. He came home in the afternoon looking a little startled at his own impetuosity and announced that he'd taken a job as lorry driver with a local contractor.

His motor cycle had been unserviceable for some time and the evening before he started work I drove him to the depot to pick up his lorry. I followed him home, marshalled him round the farmyard, put the van away, then went to see why his engine was still running.

"I can't find out how to stop it!" he shouted.

In the end he was forced to stall it, a method which he employed the following day until he lifted a blanket and found the control on the engine cover.

He was laughing as he came in the door that first night. He couldn't stop talking about his day. Although he revels in speed, like me, when in control, he took a great delight in slow smooth power, in the skill and judgement needed to manœuvre heavy lorries in farmyards and through gateways built for carts. To scrape a wall or touch a gatepost was a blow to his pride. And later, when Sheena and I went with him to pick up a load in Barrow-in-Furness, and were bored to tears with the slow grinding progress on the return, he was absorbed in the sound of his engine, in his gear changes, in the feel of sixty or seventy horses pulling a load of cattle food.

He discovered remote farms hidden away in folds of the hills. He told me about old barns and ancient pack bridges, about the birds he'd watched as he ate his lunch on the grass verge. He brought home bunches of flowers to identify in the evenings. He was intrigued by a new vocabulary. A "laal lonnen" was a little lane and "yak" was oak. On his first trip he was loaded with some kind of fertiliser, loose, and told to tear away. He had a vision of himself tearing out of the depot gates and belting for home in a cloud of dust, but the reference was to tare weight: the difference between the lorry loaded and unloaded. "Tare away" meant to put his vehicle on the weighbridge.

He carried cattle cake, fertiliser, lime, basic slag. Slag had to be spread on the fields. Although it was loaded from a hopper it was transferred from wagon to spreader manually. On windy days he came home looking like a miner before the days of pit-head baths.

Cattle cake, anything in bags, were other items which the driver must unload himself. There were men of sixty loading at the depots: small men who used craft instead of brute strength, but they had been at it for most of their lives. Middle age was a bit late for this kind of lark, he said ruefully, lying on an air bed in the yard at the weekend, letting the sun soak into his bones.

He had fractured his spine in a fall ten years ago and, since leaving the R.A.F. had suffered from it intermittently: at Ullswater after bending to repair a canoe, at Applecross after twisting at local hops ("Well you do ask for it don't you?" I said when he complained of being prostrated on Sunday mornings). Now I suggested he should tell the contractor he couldn't do the unloading but he maintained that a rest would make him supple again and, although he walked a little twisted on Monday morning, he returned to work.

Crossing a high moor he turned to look at an Alfa Romeo abandoned on the verge.

"I was only doing twenty," he said peevishly, "and the next thing I knew, *I* was in the ditch."

He was loaded with lime and a following lorry was unable to extricate him, so he telephoned the contractor. That gentleman came out, ordered the lime to be abandoned, pulled the lorry out — and all this, Johnnie said with a kind of wonder, without a word of blame.

He learned about brakes and the pushing power of a load. Coming down Brough Hill he was unable to stop and ploughed into road works.

"You were going too fast," the Council foreman said, picking up the bent road signs.

"You were going too fast," the contractor said when Johnnie, knowing it would be reported, told him.

I said nothing. I knew the point had been taken.

The pay was reasonable. In a good week, with overtime, he brought home fifteen pounds. I was saving for my new car so we didn't have fresh meat but often he brought home dead rabbits he'd picked up from the road. At first we fed these to the cats but the night he brought an enormous hare, still warm, we realised the cats were feeding better than us. Next morning I paunched and skinned the hare on the bank of the beck and left the cats fighting over the offal. That meat lasted us three days and now the cats were given only the mutilated carcasses; we kept the good ones for ourselves.

Another source of income was the innumerable beer and cordial bottles he found in lay-bys and for which he was paid handsome sums by the pubs.

We established an elastic routine. At first I had driven him to work when he didn't bring the lorry home at night but after a few days he had his motor cycle on the road again and, although I missed the dawn drives, I had more time for writing. He left early, sometimes getting up at four to start at five. I worked from eight o'clock until he telephoned in the evening.

Then I'd put the meal, already prepared, in the oven and he'd be home in half an hour. In the evenings he sat by the fire and refused to move. This was what he wanted, he said, home life, an understanding wife, a good fire, and the cat on his knee. I did understand so I stayed with him, studying my current subject, criminology, and we listened to records and only went out on match nights when he played for the local darts team.

Shortly after Johnnie started work Sheena came home for the summer holidays. She was to work at the Old Dungeon Ghyll during August and it occurred to us that in Langdale she would be climbing with people other than ourselves, and possibly pushed into the lead. Until now she had always climbed behind us or our friends, not because we didn't want her to lead but because no one thought of it. We decided that we would go to Langdale for a weekend and that she should lead us up moderate routes. I wanted her to experience that peculiar loneliness of the climber who is out in front with no rope from above. The difficulty of instilling in a teenager respect for rock seems, to the parent, insuperable. You can learn where your limit is only by making mistakes. You know when you make a mistake on rock when you're afraid or when you fall off. How could we show Sheena where her limit was without such tests? Johnnie and I had made too many mistakes and broken too many bones not to know that we'd been lucky; it seemed too much to hope for that a third member of the family should have the same good fortune. There was another factor that contributed to our survival. Johnnie and I started climbing when we were twenty; Sheena was not yet sixteen.

We went to Langdale one murky August morning and she led me up Rib and Wall, a Difficult route on Tarn Crag while, from sixty feet below, I watched her pause at the hard move and let her find out for herself where the handholds were and how to place her feet. It was now that I realised another great problem of climbing parents. I had been aware since Sheena started to walk that it was not implicit she would have the same passion for rock and ice as myself. Aware too, that unless she took to it of her own accord, she must never be pushed. And when she did ask to come out with me, I tried to make it enjoyable, not a course of instruction. The slightest hint of this can make a child rebel: "just another *lesson*; to hear them talk I thought it was fun!" I had hoped that rope work, choice of belays, the placing of runners, would be assimilated unconsciously. I had forgotten my own novitiate when, for a few weeks, I had climbed and walked always behind someone else. When I broke away and was in the lead myself, I wasn't bewildered by a profusion of belays or the lines on a cliff; I was hard put to it to find either. I had been completely dependent on another person and had followed blindly. When I saw Sheena going past spikes which were obvious and well-placed for running belays, I wondered if she should have been forced to learn techniques, and then I remembered her strong opposition to Johnnie's insistence that she should study relevant articles and books on map reading and navigation. Now, too late, I realised what we should have done: sent her on a course with a reliable guide. I could only hope that the quiet common sense of our friends the Crosses at the Old Dungeon Ghyll (who were expert mountaineers) would counteract the reckless attitude she might meet among her contemporaries.

We led through on Cook's Tour on Pavey. She climbed neatly and confidently, stepping too high occasionally, missing small holds, but this was a superficial fault. If I was being perfectionist I wasn't after style but safety.

She had never descended a climb so we said we would go down Gwynne's Chimney — but I had forgotten that as we came up the screes to Pavey we had seen a sheep trapped on the cliff. I found it as I climbed down to the top of the chimney, and there was a lamb with the ewe.

I returned to the others wondering whether we should leave the animals to someone else to rescue or try to do it on our own, Johnnie and I.

The others saw no problem: we would all take part. Now there are two important jobs on a sheep rescue: the man who

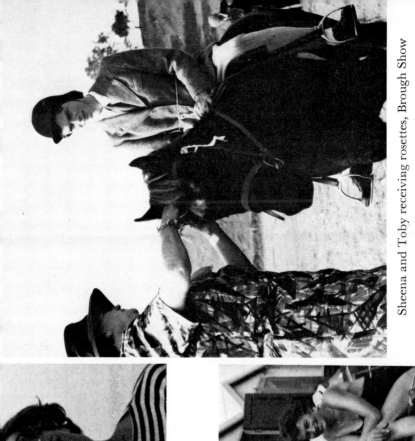

Sheena and Toby receiving rosettes, Brough Show

G.M. and Sheena

Sheena, Mother, Father and G.M., 1966

Johnnie on Ardus, Borrowdale

catches the animal (and here there were two) and the man on top holding the rope. Sheena was neither experienced nor strong enough for either, so where should she be?

"She can come down and help me," Johnnie said.

"But I can't hold two ropes! Suppose you both fell off at the same time?"

I had visions of all five of us (including sheep) being catapulted over the edge and landing on the screes four hundred feet below. Sheep are imbued with the death wish when you try to catch them on tiny ledges; rescuing them is far more dangerous than rescuing any but a delirious human being. Ideally two men are needed to catch one ewe – and a team on top to hold the ropes.

We compromised. Johnnie should go down on one rope and Sheena should go partway, tied to that rope with a sliding knot. She could play an important part because the belay was a long way from the top of the chimney. She would be able to tell me what was happening, a necessary procedure when Johnnie, perhaps at a critical moment and teetering on the edge, wouldn't be able to shout for fear of frightening the ewe. But one man to two animals! This time, I thought as I belayed myself, we are going to lose a sheep – and I knew how upset Sheena would be to see it going over the edge.

They left me. Sheena stopped on the lip of the cliff but Johnnie disappeared. The rope stopped running out and I waited, tense, for my instructions. When they came I realised how dependent we were on Sheena. I could see and hear nothing of Johnnie. He was whispering to her and she relayed his orders in a normal voice. There was a lot of: "Keep the rope tight! . . . Slack! . . . Keep it *tight*, Mummy!"

I worked grimly and silently, sweating profusely. At any moment I expected to hear a wail of horror as a sheep went down.

There was silence for ten minutes or longer. Sheena leaned

out over the edge, staring at what was happening below. She was rigid with concentration. Then she moved . . . she was going to help.

No, I thought, *don't take the rope off! Stay where you are!*

I didn't say anything.

She relaxed and turned to me laughing.

"He's got them!"

"What, *both*?"

"Oh, yes; it was quite easy. One in each hand."

I admired her compassion. Obviously one had jumped off and she was trying to spare my feelings. They shouted for another rope for the ewe. So it was the lamb had gone. But Sheena was leaning down with outstretched arms to take something. She had the lamb!

Afterwards they told me about it. Johnnie had gone down to a point below the sheep's ledge and climbed up to it. The ewe had eaten all the grass and only a few twigs of heather remained on the lip. Using these as handholds (that was when I had to keep the rope tight) he traversed till he could work them back into a corner. He'd brought a bunch of grass from the gully and he held this towards the ewe while he talked to her in that reassuring monotone which I'd taught him. I'm certain that this is better than a silent sinister approach; it diverts the sheep if it doesn't hypnotise her. A frightened animal will stare and snort and eye the edge, but while you talk the sheep watches you — so you keep talking: anything, just keep muttering away about its stupidity, its lack of survival sense; you tell it that suicide is irresponsible, it must think of its lamb, control itself: "Show an example, there's a good sheep, there's a silly old stinking ewe, *tight rope*! Nice ewe, stupid nit, *bloody rope tight*! Move back a bit, go on, just another inch, gently, *I'm almost there, tight when I jump*!" All this in the same pitch, the same tone, and then you move fast, sinking the fingers deep in the wool on the back (these are often "rogue" ewes which escape shearing) throwing her over with her legs in the air. Once you've got them down, it's over — unless they're strong and they struggle and the ledge is sloping . . .

The ewe stood across the corner with the lamb behind her. Johnnie caught and threw the mother one-handed and as the lamb leapt away he fielded it in mid-air with his free hand. When the second rope came down he wedged the lamb in the corner with his knee while he tied the ewe in a cradle.

They climbed up to me, partly under their own steam, partly with pulls from the rope. Sheena would ascend a few feet and Johnnie handed the lamb up to her. He was very light and could be tucked under one arm. But he was lively too for he was still at the suckling stage and the ewe had milk. He was hungry all the same. As they passed him from hand to hand he gurgled and squelched like a hot water bottle.

As they approached me they were preceded by an odour of sheep that was almost tangible.

I untied, and climbed the gully for sixty feet to the next belay — so I missed the next part of the performance. The four of them were avoiding a cave pitch by climbing the gully wall. Halfway up this, they were standing on a ledge, Johnnie with the ewe at chest level, Sheena beside him with the lamb under her arm and purchase for only one foot, when she realised the earthy ledge was crumbling. There were frantic cries for tight ropes and I was fighting like a puppet master with tangled strings and wondering what they were bleating about; surely they were safe in the gully?

We reached the summit and sat by the cairn, the ewe feeding quietly but with little starts of astonishment when she realised she was still on a lead. We couldn't let her go; she would kill herself on fresh grass; she must be taken down to the farm to be fed small quantities slowly.

A Boy Scout approached through the mist, so preoccupied with finding his companions that he seemed to notice nothing odd in the composition of our party. Sheena and I exchanged looks and, leaving Johnnie to deliver himself of his mountain safety lecture ("Haven't you been taught that a party never separates in mist . . . ?") we started down. We had our own troubles.

The rocks were greasy, and the ewe, hearing her companions in the combe below, pulled me down through the boulder fields at high speed. The mist was dropping now and we were invisible to Johnnie who was descending the cliff to pick up the rucksacks. He said afterwards that he could follow our progress by the curses and knew, when they stopped, that we'd reached the grass.

We collapsed on the shore of the tarn. We moistened the ewe's lips with water and loosened her harness. I swathed my toes with sticking plaster for I was wearing climbing boots which fit like a glove. One can walk sedately in them but they are not designed for the wearer to be dragged through boulders by a homing ewe.

Johnnie joined us at the outlet from the tarn, which was fortunate; the last mile to the farm was steep and the path covered with scree. The sheep wrenched and dragged us down the slope as if they were wild horses (surely that torture of tying people to horses which were whipped in opposite directions was superfluous? One horse was ample). Again and again I picked myself up with the now familiar glance at my rent slacks to make sure the bone wasn't sticking through; then Sheena would go over with a sickening jolt and, rising, tuck the lamb under her arm again and continue without a word.

The farmer put the sheep in a pen and reiterated his assurance of free milk. It was the second of his ewes we had rescued this year. At the hut Sheena and I compared bruises. I looked at her legs in wonder. We had started out with my being dubious about her leading easy climbs and now she looked as if she had fallen fifty feet: black and blue and grazed — and she was amused. She'd do, I thought grimly, but with confidence.

CHAPTER 17

Survival

JOHNNIE STILL HAD hope of a professional guiding business. He answered business letters on paper headed *J. R. Lees and Gwen Moffat. Rock Climbing and Mountaineering Guides.* He was thinking in terms of his own mountain school, staffed by his friends. Meanwhile he accepted those engagements that came his way and the contractor allowed him time off during the week to climb.

In September we were instructing officers and N.C.O.s from the Army Apprentices' School at Carlisle. It was wet and greasy that first morning in Borrowdale and as I stared through the dripping trees at the green rock on Shepherd's Crag I reflected that it would be just my luck to find that all my clients weighed sixteen stone.

This wasn't unduly pessimistic. When a car drew up and the men emerged I saw with dismay that they were all large and heavy and even if I had increased my weight I was still around seven stone. There were four men to train each day; I studied them intently, trying to pick out the two lightest, but my deliberations were wasted: Johnnie was the boss.

At the foot of Brown Slabs I stood idly at ease while he expounded on knots and paying out rope and the correct climbing position.

"Right," he said, turning to me, "demonstration!"

It was a good way to do it: having one guide climb for forty feet while the other commented on her progress, but I found it disconcerting:

"Now watch her feet, see how she's not stepping high —

well, not too high; she's standing out from the rock, keeping her hands low . . ."

I admired his loyalty – which was stronger than his veracity. The holds were polished and I was in nails; I was clumsy and I knew it – and he knew it. Damn him, I thought, why couldn't he have climbed and I do the commentary?

As the distance between me and the ground increased so did my confidence. By the time I reached the tree and tied on, and I'd looked down and seen the diffidence on their faces, I knew that for the rest of the day everyone would be so concerned for himself that I would be nothing more than an object that kept the rope tight.

We were lucky in our men. The N.C.O.s were well-disciplined. They did exactly what they were told and no one dared to come off. That, said Johnnie with the air of one discovering a fact of life, was the advantage of having a female guide in the party: the men were on their mettle.

The rain came down in sheets in the afternoon. I was a redhead at this time and more concerned with my hair running than in what I was doing. I put up the hood of my anorak and kept bumping into all the overhangs. There is a strong feeling of claustrophobia climbing in a hood, and this results in the impression that the rock is closing in on you at the same time as the drop is opening out.

On the second day we had different men, the sun shone and we climbed in vibrams on dry rock. There was no embarrassment with this party.

"Don't make it too easy," Johnnie whispered as I stepped off the ground, but I ignored him and went up Brown Slabs deliberately missing out the big holds and using only nicks for my feet, secure in the knowledge that they'd be watching the lower half of me, unaware that my hands were on the incut jug handles.

It was so pleasant that taking them up Little Chamonix (after a muttered conference at the bottom when we decided

they were equal to a Very Difficult) I strayed absent-
mindedly on to the exposed top pitch of Chamonix instead of
finishing by the easy crack of the original route. I was thinking about Jet's cough and wondering if I should step up her
daily dose of cod-liver oil. Then my foot slipped and,
trembling on one leg, I raked the road to see if anyone were
watching. The road was empty and I was out of sight of my
own party (and Johnnie) and my honour was intact. I
remembered the Welsh guide, George Dwyer, telling me how
he'd once fallen from the first pitch of Holly Tree Original
above the Idwal Slabs: "the trouble was, I'd done it so many
times, I wasn't thinking . . ."

We took the Army to Langdale and I led the two best men
up Route I, a Severe on White Ghyll slabs. Johnnie, watching with the officers from the other side of the ghyll, said it
was as good as a Marx Brothers film: seeing us perched on the
stance ninety feet above the screes with the men standing at
attention on the inadequate ledge while I climbed round and
under and through them, fixing their belays and sorting the
ropes, turning them round like roasts on a spit, inspecting
their waist knots . . .

"Why didn't you tell them constricted stances were *fun*?"
he asked.

"They wouldn't have appreciated it. Besides, you've
always said I must be aloof with my clients."

October came with the swallows and martins congregating,
and suddenly we woke one morning and they were gone.
Salmon came up the river to spawn, leaping the falls, landing flat-bellied and being swept back, returning with one
great curving bound and clearing the white water. Quail
appeared on the common – and the first dusting of snow on
the higher hills. By the middle of November they were
covered and all the high tarns frozen hard.

We went to Patterdale one bleak Saturday after a week of
rain at Bloan and we woke on Sunday to find the sun was

shining and the snowline down to fifteen hundred feet. We climbed a gully on St Sunday Crag where the snow was powdery and the ice poor, but thick enough for us to need to cut steps. It was the first snow climb of the winter — the first of many, we said happily as we came down the ridge in the sunset with the snow squeaking under our boots.

The lane was blocked again, not for the tractor and my new estate car at first, but for Johnnie's motor cycle. This had a side-car attachment which was too light and low to negotiate the drifts. He left it in the village and walked home in the evenings. One night he telephoned and he sounded tired. I told him I would come up and fetch him if he waited in the pub.

He had to wait a long time. There had been a heavy snowfall since I'd last driven up the lane and the tractor had compacted the drifts with its sump. Before the right-angled bend, where a stream crossed the track and the ruts were deep, I stuck fast with a pile of snow in front of the grille. After two hours of digging and reversing and shooting forwards, trying to rush the drifts, I abandoned the car and walked to the village. We had to reverse the Cortina all the way to Bloan, and now Johnnie must walk home again. He never realised the danger implicit in this where he passed under a Scots pine with a huge horizontal bough. One night, greatly overloaded with snow, it cracked like a field gun and fell on the track a few yards behind him.

On his way home he would call on old Mrs Donald and carry coal and water for her. He also lagged her water pipe that winter so that there was less chance of it freezing solid in hard frosts. We were acutely conscious of her vulnerability, always looking to see if her chimney was smoking in the morning, glad to see her light shining at night. But the light itself worried me. It was an oil lamp and she left it burning in case she had to get up. Several times she told me she'd fallen:

tripped over the cat or a rug. I brought new batteries for her torch but I noticed the oil lamp still burned at night.

She took great pride in her home and her independence. When she told me the district nurse, the doctor and "the chapel" were trying to persuade her to go into a Home and asked my advice, I found the problem disturbing. My instinct, or part of it, wanted to tell her to stay, with her cabbage patch (which, in her eighties, she still cultivated), her raspberry canes, to stay on the common where her husband had kept a goat and his few sheep until he was killed on his motor cycle many years ago. I wanted her to keep her dark little cottage with its shining range and the geraniums in the window — but I remembered the oil lamp and the black cat on a black rug before an open fire, and I talked about company and television and having a trained nurse on call but, for all my fear of third degree burns, I felt like a traitor.

There was a sloping field at Bloan called Whinney Hill. On good days after a heavy snowfall Johnnie would ring in the middle of the afternoon:

"Are you out?"

"Yes, I'm answering from a field telephone."

"You said you'd go out!"

"I'm busy."

He said he would keep ringing till I'd gone. I went for the sake of peace.

There was a shallow gully running down Whinney Hill. The top of its bank had a two-dimensional slope: into the gully and down the hill. I could get in five parallel turns here, six if I kept the traverses short.

They were glorious hours with the sun glittering on the snow and the bare black trees fretted against a cloudless sky. Johnnie told me to forget his meal and I did, ski-ing until the sun sank red beyond the far ghost of Blencathra and the moon came up and the snow froze so that where the turns had been slow and soft with a spume of dust, now they were

hard and fast with the grating rasp of steel on ice. And then a
light appeared in Bloan and I came down in a straight run to
the gate, putting up the mallard which went winging across
the sky in two black arrowheads, wheeling and coming back
to settle by the beck.

At night in winter the duck came downstream to feed
under the bedroom window. If you woke you could hear them
talking quietly in the darkness. It was a companionable
sleepy sound; the nights at Bloan — when the air was still —
were very friendly. It was a different matter when the helm
blew. With the windows closed tightly and the panes glazed
with ice, the curtains billowed in the draughts and we'd wake
to find drifts of snow dust inside the room in the morning.

It was a white Christmas. We went to Langdale where
Sheena was working at the Old Dungeon Ghyll again. There
was hard snow on the tops, frost in the valleys, but by day the
sun shone brilliantly and the rock was dry and warm and
almost empty of people.

Johnnie had been looking forward to the rest. His back had
been troubling him again and he'd strained his ankle. The
snow had made things hard for the lorry drivers. With the
farm roads blocked, foodstuffs had to be left at gateways and
often there was no one to help with the unloading. At
Christmas he wanted to climb on accessible cliffs where he
wouldn't have to walk far from the road.

We spent Boxing Day on White Ghyll and came down early
for tea at the hotel. A rescue was in progress, Sheena told us:
on Bowfell, two thousand feet above the dale. I followed
Johnnie out to the car.

"You won't carry the stretcher, will you?"

"No. Don't stand there. Get a move on!"

A short distance from the hotel he realised he'd forgotten
the crampons and ran back in the dark. He'd been trying to
move slowly this holiday. I was unhappy. I knew he would
help with the stretcher.

The trudge up the steep hillside from Mickleden seemed

never-ending. Far above us we could see lights in a snow-filled gully. They seemed terribly slow descending. I wondered how much Johnnie's back was hurting, what he'd be like tomorrow. It was no good saying I couldn't go on; he would know I was shamming – or would leave me and continue alone.

When we did meet the rescuers we learned that the casualty had died. He had slipped at the top of the gully and fallen to the bottom. In the dark I lost sight of Johnnie among the people and I dropped back. There were stragglers coming down the hillside without torches. They converged on me like clumsy moths, following my light.

It was a curious evening. Dinner was delayed because Sid Cross had been leading the rescue party and many of the residents were on the hill. No one mentioned Bowfell until Peggy Robinson, the *Daily Express* reporter, came in and said she'd telephoned her story to the office. Still in our climbing gear we stood and watched the dancers: colour and light and laughter . . . the Christmas party at the Old Dungeon Ghyll. Outside Bowfell would stand austere against the stars and here Johnnie talked with animation to the girls but he leaned on the wall in the curious position he adopted to ease his back.

"Don't worry, Gwen," a voice called, "it may never happen."

He was splitting logs one weekend and the axe jammed on a knot. He whirled axe and log over his head and the damage was done. He came in white and breathing hard, in great pain. After the electric blanket had been on an hour I got him to bed, but on Monday morning, twisted like an old tree, he left for work. In ten minutes he was back. He couldn't drive the motor cycle.

The doctor ordered a week in bed and hot baths daily. During the first few days Johnnie was anxious about his job but towards the end of the week he was worrying about the future. He didn't work for three months. The weather was cold and grim and he was acutely depressed. He lost his job but he'd known he couldn't go back to the heavy work of lifting hundredweights of foodstuffs, of shovelling fertiliser. Financially we were keeping our heads above water. During the previous autumn and about the time he was scouring lay-bys for empty bottles and we were eating the cats' rabbits, I'd remembered that four-day stint last Christmas when I earned a hundred pounds. Four days was too short but I thought I could do it in a fortnight. All it needed was self-discipline, I said. So I put my back into it and made over a hundred in the first fortnight, but it was heavy going. The following two weeks it was eighty pounds, then sixty and then the Christmas holidays intervened. Now that the cheques were coming in from that six weeks' work, encouraging me, I set to work again. There was none of the frustration I had experienced at Ullswater when Johnnie was ill and I was trying to finish *Two Star Red*. Now we appreciated each other's needs: he wanted company, I wanted solitude. Reconciling the two was simple. I got up in the small hours and had done a full day's work before he woke. Then I cooked and cleaned and he didn't mind that; I made a lot of noise, played records, talked to the cats. Silence was what he hated, with my working behind a closed door. I borrowed piles of thrillers and lay on the bed beside him with the bedside lamp on (it grew dark early) and the oak panels gleaming. He was contented then; it was the mornings when he was depressed, when the mail came with another cheque for me. My success underlined his own sense of inadequacy. He was ashamed to be supported by me. I pointed out that the situation was only temporary, that there would be long periods in the future when I would write books and we would live on his salary. But it was the future he was thinking about: what work would there be for him when he recovered?

A friend telephoned from London. Had we seen the job advertised in *The Guardian*? A Wardens' Service Officer was wanted in Derbyshire, something to do with the National Park; wouldn't it be ideal for Johnnie? Yes, I said, but he'd been offered a job in Derbyshire already and he'd said there were no mountains there and refused, but thank you, and I would give him the message.

Johnnie reacted as I'd thought he would. No one wanted a cripple; I'd got to support him.

"All right," I said, "it may not be too late to apply for that B.B.C. job."

Manchester had been advertising for a Talks Producer at two, or perhaps it was three thousand pounds.

"I would have to take a flat in Manchester," I said.

"All right."

"But what would you do?"

"Come and live there of course."

"What about climbing?"

"Derbyshire's on the doorstep."

He began to enthuse about the gritstone edges an hour's run from Manchester. A few evenings later I said,

"I decided that the B.B.C. job would mean too much work at weekends. I'm going to apply for the Derbyshire job. I've got the forms."

"You can't!"

"Why shouldn't a woman apply? *Wardens' Service Officer* it says. 'Experience in climbing, rescue, ski-ing, pony trekking, caving, administration.' I can be a bit ambiguous about the caving."

"What do you know about administration?"

"Couldn't you help me?"

"Yes. Yes, I could. I could advise."

"You'd be an *éminence gris*; I'd be a figurehead."

"Yes, you know, I think you stand a good chance."

"With you behind me."

"Of course."

"Then why don't you apply?"

He started to speak and I knew he was going to talk about

cripples, then he stopped. I'd won. He wasn't going to see me get that job.

If our lives seemed full of ups and downs that's just how it happened, and now things went to extremes. He applied for the job and was short-listed. He went to Bakewell for his interview and another man was given the post. He returned to Bloan downcast but certain that the result had been very close. It was. Within a few days the successful candidate withdrew and Johnnie was offered the position. At the end of March he left Bloan for Derbyshire.

Sheena and I were ski-ing on the last of the snow. Outside the run the moor was all brown and heathery but the slope was white, marked with the patterns of our turns. Standing at the top I looked out towards the Lake District and remembered that from Bloan I could see Blencathra. For twenty years I had lived in mountains: high jagged peaks: Snowdonia, Skye, the Highlands, the Lakes. Now, in a few weeks' time I must pull up my roots again and go to live in a county where there was nothing but moorland at two thousand feet, where the rocks and the walls and even the sheep were black from industrial dirt. And suddenly I realised that all the larks were singing on the summit and Sheena was waiting for me. Before I started down to lose the lark song in the sound of the running skis and the sweet swing of the turns I remembered that the Lakes and Wales were only an evening's run from Derbyshire, that perhaps I could come to tolerate moors and gritstone crags — and there would be larks on the High Peak too.

CHAPTER 18

The High Peak and the Pit

I MOVED TO Derbyshire in a heat wave, driving down the motorway with all the windows open for the cats to have air. They were quiet on this journey. Jet was in an orange box behind my seat and occasionally a soft paw, claws sheathed, dabbed my neck. There was a wild tabby queen called Bertha in the cat basket. Her mother, Pushkin, had died under the anaesthetic when I took her to be spayed. My kindly vet in Penrith had been upset when he telephoned me: a very nervous cat, he said, and it happened so seldom; he refused to submit a bill. I was glad I hadn't been fond of Pushkin. She left four kittens. I found homes for all except Bertha and she was too wild to go to a strange house. When we moved we had to entice her into a shed and go in to catch her wearing thick clothes and gauntlets.

The new house was a small lodge close under the moors outside Buxton. Although it was at a thousand feet it was surrounded by fields and woods. There was a short-eared owl, lapwings nested at the back—and on my first morning I thought I heard a buzzard mewing. Yes, our landlord said, there was one in the next valley.

Our luck had held through the rigours of house-hunting. Johnnie and I had scoured the county: he for months and I for one busy week after the Easter holidays. He was living with his friends Don and Valerie Aldridge at Hathersage. Don worked for the Peak Park Planning Board as its Information Officer. Near the end of my visit, when I must return north for some broadcast or other, Don was talking on the telephone to a man who owned land at Buxton. At the end of the conversation he mentioned our unsuccessful search for a house. The man said that if we were interested he had a lodge which would soon be empty. We went to Buxton the following evening.

We passed the lodge as we went to call on Ivor Morten, who, I hoped, was our potential landlord. We knew the lodge was suitable for the lane was a cul-de-sac and there would be few cars. Anything would suffice that had a roof and where the cats wouldn't be run over. I was putting down no more roots, I told myself sternly. We turned up a rough track and came to a big, square, uncompromising house. On the slope in front of it were pheasants: gold and silver, peacocks, guinea fowl, Muscovy ducks. "Oh, look," I said, "silkies!" Johnnie stared at the hens which looked like fat barmaids in white furs. Bantams scattered in front of the car and at the back door there were a pair of Chinese geese, slim, brown and beautiful. A young springer spaniel barked at us furiously.

Ivor Morten opened the door: a large middle-aged man with the confident bearing of one who has been born in this house, lived on this land all his life and whose family, we were to learn, had farmed here for four hundred years. He roared at the spaniel – who was called Haggis and took no notice – and showed us into a large dim room where the centre light appeared to have a skirt draped round it. Under this, and dimly illuminated, was a huge table covered with books, photographic material, a clean China tea-service, old letters bearing threepenny stamps and an aerosol for moths. Later, seeing my interest he disinterred from underneath this curious collection an Irish shillelagh, reindeer bells from Lapland, a pair of cockfighting spurs and a set of wooden English cowbells that were two hundred years old.

Before I sat down I removed a stack of records to a safer place on the sofa, prompting the information that a relative had composed the score for "Chu Chin Chow". Ivor himself had taken his degree in agriculture at Bangor. We talked about Wales, the High Peak, sheep, photography, mountaineering, youth work. The telephone rang several times. "For Heaven's sake," I whispered to Johnnie as Ivor left us again, "what about the *house*?"

"Ah, yes," Ivor said on his return, "I think we'll put in an immersion heater" (he was a bachelor but always he used the plural) "and they tell me there's something wrong with the lavatory bowl. We'll have to look at that. Do you know Exmoor? I'm going there to look at the National Park; I'm looking forward to it."

On our first evening at the lodge, when the removal men had gone and the neighbours, complete with lorry, had driven away with Johnnie to store all our superfluous furniture in Ivor's stables, I was sitting in the living room among the piled packing cases when Jack Longland arrived from his home at Bakewell with bottles of whisky and sherry. Then Johnnie, sent out for fish and chips, returned with Ivor:

"We met in the town and he told me where the best fish and chips were."

It must have been after midnight when they left. We had a proper house-warming two weeks later. We dressed correctly and we had glasses for the drinks and canapés. It was fun but it wasn't like that first night, sitting among the packing cases, drinking whisky out of teacups.

I didn't climb for ten days after our arrival although the edges were all around us. I had climbed on gritstone twice: some years ago when a local club took me to a crag one wet winter Sunday and I found a moderate route surprisingly hard, and recently when I had been house-hunting and Johnnie took me to Stanage Edge. The shortness of the routes (most were one-pitch climbs), their preponderance of steep cracks, the rounded holds, all these were so different from the general run of mountain climbs that I was intimidated. I felt

o

that I could never enjoy this kind of climbing. Nor was I interested in the moors. I had walked on the Northern Pennines in winter (when they were most dramatic) and come to love and respect them, but a few miles of upland country between Manchester and Sheffield! Eventually I would climb on gritstone if only to keep myself in training for weekends in the mountains, but these moors were for trippers, not for me.

On the second Sunday after our arrival we drove to Raven Stones, across a valley from the Manchester–Huddersfield road. With distaste I listened to Johnnie's information that from here we could practically see where the bodies of children were found after the Moors Murders. Perhaps it was this that made me look at the dank black rock of Raven Stones with hostility. Nursing my resentment of this hateful place I said I would walk to Crowden alone and meet him there later.

"You've got your compass?" he shouted as I moved away.

I ignored him. Ahead of me was a two-mile walk before I struck the Pennine Way which would lead me down to Crowden. Visibility was perfect and the moor didn't exceed seventeen hundred feet. His facetiousness was salt in my wounds.

After a few steps my training asserted itself and I turned to reassure him. He was gone. I glanced round, trying to locate the top of Raven Stones. Everything was the same: all cotton grass and heather – and no tracks.

For a moment I was so astonished that I couldn't think. Then I recognised that I was lost to the extent that I didn't know where I was, in which direction the crag lay. Johnnie was so near I could have summoned him with a whistle, and yet I had no idea from which point of the compass he would emerge. Then a bird called, a golden plover, and there were curlews. There were clouds over the sun but I could see faintly where it was. My course lay due south, so I walked south and I topped a rise and saw the hills: long grey ridges completely featureless. Then I knew that this was no country for trippers but for mountaineers.

I came to the groughs: deep meandering channels in the peat with steep sides and overhangs of sods and heather along their lips. First I tried going straight down one side and up the other but the peat was greasy and I slipped – and longed for an ice axe. After that I treated them like snow, kicking steps, looking for easy lines up the dark brown banks. What must they be like in winter, I thought, with the peat frozen and water under ice in the bottom?

The cloud dropped and I thought of mist. I must find a landmark before all landmarks were hidden. I looked from the map to the featureless hills and at last, to the east, I saw the television mast of Holme Moss. Then, compass in hand, I walked my two miles to Chew Reservoir: walking on a bearing in good visibility.

New country is like a new lover. I never gave up my old loves because I knew my absence was only temporary, nevertheless there was an element of disloyalty, not in leaving them but in giving my love to another. At first in strange country I would be hostile and wary and plead all kinds of excuses for dislike and suspicion. But I had to succumb in the end for any place that has steep rock, whether it's eighty feet or eight hundred, anywhere that there are redshank and golden plover and a thin wind on the uplands is mountain country. But I still resisted and told myself, after the walk to Crowden, that I would go back because the walking was rougher than any I had known, because navigation was more hazardous, because there would be people to rescue and I must be competent. So I walked on Kinder and Bleaklow, first alone and then, when the summer holidays came, with Sheena. I found ravines, called "cloughs" here, where streams ran clear over orange slabs and there were flycatchers on the wooded banks. With Sheena I went to the Downfall on Kinder where the river drops a hundred feet over a broken cliff and we climbed the moderate route in shorts and shirts and were drenched to the skin. We went in the middle of the week for Kinder was popular at weekends and best avoided then. I preferred Bleaklow at all times: a wild high plateau with its sculptured stones on top, its acres of peat, its deep and twisting cloughs, wooded in their lower reaches, rocky and bare in their upper sections, where you could walk all day and see no more than the occasional solitary walker like yourself.

I was asked to join the Edale Mountain Rescue Team, a group of wardens who trained one evening a week and sometimes at weekends as well. I had never been in a civilian team which turned out so conscientiously for exercises, some of which were as arduous, or more so, than many rescues. We climbed, we lowered stretchers, and we practised sweep searches.

The fact that a sweep search is called for at all indicates that the ground in question is rough, full of boulders or hollows or wooded gorges or all of these. On easy ground a lost man can be found by a handful of people with field-glasses. On the High Peak with its groughs, its deep heathery hollows, its rocky cloughs, teams may search for days without finding and, in winter when every drift may cover an unconscious man or a body, their task is infinitely greater.

A sweep search is designed to comb the ground meticulously. The team, perhaps thirty strong, spreads out in a long line with a man at one end as marker who navigates on a bearing. The distance between each man is determined by the ground, the weather and the amount of light. It is the distance that you can see anything which you need to see: not necessarily a huddled figure but discarded clothing, for often victims of exposure, still moving, remove hats or gloves, even boots. In mist, at night, among boulders, the line closes up; in good visibility, on easy ground, it can afford to open out. The sweep advances on a straight line; distance must be kept so there can be no avoiding of obstacles. The groughs cannot be circumvented nor followed unless they happen to coincide with one's undeviating line. If a channel runs at right angles across your path you go straight down and up the other side and at the same time that you are keeping your place, neither shooting forward nor lagging, you are searching. A sweep search on the plateau in good weather is extremely arduous; at night in a gale it's hell.

On a big search several teams may be taking part and the operation is supervised by experts at the base who keep in touch with the teams by radio or runners. The area to be searched is divided into sections, usually strips, often based on natural features such as watersheds or streams. The strips vary in size but some are roughly one square mile in area. Those where the ground is rough may be smaller; a larger section will contain easier ground. Each team is allocated its area and the section is searched, going up and down the strip on parallel "legs". These should not overlap but no ground must be missed. The Edale team uses flags on bamboo poles to mark the boundary of the leg and these are collected on the return course. Sometimes lime is used if flags or other signs are not available.

The man responsible for the idea of dividing a search area into sections was Fred Heardman, a lively septuagenarian who lives in Edale and was for many decades one of the great Pennine walkers. He still thinks nothing of twenty miles a day.

The Peak District teams train not only among themselves but periodically together on large-scale exercises. One of these took place in October of that year when eighteen teams were to assemble at Crowden to find "casualties" supplied by the Territorial Army. Johnnie, now on the panel of the Peak District Mountain Rescue Organisation, had been eager to go out on this exercise as an observer but his back was giving him trouble again and his doctor had banned all mountaineering temporarily. So, having had a special dispensation from the Edale team leader, I went instead, thinking that thus I was avoiding taking part in a sweep search and that I might have an easy time. The previous day I had walked fifteen miles on Bleaklow. It didn't occur to me until I left Crowden that Sunday morning that since all the teams were starting out at the same time, many would find their quarry within a few hours and, the casualties being scattered over undulating moors which measured roughly six square miles and included two river valleys and all their side cloughs, I was going to have to move fast to observe more than two or three "rescues".

I was out for six hours. I had been given the map references of the casualties in advance and by late afternoon I had seen what I hoped would be enough: six men found and evacuated. I came down behind the last team, my last — there were others still out — very wet for I couldn't pick my ground as I ran up and down the slopes but must go straight through the bogs and streams. I regretted now that I had brought no dry clothing, but the operation was nearly over and we would soon be home. Not a bad day's work, I thought, drinking tea at Crowden and hoping that I could write my notes for Johnnie in an hour so that we could have an early night.

At five-thirty all the teams had dispersed and there were three of us left in the Briefing Centre: Johnnie, Ken Drabble, his assistant warden, and myself. It was at this moment, when we were about to leave, that a message was telephoned to Crowden saying that two people, a man and a girl, were missing on Bleaklow. The man, aged fifty-seven, had fractured his leg some time ago and the plaster had been removed only recently. He was reputed to be a good walker but little was known of the girl's competence. We thought of coronaries and another fracture, and we wondered why the girl hadn't come down. They had last been seen on top of Bleaklow at two o'clock that afternoon.

Since they had been intending to return to Glossop which lies in a south-westerly direction from the range this was the most likely area to look for them first. Johnnie drove to

Glossop Police Station to set up a base there and to alert the teams, while Ken and I and four or five others went up Bleaklow with a pressure lamp, hoping the missing pair would see the light and blow whistles.

That first drag up the hill was tiring. I had not yet accepted the situation: that we might be out many hours, possibly all night. I still thought we would meet them as we ascended, one with some minor injury like a wrenched knee or a sprained ankle, being supported by the other. I was still thinking of a good meal and dry clothes and bed. After all, it was only six o'clock.

Ken Drabble, who had been a Commando, went very fast. Two of us managed to keep up, myself with difficulty and only through pride for the other was a long-legged blonde called Linda who moved like a good guide in a hurry. Behind us the men strung out and I thought how much easier it would be for me if only Linda would drop back. Through the blood pounding in my ears I could hear her *talking* to Ken.

On top of the rise called James' Thorn, at eighteen hundred feet, we put down the lamp and shouted in unison. We moved half a mile to Higher Shelf Stones and shouted again but there was no reply. It was here that they'd last been seen and one enthusiastic lad dropped down and nosed about the path until he found tracks of nailed boots. This didn't help. The man had been wearing nails, but we could follow the tracks only a short distance. They led east towards Hern Clough, and there was no light, no sound from Hern Clough.

As we turned for home we saw the Edale team coming up from the highest point of the Snake road. We knew it was them because Edale has a very strong arc light, like a miniature searchlight, which the tallest member, Dave Forshaw, carries strapped to his chest. We met and passed them, telling them we had found nothing. As we continued we saw that now there were lights in several places on the tops. There was even, we saw with annoyance, a party following our own route to Higher Shelf Stones. Back at Glossop we learned that this latter party was with Johnnie and that they were carrying a stretcher. My annoyance changed to anxiety: Johnnie had interpreted the doctor's ban as one on mountaineering for *fun*.

There was a friendly, helpful air about the police station. It is in the charge of Inspector Watson who is not only interested in mountaineering but in rescue as well. This night it was crowded with teams standing by, while a police-woman and the Edale girls made tea and sandwiches. We were very hungry. Few people had eaten much since break-fast time.

A small brown man came in wearing ginger plus fours. He was immediately at home: listening to reports, consulting maps. They were his maps: this was Fred Heardman. No one seemed to think it unusual that he should have driven over from Edale late at night to offer his services. He was the guiding light behind the rescue. Johnnie was in charge but he turned to Fred for help and advice. Until he arrived there had been talk of calling off the search until dawn. The rescuers were against this; it was a fine night (but it might deteriorate) and there were definitely two people out there, waiting for us – if they were still alive – and surely at least one was alive?

The Edale team came in having found nothing, and were sent back almost immediately to do a sweep search up the Yellowslacks Brook. I went with them, reflecting that a sweep, being slow, wouldn't be nearly so bad as trying to keep up with Ken and Linda.

We started through bog and fields, climbed a wall and came out on ground which grew steeper and rougher as we worked up towards the plateau. There was a lot of loose rock on little cliffs. It was difficult to keep your footing while you swept the torch beam round, searching, looking to see if you were still in line with the next man. The searcher in the bed of the stream was in a vulnerable position with the rocks coming down and no crash hat. I know: I found myself there several times.

Occasionally the line stopped while Dave swept the shattered cliffs with the arc light. He had the most arduous job for the light protruded far beyond his chest and it was impossible for him to see where he was placing his feet. He is a very tall young man, about six feet four, with a zany sense of humour.

It was cold when we stopped at the head of the brook and George Garlick, the team leader, called us in for a rest. Some of us were wearing duvets and weren't really chilly, but we came in close to the light and lay there, almost silent, looking out at the night. At these times, in a potentially tragic or dangerous situation, there is a strong sense of security engendered by your own kind: "here is the herd, burrow into it and be safe." But the lamp is the focal point and some of the feeling one has for it extends to its bearer. After that night I tried to explain this to Jack Longland: the curious ambiance that seemed to surround the lamp: an asexual love, but deep and primitive and not unmixed with awe. "Of course," he said, "the light is God."

On top of Bleaklow's watershed we stopped at some rocks and I recognised the piled gritstone pancakes of Wain Stones. We saw the lights of another team coming up Torside Clough from the north. It was a little misty now but with a moon behind the cloud. It must have been about three or four o'clock in the morning, but on the hill I lost all sense of time. We started up Yellowslacks at one o'clock in the morning and we returned to the police station at five-thirty.

Big Dave stood on top of Wain Stones and, slowly revolving like a lighthouse, sent the beam in all directions. No one laughed. No one thought it funny. As the beam swept the moor we listened for shouts or whistles but there was no sound. We were worried now. All night we had thought of bodies under waterfalls, of a paralysed man dying of exposure.

And always there was this recurring thought: why hasn't *one* come down?

I was feeling tired. I had a torch but the battery was failing. Stumbles and the strain of staring at the ground increased my fatigue. I had left home in my old walking boots which leaked abominably, and one pair of socks. My feet had been wet all day (and all night) and now the soles were very tender. It was fortunate that I had my duvet with me; its warmth made me forget that my breeches were soaked from the bogs and splashing up the streams.

As we came back down the long Snake Hill we passed fresh teams going out. In the police station others, like ourselves, were resting, sitting on the cement floor, propped against the walls. The Edale girls were sleeping in the cells.

As dawn approached it was decided to move the base to the summit of Snake Pass. I borrowed a blanket from the police and drove there in the Cortina. The cloud was down now and the air was sticky but very cold. It would be a dirty dawn.

I put the Cortina in the lay-by and asked Johnnie if I were needed. No, he said, I could snatch some sleep. I was too tired to put the back seat down. I curled up on it, took off my boots, hesitated about wrapping my filthy feet in the police blanket, decided it was justified — and slept.

Someone was tapping on the window. I woke feeling hot and dirty and ugly. A clean fresh face peered in at me. A hand appeared with a mug of something that steamed: coffee in bed on Snake Summit!

I sat and drank and caught up with events. There was nothing except the movements of teams. The Edale members who arrived too late to go up Yellowslacks had been sent out when we returned, taking with them the girls who had been sleeping in the cells. They were out there now.

Visibility outside the car was only a few feet. I turned on the radio and we listened to the weather forecast. It was for rain.

Breakfast was sandwiches brought by the Women's Voluntary Services from Buxton: efficient, cheerful women in tweeds and sheepskins and sensible hats. They had set up a trestle table on the verge from which they dispensed sustenance as if they were serving tea at a garden party.

Johnnie (who had been working while I slept) said I must go home and bring back dry clothes and sleeping bags and food. We might be here another night, he said. There were now forty or fifty vehicles parked along the road. Many teams were involved in the search. We had been worried enough at night and we had searched diligently, but it had been a fine night. Now that the weather was deteriorating (the rain that was forecast could be snow on the tops) there was a new sense of urgency. I watched the long lines leave the road, searching immediately they left the tarmac, and, knowing that they would sweep clear to the watershed, I felt that surely they would be found soon. But with the possibility of snow and drifting there could be a chance of missing them.

"Go back," Johnnie urged, "and get sleeping bags and food quickly. We'll need everyone we can get if they're not found by midday."

I drove home fast, fed the cats, took all the food in the house, piled sleeping bags and quantities of dry clothing into the car and started back. On the way I listened to the news. They had been found – alive. I eased my foot on the accelerator and drove slowly, not feeling anything. A moment ago I was tense, anxious, stimulated, keeping myself at a pitch where sleep and food and shelter were superfluous, where a storm-swept moor must be my world until the job was finished. Now, suddenly, the rain which lashed the windscreen was merely something that affected driving; I could look forward to food and dry clothes and a proper bed again. Bleaklow was just a moor outside the car.

Johnnie told me the story. The man had injured his leg and he hadn't wanted the girl to go for help at night alone. They had seen our lights on Higher Shelf Stones and heard our shouts. They blew whistles and shouted but either the wind had been in the wrong direction or they hadn't been powerful enough to attract our attention. But they had the assurance that we were looking for them. In the morning the girl came down but before her information could be acted upon the man was found by the R.A.F. team from Stafford.

November came, wet and dismal. Snow warnings were forecast but no snow came. Gales took the last of the leaves and I tried to lose myself in work for there was no climbing. In the middle of the month Johnnie saw a specialist.

I was shopping in Buxton one morning and I heard his voice. I turned and saw him at the wheel of his Mini looking white and shocked. I went and sat beside him and he told me he must stop climbing. "For how long?" I asked, thinking that the weather was so poor it didn't matter very much.

"For good."

He had been putting too much strain on his back for twelve years: every time he carried a load, lifted a weight, even when he bent to fasten his shoes. Now he must lead a sedentary life, resting for months, and then perhaps he could take gentle walks on the level. Climbing was out – unquali- fied – for the rest of his life. The slightest jar, even a second falling and his having to take the shock, could result in his becoming a paraplegic.

His shock took the form of acute depression, a morbid fascination with the picture of himself in a wheelchair being supported financially and physically by me. I said nothing for two days waiting for him to ask me what I would do in his place, although I was not sure that my reaction to such a verdict on myself would be the right one for him. I told him this when he asked me and inevitably (for Johnnie always takes the opposite side to me) he argued. I wasn't worried. I knew, and his friends knew that he would fight.

After a few days he said that when the spring came perhaps

he might try little outcrops, close to the road with no walking and no loads to carry.

"Yes," I said, "and we'll go to the Alps in a year or two, when we've got some money, and employ a porter."

The Alps were out, he said, that was definite.

I mentioned the Weisshorn, the traverse of the Matterhorn, all those great routes I wanted to do. No, he said, never again.

We lay in bed one night, awake but silent. I thought of the Alps again.

"What about the north face of the Badile?"

"Oh, well—the Badile. That's different. Yes, I could manage the Badile all right."

CHAPTER 19

Rock

WE DIDN'T FIND the enforced inactivity of that winter unbearable. We accepted it because we both knew now that it
was only temporary. Our evenings and our weekends and, to
a great extent, my days were fully occupied. We made new
friends and old ones rallied round. I realised more than ever
that it is in emergencies that the sheep are separated from the
goats.

Ivor was interested in anything connected with the open
air, in history, in people. With him we attended lectures and
local dramatic performances. We spent evenings showing
slides and watching those of other enthusiasts. We enrolled for
First Aid lectures and gained our certificates. We gave lectures ourselves, attended dinners of mountaineering clubs —
and visited the local cinema. Johnnie wrote technical articles
for *The Climber*. It was difficult to find a free evening to read
the latest Rex Stout or Simenon. We had considered renting
a television set but decided that we would have no time to
watch. The Longlands invited us to Bakewell at weekends
where the talk was all of climbing and rescue and safety — and
one night that winter, a wet Sunday night, coming home
through the bright empty streets of Buxton, Johnnie said,

"You know, I'm happier than I've ever been in my life."

I had fun, associated not with mountains but with gathering material for stories. Until I came to Derbyshire I was still
finding it difficult to widen my field: to break away from
subjects associated with country life and travel. I had
followed editors' suggestions that I should write on the wider

social problems: juvenile delinquency, capital punishment, birth control, but I had neither the mind nor the facilities for that part of the research which would involve paper work and statistics and I started out with a disadvantage: there was too much competition in the field. Thinking about my advantages and how to use them I realised that there was one place, outside of mountaineering journalism, where I might have the edge on my competitors. I would trespass on the male preserves and write about them from the woman's angle. It was surprising that other women journalists weren't doing this. Perhaps they thought the rewards didn't justify the time and work involved. But the interest of working with my subjects was part of the reward; I derived far more from my chosen jobs than an article and a cheque.

I researched and wrote a feature on long-distance lorry drivers, I worked with motorway police patrols – and did one hundred miles an hour, legally, with the emergency services. I was tracked and held by police dogs, and was lost in wonder at their intelligence. And one day, on a new tack, needing material for a book which had been in the back of my mind for two years, I went to a quarry and saw one of the most dramatic sights of my career.

The manager drove me to a place from which we had a perfect view of the face which was about to be blasted. I had all the statistics: the composition of the charges, the timing, the amount the explosives expert earned. Now I waited, through interminable minutes, for the climax. The face was about one hundred and sixty feet high and over two hundred feet in width.

The manager stopped talking and we stared at the rock. I knew he was excited too. Suddenly and without a sound the whole face came forward, in one piece, horizontally. Then there was a dull boom which went almost unnoticed after the visual shock. The face dropped, fell a little but only a fraction out of shape. Then it crumpled and clouds of orange smoke filled the quarry.

Over a quarter of a million tons of rock had come down – and I felt no guilt. I should have felt it; I deplore the ravages that quarrying makes in the hills, but although I would take a stand against it on principle, although I saw a fine rock face devastated, the impact of that moment when the hill leapt out in silence was one of strange and overwhelming beauty.

At Christmas we were all at the Old Dungeon Ghyll. I envisaged a quiet holiday, motoring round the dales, taking photographs, visiting friends. Christmas Eve was dry and cold with snow on the tops and a bitter northerly wind. Sheena was on Middlefell Buttress behind the hotel, fastening the traditional balloons to belay spikes.

"Let's walk up to Raven Crag," Johnnie said in the afternoon, "we'll take a rope, just in case."

We went up the scree very slowly. He rested often, unable to breathe deeply, constricted by the rigid back support which he had to wear.

We reached the foot of Raven and a blue balloon lay in the grass, blown off Middlefell.

"That will have to go back," he said, looking up the line of Original Route.

He was happier on the rock than he had been on the screes. At first I watched every movement anxiously but he climbed easily, confidently, and I relaxed.

I tied the balloon to a spike on the top pitch.

"We put your balloon back," I told Sheena later.

"We?"

"Johnnie and I."

"Where?"

"On the top pitch of Original."

She nodded approvingly.

There were no accidents to spoil that Christmas, no party where I hadn't time to change and stood at the side in breeches and boots. On Christmas Day the sun shone brilliantly and I suggested Kirkstone Pass as the most acces-

The Edale Mountain Rescue Team on Kinder Downfall –
the wind is blowing the waterfall upwards

Sheena on the Inaccessible Pinnacle, Skye

Sheena on the White Slab Direct, Skye

sible place to obtain wintry photographs for the snowline was
high. But when we reached the highest point of the road we
saw that the best snow was in the top of Kilnshaw Chimney, a
thousand feet higher.

"You carry the gear," he said, "and I'll go ahead."

He had about ten minutes' start. By the time I'd fastened
my boots and packed the rucksack he was well ahead, moving
steadily today where yesterday he had paused every few
strides. I didn't catch him until he was at the cornice.
Neither of us made any comment.

We had little snow that winter. After Christmas we returned to Buxton, followed by one of Sheena's friends, John
Hammond, who slept on the floor because we had no spare
room and was entranced by a place full of climbing gear and
books — boots and axes in the living room, maps on the walls,
skis in the bedrooms — all the clutter of a house where there
is no non-mountaineer to say "gear must be kept in your
room out of sight" and no one worried about boots on the
carpets.

I drove them out each day to climb, and then came home
to write. They asked me to go with them but they were doing
hard routes on limestone and we had not yet climbed on
limestone. The combination of their youthful prowess and
rock that was an unknown quantity intimidated me.

There was a light snowfall which melted and left nothing
but a skin of snow on Bleaklow. Sheena and I found this only
by dint of driving about the Peak with the skis ready and
waiting on top of the car. We carried them to the top of
Higher Shelf Stones and came down slowly with careful turns,
through the heather and, hilariously, across the groughs and,
with tremendous effort, managing to skate the last level
stretch of moor to the road so that we could say we had skied
from Bleaklow to the Snake.

With no winter worth mentioning, little ski-ing and no

P

snow climbing, I found myself, like Johnnie, longing for the spring. It had come to mean more to us that just warm dry weather; it was the time when his enforced rest would be over, the support might be discarded, when the specialist might be persuaded to give a different verdict.

February came with a fine cold Sunday and a meeting with Sheena on Froggatt Edge. Apart from the climb on Raven at Christmas Johnnie hadn't touched rock for four months, but he had persuaded the specialist to agree to "little outcrops not far from the road, so long as you don't subject your back to any strain".

On Froggatt we went straight to Severes: hard cracks, delicate slabs: "I'm keeping my back straight; I'm not stepping high . . ."

In the weeks that followed there were sudden furious out-bursts – as when we went to Burbage Edge in a wet gale and I wouldn't climb so that I might stop him doing so, and he went solo, saying that he had been solo-ing for weeks without my knowledge, and I was torn between pleasure and retro-spective fear, for who would have known his whereabouts if he *had* fallen? There was the time he came home and told me, laughing, that, again solo, he had slipped on a greasy Very Severe, had managed to retreat but had been shattered when he reached the ground.

We went to Wales one Friday, stopping the car in Llan-beris Pass and climbing a strenuous route called Ribstone Crack where the wind was so cold my hands were numb, but he climbed as he used to climb: slowly, neatly, with the utmost confidence.

Easter came and for seven days he was on the hill without a break. Some weeks ago we had gone to limestone and, on a greasy day in Chee Dale, had been defeated by a route which Hammond and Sheena had dismissed as innocuous. On the first day of the holiday we chose a place with a more gentle ambiance: Water cum Jolly, where the limestone cliffs rise white out of the wooded gorge and the river runs deep and green between banks of sedges.

We climbed in the sun amid bird song and the occasional cry of a moorhen. Coltsfoot grew like an alpine on the screes and it was hot on the stances. Here we found steep and strenuous rock with holds and belays that were reminiscent of mountain rock, small but firm and spiky.

Johnnie worked on Easter Saturday, patrolling the tops east of Bleaklow. He carried a pack and walked a long way; he saw golden plover and the first buds on the bilberries — and returned with no more complaint than the stiffness in his thighs.

Next day I went with him and Ken Drabble over Bleaklow where the mountain hares were still in white, looking huge and conspicuous against the brown moor. These hares are not native to Derbyshire; they were introduced in the nineteenth century from Inverness-shire. Fred Heardman told me that they weren't shot: the keepers protected them. I asked if this were through superstition; many of the Pennine keepers are Highland men. No, he said, it was affection; they liked to see white hares on the moors.

On Easter Day we climbed at Yarncliffe Edge between snow showers and, coming down late in a red sunset, saw kestrels rise like phoenixes out of the fiery quarry.

We found the first primrose below the cliffs of Ravensdale and wild chives for our sandwiches — and lay on the top in the sun and planned our summer.

Now that the winter was over I was aware of a new security. I was halfway through this book, Johnnie was climbing, and climbing well, Sheena was at college studying domestic science — although we never heard about her studies, only about the weekends in Langdale or Llanberis or on the fierce cliffs at Malham. I didn't have to think about school fees and how to pay them. And along with this conscious awareness there must have been some subconscious feeling of release. I was no longer afraid of falling, of being incapacitated, because there was no necessity to earn my own living. Consequently I climbed better and, without that overwhelming compulsion to make money, I enjoyed my work again and made good sales. *Argosy* had recently bought one of my short stories and I seemed to have broadcast every month for a year.

With the spring came a new kind of relaxation. Once again I could revel in things for their own sake. I had come to like gritstone climbing last summer when I found I could cope with it, and then I had suppressed this liking for months for, if Johnnie couldn't climb, then neither would I, but now my relief at his successful comeback and my release from financial strain combined to bring me back to gritstone with a kind of passion which I had not known for years.

I have never counted the number of crags in the High Peak. There must be dozens. We visited many in our first season and now we returned and, in my new awareness, I saw that each had its own character and atmosphere. Some were finest at one time of day, others were seen at their best at night. Some were wild and windswept, others lay snug in trees – but still presented fine cracks and overhangs where you could play when bad weather barred the tops.

I had no favourites, only those which I preferred under certain conditions. An outcrop like Cratcliffe Tor, monopolised by hard routes – overhanging laybacks and ferocious mantelshelves – this was not for the evening after wash-day. Then we went to the Roches: an extensive crag where the climbs had incut holds like mountain rock and of all standards. It was here I started climbing solo again and Sheena led me up her first gritstone Severes. I felt at home here, back in the mountains, even though the lights of Leek gleamed through the dusk and the sun hung like an opal fruit in the smoke. But in the mist, with the tips of the pines clearing the cloud, you could have been anywhere. On a good evening with the sky pale and the moon rising, the overhangs loomed like prehistoric monsters and then you could be nowhere but on the Roches. There was Hen Cloud, a little way to the south, which rose like the prow of a battleship out of a bilberry-green sea and the grouse chattered anxiously in the background. Driving home, up the long moor road to Buxton, the rocks of Ramshaw rose on our left and, with nothing to give them scale, could have been strange desert pinnacles in the middle of an unmapped continent.

There were evenings at Stanage where, after the ring ouzels had stopped their clacking, the bats came out in the twilight, first one, then others, and later the swifts appeared until the air was full of bats and birds flitting and gliding with incredible speed, hawking through each other in complete silence.

On Laddow, that isolated cliff which looks out on a glen that could be in Scotland, I had my first experience of a really nasty storm. We had climbed all day with thunder muttering in the south and the occasional desultory shower, and we were tired and demoralised by hard climbs on wet rock – and perhaps we sensed the potential danger in the air. As Johnnie retreated down a delicate pitch I stood at the bottom taking in the rope and I looked out at the valley and saw lightning like snakes' tongues flicker against the grass. I was most uneasy and, although it might have been better to wait, I advocated leaving now, before the storm came closer and lightning struck the crag.

We saw no more strikes as we descended the valley and this was a coincidence more fortunate than we knew at the time, for that afternoon a man was struck and killed a few miles to the south and a party of three was injured in a field at Edale. I wasn't surprised when I heard this. Those little flickers *below* me had been in a different category from the glorious explosions on the Meije. Then I had been happy; below Laddow I was very much afraid.

For years now I had climbed almost exclusively with Johnnie. This meant that I was usually following hard routes, seldom leading. I had guiding engagements this summer and

I knew it was high time I climbed with my equals — and led. In my training with the Edale team I had led nothing more than easy routes on gritstone.

The Longland family arrived one Sunday afternoon when Johnnie was working and dragged me, protesting, from my book. We went to Windgather Rocks and I led all afternoon and towards the end I walked along the foot of the crag and looked up at Green Crack: a short steep Severe, an over-hanging fissure.

"Just hold my rope," I said to Jack.

It had something of the old and almost forgotten quality of my first Severe lead: the careful working out of moves, individually and in sequence, the feel of the good rough rock as my fingers moulded to it, someone watching in silence knowing that this was yet another small milestone, of seeing the top approaching and going a little slower, a little more carefully, stepping over the edge with a mist in front of my eyes — and then remembering the others suddenly, finding a belay and shouting down: "Who's next?"

Johnnie had to go to Keswick for a conference. We went together and parted in Langdale. I climbed on Gimmer with two girls and all day we led through on Severes, coming down to the foot of the cliff through violets and lambs, only to go up again with the deep gullies dropping away below the climb so that the exposure was there as soon as you stepped on to the rock. We had all been trained by men and, like the hard men who climbed the great routes parallel to us, we used the same methods. We wore crash helmets which I first wore to protect me from falling stones but which I knew now could save a fractured skull if I fell. We used nuts and spuds and crackers. As with many innovations I had laughed the first time I saw these: it was all very well for Joe Brown and his followers to carry up stones to insert in cracks and thread a sling round for a runner, but to manufacture them de-liberately on a machine, or to use old brass or steel nuts having drilled out the thread: this was going too far. But

Johnnie succumbed, then Sheena — and now I had my collection threaded on spliced slings — and how could I have climbed without them? All those cracks I must have passed on long unprotected leads, cracks an inch, half an inch wide, narrowing as they descended: just the place to insert a nut with its attendant sling and the friendly carabiner to clip the rope into. There were still reactionaries, fast dying out, who protested that thus we pushed our limit, that what you couldn't climb without these artificial chockstones you should leave alone, but I prefer to fall ten feet on to a runner rather than a hundred feet without one.

Another thing I had learned during my year in Derbyshire was to jam. Gritstone, being steep, is mainly crack climbing (which is where the nuts are useful too). Since many of the harder cracks have few if any holds the only way to climb them is by inserting the hand, thumb into the palm, crooking the knuckles, then moving up on the jam. Sometimes the hand is so secure that you have considerable difficulty releasing it, sometimes it moves slightly when it has to take your weight. At first my hands were covered with old scabs and new grazes. This is the mark of the novice; the gritstone expert places his hand correctly and it stays there and the jam leaves no mark on the skin. Another sign of the novice is having the right hand more scarred than the left. The best climbers are ambidextrous.

We hadn't had a holiday, not a proper going-away holiday for years. When each spring came round we would say, "now this summer we will go to Zermatt — or the Bregaglia — or the Dauphiné", but always there was the lack of money. The last time we had been to the Alps was six years ago. Johnnie was due for three weeks' leave now but, wanting to repay our debts, he had accepted a fortnight's guiding engagement in Langdale. I was worried: climbing for fun was very different from *having* to climb, every day for two weeks and in all kinds of weather. And what about our holiday? He would have a week of his leave left, he told me; we couldn't have gone to the Alps, anyway; he wasn't fit. When it was quite obvious I was winning the resulting conflict but that in the long run it was checkmate because he was committed now to guide, he tried to placate me with a promise of a week anywhere I wanted to go, even limestone in the south of France, we could fly there. Extravagant, I said. We would go to Wales then; he had to write an article on the Rhinogs in Merioneth. I told him what I thought of the Rhinogs. He mentioned Nevis. Yes, I said, and climb on that north face in the shadow all day while the sun is shining elsewhere. Arran, I said, wanting somewhere new. Not Arran, we would have too far to walk to the climbs. Skye then; we had never climbed in Coire Uisg (but that would be in shadow too). No, there were midges on Skye. All right, I said, Cornwall — because he loved Cornwall and there would be no walking and no midges.

He went to the Lakes and came back bored with easy routes, a little stiff and tired but fascinated with the new Cornish guide book which my mother had given me for a birthday present.

My mother was staying with us. A few days before our holiday I drove her home to Sussex by way of North Wales. We stayed two nights with my friends, Mabel and Mary, in the Machno Valley. On a glorious day we drove past Snowdon and down to Aberglaslyn then back over the Crimea Pass and down the Lledr Valley. I looked at my mountains and I didn't want to climb on them. I could afford to wait. But when I woke a few hours before I must drive to Sussex on that last morning and realised that there were two hours to spare before breakfast, I slipped out of the house and drove to Ogwen.

The north ridge of Tryfan was grey under low cloud and as I came out on the slanting platform below the last steepening I was met by the wind. From the summit I caught a glimpse of water through the mist: the little lake in Cwm Bochlwyd. In the cloud were the angular pillars of Glyder Fach, the ridge of Bristly — and the sea would gleam beyond the coastal flats. I couldn't see them but they were there. It was over twenty years ago that I climbed my first route and emerged on this summit. Now I climbed down South Gully so that, if I didn't come to the mountains for another month, I shouldn't miss the saxifrage in bloom.

"You've been climbing!" they said as I came in the kitchen, pushing the dogs aside.

"I've been up Tryfan."

"There! We said so! We told your mother. She's gone climbing, we said, she'll have gone up Tryfan."

CHAPTER 20

Exposure

UNDER AN ANAESTHETIC I dreamed that I'd died and
there was an island to which I was being drawn very swiftly
on a kind of umbilical cord. I heard the singing sound of my
progress. I came to the shore and the air was soft and bright.
I went up the sand knowing everything there was to know
and remembering – now – that I must go back to the hospital
ward but determined that I would carry the meaning with
me. I woke to the bustle of visiting hour and tea cups. The
meaning was gone but the quality of the light and the silence
of my island stayed with me, so that when I woke this morning a decade later, and before I was aware of the difference of
Cornwall, there was a moment's deep sense of arrival, of
familiarity.

Dismissed as soon as I saw them were the rumpled sleeping
bag, the luggage, Johnnie slumped in the driving seat. Outside the open windows was the grey face of the climbing hut
with its sleeping bedrooms. Everywhere there was this great
shining light and the profound silence. Even the larks were
still. The air smelt of the sea.

It was a quarter past seven. Johnnie went inside and made
coffee and brought it out to me because I knew that if I left
the sleeping bag I must unpack and all I wanted to do was to
soak in the light and heat. Each cup of coffee was accompanied by outraged protests from himself concerning the
filthy condition of the hut. I wasn't disturbed. What did a
few dirty saucepans matter in the face of this world outside
the walls?

· · · · ·

I swept an empty bedroom and shook the mats; I unpacked and, despite his resentment, I walked out and through the bracken towards the cliff. I remembered that the ground was riddled with old mine shafts and I walked carefully, putting my feet down only after I'd parted the bracken. And there, on a bare rocky place in the track, was a fine fat viper coiling slowly out of my way, olive with the dark zigzag down the back. Suddenly I was aware of my vulnerability: in sandals on a cliff top in July. A snake's bite could lose me a day's climbing at least. I turned and, doubly wary but making a ridiculous amount of noise, I went slowly back to the hut.

We drove through narrow flowery lanes to Chair Ladder. I wondered how I would react to climbing above the sea again—not a rough sea today, not the stupendous striking swell that we'd had on our last climb here with Sheena, but not smooth either. The tide was nearly full and the cliffs dropped into foam. I remembered the terrifying sense of exposure which I had experienced four years ago when half my world was in tumult. Would I go right back to the beginning and feel sick as I started to climb down and saw the movement below and heard the breakers?

We left our rucksacks at the top and descended a gully. As we approached the water I was expectant: watching myself objectively—until the gully ended in a chimney and I was absorbed in roping up and the concentration of descending on holds.

I belayed and Johnnie came down. To our left was Wolverine Chimney, starting at sea level. He had to wait for a wave to subside before he could reach the foot of the climb. The spray touched my face. When it came to my turn I traversed high, above the broken water, and came to a giant's step: a short steep wall where I was angry: the pure anger without fear that results simply from being too short to reach a hold. Once I fell off and landed on my starting ledge —and turned and surveyed a slab at the side. I climbed this and, afterwards, looking at my route from across the gully, Johnnie said, "But that was *hard!*"

In a few hours my whole attitude changed. There was a kind of sequence of milestones through the day: the dawn wakening at Bosigran, climbing down towards the sea, wary, then climbing up away from it, taking my own line with the specialised knowledge that I could follow that line, and then the sudden compulsion, the joyful eagerness to go down again and know the stimulation of the coloured moving water and its noise and the gradual fading of movement and sound as I climbed higher. Slowly the sea gives way to the rock until you are left with nothing but a whisper far below and the hard granite under your hands, and the scent of flowers.

There were young gulls on the ledges: fat and speckled, in full plumage but for little grey downy heads like elderly Negroes. We went out of our way to avoid them. The parents swooped at us silently with great power. I tried to face the frontal attacks but as they came in with the yellow stabbing bills aimed for my eyes I flinched and jerked aside. The fact that every time they veered before they hit me was no pledge of security; one might make a mistake.

Cornish climbs, we'd read in the new guide book, were graded like gritstone routes, presumably because they were shorter than mountain climbs on the whole. This meant they were under-graded — as if I hadn't noticed that on my first visit. Whether we had not yet accustomed ourselves to steep granite or the guide book was a masterpiece of under-statement, we climbed two Very Difficult routes that afternoon and found them, for their standard, hard. But we knew that Very Difficult is a curious classification, often indicating large holds but with long distances between them, or tricky technical moves which are safe because they are close above a big platform. As the standard rises the holds become smaller but, on the Severes, for instance, there are more of them as the angle steepens and the climb becomes more exposed. (It is on the Very Severes that you have few holds *and* exposure.) So, late that afternoon, impatient with the rigours of "easy" routes, Johnnie suggested we look at Red Wall, a Mild Severe. I approved this cautiously, knowing that with such a name it would be steep, but hoping that, even by Cornish standards, a *mild* Severe would have holds.

The wall was forty feet high, its top a hundred feet above the sea. Johnnie was out of sight from my stance so the pitch was new to me when I came to it. There were holds, but none that was superfluous, so since the rock was vertical you had to plan your moves in advance, leaning out as far as possible on finger holds to see what was above. On a ledge at the top a snaky head craned down at me and made anxious noises. It was a young shag, unable to fly.

The pitch needed concentration and strong fingers. I came to the top and relaxed and stared at the shag. In sudden reaction he threw up, right down the rock which I'd just climbed. I had never seen such an elegant vomit; I was full of admiration.

In a good summer Cornwall has everything. Apart from the climbing and the sun it is like being in a cliff-top Kew and a big game reserve. Everywhere you look there is something to see: not animals used to being gawked at and which one feels are something of exhibitionists, but animals for the most part unaware that they are being watched.

The following day we came to a headland and looked down across a bay of jade and sapphire and there, rising even at a distance high out of the water was a shining fin – and another, a different shape, behind it. Even as I realised the distance between dorsal and caudal fins, I saw the huge flattened shape below the surface, and others near it: six in all. The basking sharks were feeding in the bay.

We watched them for a long time, through binoculars and with the naked eye. I saw wet fins flap, catching the light as the fish moved.

"How big are they?" I asked.

"Fifteen feet — twenty-five. There's no scale. You could swim out to them."

"They only eat plankton," I said.

"Swim out to them and we'll get exact measurements."

"Well," I said, "we aren't zoologists. We're only almost sure they are basking sharks, that they eat plankton. And suppose the water was cold and you were tired by the time you got there and one swiped you by accident with his tail?"

We left the sharks and went down the rocks to climb. There was an island called Bosistow and caves where hundreds of gulls stood on ledges with their chicks. There was a zawn up which the seals came to breed. I stood on a platform in a corner a few feet above the sea. It was calm here, the water lapped the rock.

I paid the rope out idly. It ran up across the rock face diagonally. I looked down from Johnnie to the sea and there, a few feet away, was a seal following the line of the rope with great interest.

The head disappeared but popped up again in a few moments. I laughed. Startled eyes slewed round to me and there was an explosive splash as he up-ended and dived. I saw the spots of adolescence but even without them I would have known he was young, the dive was so ridiculously clumsy. Thirty feet away he came up again and I hissed at Johnnie. He was fastening a runner, looking down. He was determined to have a picture of a seal. He should see movement out of the corner of his eye. I waved my arm wildly, hissed like a goose. I failed to attract his attention but the seal was vastly intrigued.

A day or two later we were on a hard climb above Pendower Cove. The crucial pitch started with a strenuous mantelshelf far out of reach. Johnnie accomplished this by lassoo-ing the shelf with a sling and standing in the loop. I made several efforts to climb it free but in the end I had to use his method. These unsuccessful attempts took most of my strength and a steep final crack accounted for the rest.

"Look," he said as I moved up to him, "look at the seals."

"Watch the rope," I said between my teeth, "I'm not up yet."

"Look, they're *playing*!"

I glanced down and there were two adults chasing each other, looping the loop as they went, their pale bellies gleaming as they wheeled.

There was the biggest shark we'd seen nosing round the foot of the slab we'd just climbed to the top of Hella Point and, at the same time, a school of fifty porpoises travelling in line parallel to the shore: a line that must have been half a mile long, of arching backs and spurts of spray.

Sometimes, in the evenings, even after the sun went down and its rays struck upwards from below the horizon, it was still warm as it would be in the south of France. Sunset colours were a muted spectrum, paling through rose and lemon and orchid-green to lilac which shaded to cobalt over the inland moors. The lanes were full of the smell of cut hay and honey from the heather.

The tops of the cliffs were covered with flowers. Hawkbit and trefoil were everywhere, so was the thyme and stonecrop. Back in a bog, taking one of Johnnie's misguided short-cuts, we found two purple orchids with blooms nine inches long.

Sea sand spurrey grew among the rocks: a little flower like a rosy saxifrage, and there was a gentian: a stubby centaury, a brighter pink — and an ubiquitous fragrant plant which we failed to identify but which Johnnie referred to with casual superiority as "one of the umbelliferae". He saw a green woodpecker at the top of Chair Ladder, which was likely, and a kite on Carn Barra, which was not.

There are two celebrations which Johnnie insists on observing: our wedding and my birthday. This holiday had been planned to coincide with the latter and the day itself must suit my requirements: sun and steep rock followed by good food and wine. A table was booked at the Old Success in Sennen Cove and, faced with a short day, we climbed on Bosigran Face below the hut. I chose the climbs: Ochre Slab to start, I said, not wanting chimneys — and shameful grazes on bare flesh in the evening.

There were guillemots on the ledges of Porthmoina Island: little dumpy figures sitting in a kind of three-point squat, taking off with a rapid beating flight as if the plump bodies couldn't remain airborne without this hurried progress. In contrast the gulls were slow and languid, so illumined by light that they seemed transparent as they swept across the sun.

We climbed — and lay in the soft grass among the flowers. We climbed again: a route called Nameless which mounted in a crescendo of difficulty through walls and slabs to a final bulging groove with very few holds and, on the left, a crack which was a pink cascade of stonecrop.

Three days of coloured shabby clothes hadn't prepared me for the shock of seeing ourselves in white. My new pale lipstick — which had looked fine in Buxton a month ago — was all wrong, he said, I looked like a Black and White Minstrel. We had a bottle of Chianti and a lot of Cointreau. We met two married doctors, one from South Africa, with whom we talked of sharks and hypothermia and stretchers. MacDermott, the Cornish guide, came into Charlie's Bar: tanned, pale-eyed, a man fined down physically like a hunting cat. A member of the lifeboat crew "sold" me a Council house for two hundred pounds — and suddenly I remembered we would be climbing tomorrow and midnight loomed.

Driving up the steep hill out of Sennen Cove, we came on a cat lying indolent on the still-warm tarmac, washing itself. We came home through the quiet lanes to the cliff top where the Pendeen light swept silver across the sea, and our room was soft with candlelight and the scent of honeysuckle. July is a good month for a birthday.

We had one day of poor weather when, needing photographs for articles, we went to Land's End and climbed

Land's End in winter

Johnnie on Diocese, Cornwall

Longships Ridge as a reconnaissance for a good day. The tide and the wind rose as we climbed until, on the long exposed crucial pitch, I swayed as I moved. I could resist the tremendous gusts only with four points of contact; as soon as I moved one hand the wind caught me and swung me to the left. Never, I thought, would I solo this pitch for pictures: with the sea crashing in the black zawn below and the holds so small. We would forget about photographs. The climb was merely a defiant gesture against the gale.

For a time our habits clashed. I slept well and was up before eight, anxious to be out and climbing. Johnnie slept late, maintaining that he couldn't enjoy his holiday if I dragged him out early. The heat, he said, stupefied him. On the Friday, arriving at Sennen with the morning gone, we raced up and down climbs trying to take advantage of what was left of the day. I climbed badly at first, full of resentment at those lost hours, but late in the afternoon I recovered my equilibrium as I followed him up hard cracks where lay-backs needed no concentration, no mental effort, merely shoulder muscle. As we stood at the top of the last climb with the sun gone and a pennant of flame above the horizon I said,

"There are two days left. Suppose we both get up early, and during the day you sleep on top of the cliff while I climb solo?"

He wouldn't agree to sleeping while I climbed but he had to admit that this was the sensible answer to the problem of reconciling our difference. On the Saturday morning we were away before nine o'clock and we arrived at the top of Longships Ridge by ten.

The place from which to take the photographs was across the top of an earthy gully. From here the whole of the steep rocky arête was in focus with the lighthouse beyond and the sea below. I knew he would want me exactly on the skyline — or the sea-line. I wondered what the holds were like out there.

We went across and he belayed at the top of the pitch. I

climbed down to a point below where he would need me,
then up again. It was a different climb from that which we
had done in the gale. There was a slight breeze but no cloud.
The rock was hot. I was constantly drying my sweating hands
on my bikini. I found an earthy corner where I could rest
but it was so hot in there I hoped he wouldn't take long
changing films.

He threw down the rope and I passed it on below me until
it hung straight down the rock to give the illusion that someone was on the end. I waited in my corner, shifting my feet
on the hot earth. I stared idly at the zawn glinting over a
hundred feet below. The sea sucked and chuckled among the
rocks.

"O.K." he called, "start down!"

I descended, moved across to the arête, then up. Directions
came, audible when the sea was quiet, visual when the big
breakers were coming in. It was slow, meticulous work:

"Bend your left elbow . . . turn your right foot out . . . your
cheek's in shadow, look up! Go out to that knob on the edge.
Now come back and do it again . . . wait, wait; stop there!
You're *posing*! Go back to the knob . . ."

I was on the arête for two hours, then we changed places so
that I might take pictures of him to illustrate his technical
lectures. A barefoot woman in a bikini was too frivolous, in
this context, to show to contenders for the Duke of Edin-
burgh's Gold Award.

In the afternoon we progressed slowly towards Land's
End, climbing as we went, and ended right below the hotel,
descending a gully where we were entranced respectively by
the antics of a large fat mongrel and a mini-skirted popsie
who were having difficulty regaining the top.

We led through on Long Climb and then, in an unsuccessful attempt to find a route called The Vein, we made a
first ascent: rather a silly one because it started hard and
ended easy (climbs should be sustained or a crescendo) —
and the light came on red in the Longships while out at sea

the Wolf was a white pin prick. We had climbed for twelve hours.

At ten o'clock on the morning of our last day we stood above the bay where we had seen the sharks a week ago. We came carefully down the steep soft grass to a ledge above the island. Under us the cliff dropped vertical into the passage where the seals came up to breed. The tide was half out. While Johnnie assembled the equipment, I scrambled down easy rocks on the point and came to a platform from which I could look into the cove. The tide was wrong to reach the routes that started there. Huge boulders lay submerged with holes between them where we would be chest-deep if we slipped. There was a place where we could abseil but then we must leave one of our ropes behind for emergencies. We used two ropes now for harder climbs – it was safer.

As I turned away I looked upwards, above my platform, at a steep buttress with a crack running up to an overhang. It looked as if one might traverse to the right across a wall below this roof.

Johnnie came down and surveyed the cove ruefully. I didn't mention the line up the buttress: it looked too hard. Prospecting in a corner I called,

"There's a chimney up here – Severe perhaps: a new route."

"Come and look at this," he shouted.

I went and stood beside him, staring at my route to the overhang. About fifteen feet up was a kind of plate stuck on the wall: the only good hold in sight. You could reach it but the next few moves would be committing.

As I watched him trying to jam his toes in the crack above the plate I realised that I'd been right. These moves couldn't be reversed and he couldn't afford to fall even twenty feet on to his back. Then I thought that he would find a place for a nut in the crack. Without being aware of the transition I was thinking like a technician, not like a wife. It was the first time this holiday I had worn my gauntlets; I would be able to hold him.

He reached a niche below the overhang and put on two more runners (he had inserted a nut as I'd hoped, above the plate). He explored to the left, in the shadow above the shadowed cove. I looked right where the traverse lay in the sun, where I could watch him. I didn't want him out of sight. He came back to the niche and looked over the corner to the right, then down at me.

"If you descend ten feet," I called above the noise of the sea, "there may be an easier line out right."

"It's a swing," he shouted, looking at his higher line, "you've got to throw yourself at it."

I waited, saying nothing.

He swung out of the niche and on to the start of the traverse. He moved quickly—indeed, his unusual speed amazed me until I realised that this was no climb where one could afford to linger. He shouted that the holds were getting bigger; he reached the end and moved up. I relaxed a little and felt the sun scorching through my jeans and my woollen shirt.

The halfway mark on the ropes passed through my hands and up the rock out of sight. The pitch was over seventy feet.

There was a moment when I stood at the foot of the crack that habit asserted itself and I thought that what he had found hard I might find harder, but I didn't argue the point nor suppress the thought—it went.

I moved up the crack quickly. The first nut runner lifted out easily and I climbed slightly left and into the niche. I was aware of steepness only when I stood on those good footholds under the overhang, when I had taken off the second and third runners and the ropes ran diagonally up to him above on the right. Then, as I leaned out to look round the corner and along the traverse, I was aware of how easy it was to lean—and I looked down the line of the crack and saw the empty starting platform under my feet. No wonder he had hesitated before he swung on to the wall.

He'd guessed what I was thinking although he couldn't see me.

"The holds get bigger," he shouted, but I hadn't forgotten.

There were places for toes and hands, just adequate. In the mountains there would be no sound except that of the rope on rock; you would move in your own small world insulated by concentration. Here the sound of the sea was in your ears as you moved: the lift and wash and the strike of the ground swell in some deep cave. Through this and the hot air came the calling of the gulls. And the wall dropped in front and the holds showed in such a sequence below the overhang that you were touched by wonder that they should be so perfectly placed.

I pulled over the end of the wall and rested before climbing up to his stance. I congratulated him: it had been a bold lead in the circumstances. Like parties, the best climbs are spontaneous.

The green passage a hundred feet below was empty of seals. His disappointment for me marred his pleasure. "What would you like to do on Chair Ladder?" I asked, trying to raise his spirits. I knew he had been thinking of Diocese since he had talked to hard men earlier in the week. Terry Sullivan, an old friend from Mountain Rescue days, had recommended it. We had both talked to him, but separately. The chimney was the most difficult part, he'd told me but I, like him, would be able to get inside it. Johnnie would find it hard. There was a traverse . . . Was this as hard as Laugh Not, I asked. Nothing like, Terry said airily. Now the crux of Laugh Not, though hard is only one or two moves across a slab. I imagined something even shorter and with better holds – and Laugh Not has one good hold, sloping but right where you need it. So I'd dismissed its traverse and come to think of the chimney on Diocese as the crux of the climb.

Sitting at the top of Chair Ladder I read the guide book. The traverse was "on widely spaced holds . . . a magnificently exposed crucial pitch . . ." I blinked. That could agree with Terry's description but not with my hopeful picture. It seemed a little colourful for something shorter and easier than the Laugh Not crux. But then I could stretch far, and the traverse was only eighty feet above the sea – and I would have a top rope . . .

We climbed solo down moderate rock to the foot of Bishop's Buttress. The tide was coming in and, despite the fact that offshore the water was calm, sizeable waves broke against the cliff. Communication would be difficult.

From sea level we looked up at Diocese. The chimney faced away from us but we could see all the traverse – that is, we could see where it went. What was called a slab but was surely a wall started some distance above us (the chimney would be in its right-hand corner) and this lift of rock ran up into a tremendous roof where you must traverse left for twenty or thirty feet until the overhang ended and you could go up again. I felt nothing, only the sun boring into my shoulders. Stupefaction, Johnnie had called it, but for me it was involvement.

I followed Johnnie easily to a big square ledge below the chimney. The latter was too narrow for me to get inside (Terry must have been talking about its upper section, still invisible). The guide book admitted that this part was strenuous but there was a delicate slab over the corner on the right. The belay was our smallest nut wedged in a crevice and the sling was line: breaking strain a thousand pounds, considerably less than the shock-load of a falling man. Between the wall and the ledge was a big horizontal crack. I sat down and wedged my leg in this up to the thigh. Then I told him he could go.

"Where are your gloves?" he asked.

"Oh, my God! I forgot them!"

He said nothing. I would have climbed down and gone

back for them, and he knew it, but he was all keyed up now; he couldn't wait.

He went over the corner. The rope ran out. I couldn't see him although he was only a few feet away. He was talking about polished holds and his sweat making them slippery. The slab must have been twenty feet high. Suddenly he appeared at the top.

"You climbed that fast!"

"I couldn't stop once I was on it!"

He went on, moved left. I could see only his legs. Strange, how immobile lower limbs can be while the torso and arms are working out of sight and the brain running overtime. I saw his calves were sunburnt. I felt a crick in my neck and I looked out to sea, then back. The legs were gone. The rock was empty but for the rope.

Acoustics were strange. The crack in which my leg was wedged was part of the fault-line of the chimney. A voice mumbled up at me from the depths. This was Johnnie talking to himself thirty feet *above*. Suddenly there was a sharp outburst of swearing, this time coming more conventionally downwards. I heard the slings cursed, the chimney, the guide book, the rock. I took a turn round my wrist. With complete detachment I thought about a rope with a fourteen stone load running across my naked back. I followed through, first to my climbing down fast and pulling him out of the water after he'd hit the starting ledge, then I pondered the effectiveness of my tiny belay and my wedged thigh. Of course I would be catapulted out and with him hit the ledge and land in the water. At the thought of two fractured skulls in the sea I stopped thinking. There was no one else on Chair Ladder. I wedged my thigh a little deeper.

The curses stopped. His feet came into view again. As if I had heard nothing he elaborated.

"Terry said it was hard," I pointed out. Terry came in for his share of anathema, then he stared down at me. I looked at the gulls, searched for and found the red lattice spire of the bell buoy halfway between me and the horizon. I felt him relaxing.

He disappeared again and swore solidly for ten minutes – but the rope ran out. There was a pause and then a clear pleased voice:

"I'm near the top."

I smiled and nodded. I hoped Terry had been right about my being able to get inside the chimney.

When it came to my turn I staggered as I stood up. It was only then that I realised how tightly my leg had been wedged. I removed the little nut too easily, glad he hadn't needed to trust it – and me—and I stepped up and looked at the slab.

It was grey and pearly and smooth, but it was climbable: he'd climbed it.

As I worked my way up it I was aware that the rope wasn't being taken in quickly enough. He would be tired. I didn't say anything but knocked the slack out of the way with my elbows.

I came to the place where I'd watched his feet as he peered round into the chimney. I peered too. It was quite wide, quite big, very deep, but there were no holds. It leaned sideways gently, away from the sea.

"I faced left," he called.

This would mean my leaning forward with the incline of the rock. I preferred to lean back if I was to progress upwards by friction. I faced right and moved several feet inside.

The space was too narrow for conventional methods: back and knee wedged against opposite sides. There was only one solution: unpleasant in a bikini but inevitable.

I put my back against one wall and bore down on the rock with the palms of my hands at waist level. Occasionally I put a leg sideways and wedged the inside of my knee. For friction I used anything that came to rock, as it were: shoulders, buttocks, thighs. As in a hand-jam it was essential to place yourself carefully so that you didn't slip when – at the same time as you lost valuable inches of height — you would lose much skin. You could withstand the first shock of pain but would the grazed flesh hold a second time on rock that bristled with quartz crystals like broken glass?

I seemed to be making no progress but suddenly there was a capstone above me and I must make my way out from the depths to an incipient scoop with one poor foothold in the bottom. I worked my way sideways, still bearing down on the palms of my hands and it was here that, almost unscathed until now, I had to puncture my hand on a crystal.

From the constricted stance in the top of the chimney and under the start of the great overhang we looked out along the traverse.

"'Widely spaced holds'," he quoted, "there aren't *any*!"

I saw little things, not holds. Reluctantly we adjusted ourselves until we arrived at a state of mind where these tiny wrinkles were what we must use.

It was a strange place, dark and shadowed at our stance, sunlight on the wall — and the black roof extending outwards for twenty or thirty feet. Up under the overhang where the wall ran into it there might be handholds, but there was nothing for the feet below. We stared hungrily at the brown rock, wondering if we could swing along on a hand traverse, wondering if there were runners.

"Before you start," I said, "I want to say something."

He continued to work things out for a while then he turned to me.

"You'll be out of sight," I said, "and the sea may be noisy. If I come off, I'll grab the rope and run across the wall. I'll end on Flannel Avenue" (this was a Severe away to the left) "you'll be ready?"

He laughed. He thought it was funny but I was serious; I didn't want my tremendous falling swing to take him unawares. We were a long way above the sea now.

He started. I watched very carefully to see which holds he used. Again, he had to move fast. Halfway he shouted,

"I might go up and put a runner on for you but it would take a lot of fiddling . . ."

"It's all right," I said, "I don't need a runner."

He went on. Towards the end he made two moves at full stretch, on tip-toe, reaching high with his fingers. There I must find another way.

He reached the end, pulled out round the corner and disappeared. After a time I knew he was belaying by the way the ropes ran out. He flicked them. They hung down from the lip of the overhang vertically on to the wall, so that it was like being in a cave with ropes hanging down across the mouth, but this cave had no floor. Then the ropes came in a huge curve to me. Suddenly I realised that I must do the whole of this very severe traverse with the ropes slack; I was on my own.

He pulled in the ropes until, with the curves still in them, I shouted: "That's me!" Then I took off my belays, gave one last admonition: "Don't pull!" and tried the first move.

There was a wrinkle for the left foot, a pock mark for the right, but I didn't like the latter: it meant facing in to the rock. I wanted to face left, the way I was going. There was a hold for the tips of three left fingers, a speck of quartz for the finger and thumb of the right hand – and this was the first move. You could make it, but there was another, more delicate, to make before you reached the first good sloping toe hold. The second move couldn't be reversed; once you'd made it there was no going back to the first: you'd never find those wrinkles again. I shouted, telling him to listen to me. He pulled in some slack.

"No!" I yelled, "I'm *talking*! Listen!"

I listened to hear if he were listening. I heard a lot of shouting.

"I can't hear you!" I screamed.

"Climb when you're ready!"

"Listen! I want to speak!"

"What?"

"If I come off, it'll be on this first move. Be ready for the swing!"

"What?"

The sea was suddenly very noisy, then subsided. I could hear a long monologue from above, then:

"Climb when you're ready!"

"Climbing!" I shouted. I was angry now: with the sea ridiculing me, with my contrivances for safety, with the traverse.

I put my left foot on the wrinkle, my fingers on the holds. I drew myself up until a fraction of the edge of my right sole was on another smaller wrinkle, then I made the second move — and as I moved for the third time I reached the first good holds and I was still on the rock and the wall fell into the sea which, hushed now, whispered against the starting ledge, and I called quietly:

"Take in a little."

And so it went, all the way: a hold here and there (there had to be, people had climbed Diocese before) but in one place, perhaps because I was small and couldn't reach a hold: a sliver of quartz no bigger than a finger nail for the right hand. There, looking down for the next foothold, I realised my leg was starting to shake.

"Stop it!" I said sternly, and it stopped.

Where he went high, I went low, and came to the end of the wall and reached round and found a pinch hold. I was off-balance. I shuffled my feet a little and the pinchhold, projecting towards me, seemed like a jug handle. I was round then and resting on big ledges that would take the whole of each foot. Above me, jugs covered with orange lichen ran up to Johnnie.

We changed places on the stance. I stood straddled on an overhang, leaning outwards against my waist-line. The sun poured into this crazy haven and there was no wind. Above me he climbed the steep wall on ochre holds. Below, the sea shone blue and the white lace at the foot of the cliff was quiet.

The bell buoy tolled, the Wolf was a grey spire on the horizon and a fulmar floated past.

I thought of the guide book description: "magnificently exposed". It was magnificent but was it really exposed? I had to work it out systematically: exposure is a long drop over nothing, there is nothing below this ledge or that traverse but the sea and that's a hundred feet below. Exposure is fear or splendid soaring triumph.

"Climb when you're ready!"

I took off the belays and waited while the rope slid up the cliff. The swifts were out, skimming over the top, and all the rock was gold in the lowering sun. I started to climb.

Glossary

abseil: descent (where it is impossible or inconvenient to climb down) by means of a doubled rope round belay or through loop of cord attached to piton.

aiguille: a needle.

arête: a narrow ridge.

bealach: a pass.

belay: securing the party by tying the rope to a projection: bollard of rock, piton, etc. The projection itself. On snow the belay is the axe shaft, driven as deeply as possible into the surface. See "runners".

bergschrund: large crevasse between glacier and steeper slopes above.

brèche: a gap in a ridge.

bridge, to: placing hands and feet on opposite sides of chimney or corner.

capstone: wedged boulder roofing cave or chimney.

carabiner: metal snap-link for attaching rope to pitons, running belays, etc.

chimney: fissure usually wide enough to admit climber's body.

chockstone: stone wedged in gully, crack, chimney, etc.

col: a pass.

corde d'assurance libre! safety line free!

cornice: overhanging wave of wind-formed snow on a ridge.

corrie, coire: a bowl-shaped valley, often hanging, but can be at sea level.

couloir: a gully.

crackers: small artificial chockstones of alloy. See "runners".

crampon: metal frame with spikes to fit on boot for use on hard snow or ice. To move wearing crampons.

cwm: a hanging valley.

dalle: a slab.

Difficult: see "standards".

duvet: padded eiderdown jacket.

edge: gritstone outcrop.

étriers: miniature ladders of nylon line with alloy rungs, or knotted loops of heavy-duty nylon tape.

gabbro: very rough rock of Black Cuillin on Skye.

gendarme: rock tower.

glissade: controlled slide down snow using ice axe as brake.

Hard Severe: see "standards".

ice fall: very broken and crevassed area of glacier where the angle of ground beneath changes.

jug: jug handle: a very good hold.

lead through: lead alternately.

llyn: a lake.

lochan: a small lake.

mantelshelf: levering oneself on to ledge by hands and shoulder strength without, usually, being able to use the feet.

moraine: accumulation of stones and debris brought down by glacier.

nails: nailed boots.

nant: a valley.

névé: old hard snow.

nuts: the type complementing a bolt; used as artificial chockstones. See "runners".

parallel turns: changing direction fast, keeping the skis parallel throughout the turn.

peu difficile: slightly difficult.

pitch: section of climb between belays.

piton, peg: metal spike with eye in head which, used in conjunction with carabiner, safeguards the rope, and therefore the climber, on the principle of a pulley.

ravure: cigar- or fish-shaped cloud. Bad weather sign.

refuge: climbing hut in Alps usually at snowline. Higher ones are smaller and primitive and have no guardian.

runner, running belay: works on the principle of a pulley; intermediate belay on pitch where a sling and carabiner are slipped over a projection and the climbing rope clipped into carabiner. Chockstones, natural or artificial, wedged in cracks are excellent runners. A route with places for runners is "well-protected".

safety line: second rope used when abseiling. Prevents climber falling if he loses hold of abseil rope.

sérac: fang or tower of ice in ice fall.

Severe: see "standards".

skins: originally strips of seal skin, now nylon plush, attached to skis for climbing gradients. Skis can slide forwards but do not slip back.

sling: short loop of line, rope or heavy-duty tape.

solo: alone, unroped.

spuds: small artificial chockstones. See "runners".

stance: standing or sitting space by belay.

standards: British climbs are graded Easy, Moderate, Difficult, Very Difficult, Severe, Very Severe, Extremely Severe (with shades between) in ascending order of difficulty. Grading varies in different areas. In comparison with mountain climbs, gritstone and Cornish routes are undergraded.

stem turns: slower and less stylish than parallel turns. Made with the rear ends of the skis apart.

through-route: hole big enough for passage of climber, in chimney or gully, between wedged boulders or between chockstone and main face.

tigers: the better climbers.

top rope: rope from above.

traverse: horizontal line across rock. Climbing one side of mountain and descending by the other.

tricouni: boot nail.

Very Difficult: see "standards".

Very Severe: see "standards".

vibrams: moulded rubber boot soles. The boots themselves.

waistline: about twenty feet of hemp line coiled and knotted, to which climbing rope is attached by special knot and large carabiner.

wet: of glaciers; snow-covered glacier with crevasses filled, bridged or, dangerously, masked.

zawn: sea inlet of cliff.